Mongameli Mabona

Mongameli Mabona

HIS LIFE AND WORK

Ernst Wolff

Leuven University Press

Published with the support of the
KU Leuven Fund for Fair Open Access

This work is based on the research supported in part by
the National Research Foundation of South Africa (Grant No 81228)
and KU Leuven

Published in 2020 by Leuven University Press / Presses Universitaires de Louvain / Universitaire Pers Leuven. Minderbroedersstraat 4, B-3000 Leuven (Belgium).

© 2020, Ernst Wolff.
This book is published under a Creative Commons Attribution Non-Commercial Non-Derivative 4.0 International Licence.

The license allows you to share, copy, distribute, and transmit the work for personal and non-commercial use providing author and publisher attribution is clearly stated. Attribution should include the following information:
Ernst Wolff. *Mongameli Mabona: His life and work.* Leuven, Leuven University Press. (CC BY-NC-ND 4.0)
Further details about Creative Commons licenses are available at http://creativecommons.org/licenses/

ISBN 978 94 6270 255 4 (Paperback)
ISBN 978 94 6166 361 0 (ePDF)
ISBN 978 94 6166 362 7 (ePUB)
https://doi.org/10.11116/9789461663610
D/2020/1869/66
NUR: 731

Layout: Friedemann Vervoort
Cover design: Daniel Benneworth-Gray
Illustration on cover and p. 2: Mongameli Mabona (Private collection Family Mabona)

To Mongameli and Marta Mabona,
their children and extended family

CONTENTS

Preface	11
PART 1 - LIFE	15
1. Xhosaland: A history of confrontations	19
1. A snapshot of Xhosa life in the mid eighteenth century	19
2. Accelerated change: A typology of mounting conflict	23
3. A changing region in a changing world	25
3.1 Spread of Boers and British expansion	26
3.2 British domination and its effects on Xhosaland and beyond	28
3.3 Changes from the Xhosaland perspective	29
3.4 Changes from the broader South African perspective	34
2. (Dis)Union: The world of Mabona's youth (1910 to the mid 1950s)	41
1. International and Union politics	41
2. The economy	44
3. Separation – reserves – labour	45
4. Transkei: Culture, religion, education	49
5. Resistance nationally and in the Transkei	51
3. Enter Mongameli	53
1. Birth and first years	54
2. Early childhood in Qombolo	56

3. Life in Zigudu – Catholic background (1)	61
4. Ixopo – Catholic background (2)	67
5. Pevensey – Catholic background (3)	72
6. Early priesthood	75

4. Italy 77
1. Italian society after World War II	78
2. Everyday life in Rome	80
3. Mabona, the student and researcher	82
4. Further intellectual work	85
5. Second Congress of Black Writers and Artists: Alioune Diop and *Présence Africaine*	88
Excursion: The journal *Présence Africaine*	89
6. Preparing for Vatican II	98

5. Back home? Apartheid, St. Peter's, SPOBA 103
1. Apartheid	103
2. Apartheid education	106
3. The South African economy in the 1960s	107
4. Resistance	109
4.1 The ANC and the PAC	110
5. Life back in South Africa	113
5.1 Lumko	113
5.2 Independent ethnographic studies	116
5.3 Poetry	118
5.4 Lecturer at St. Peter's in Hammanskraal	119

6. London and Switzerland: Politics or anthropology? 129
1. SOAS	130
2. The Azanian People's Liberation Front and other politics	131
3. Family life	133
4. Continued research	135

PART 2 – WORK   139

   1. *Lux*: The first impetus   143
   2. *Présence Africaine*: Writing for a wide public   152
   3. "The depths of African philosophy" and *The outlines of African philosophy*   159
       3.1 General appraisal: South Africa's first African philosopher?   164
   4. Dissertatio ad lauream in Facultate Juris Canonici apud Pontificiam
      Universitatem Urbanianam   165
   5. "The nuclear blast of spring": Poetry   167
   6. Writings of a South African priest   170
   7. Anthropology and religion   174
   8. Interlude: The publication spurt of 1996   178
   9. *Diviners and prophets*: The last, incomplete, work   180
       9.1 Final appraisal   186

Timeline   189

Mabona primary bibliography   191

Notes on the sources for interviews and biography   195

References   197

PREFACE

After the Second World War, as most African countries were struggling through the turbulence which led to their independence from the erstwhile colonial powers, South Africa increased and strengthened the mechanisms of oppression and exploitation of its African population. Apartheid was never designed to give any recognition to – let alone support the flourishing of – black talent. In the dust of social and political turmoil thrown up by the strife of the following decades, it was often difficult to notice some of the remarkable achievements that were realised despite all adversity. Thus, it was possible that exceptional individuals could simply disappear from public view.

At the end of the 1920s in a remote rural area in the Eastern Cape of South Africa, Mongameli Mabona was born. To a great extent, the most probable path that his life would take was set by the major forces of his time. Like many of his family and peers, he would have herded cattle as a child and received a few years of primary school education (if any), before entering the labour market at a young age, either as a manual worker on a farm or as a miner far away from home. He would have married, lived mostly separate from his wife and children as a migrant labourer, and then he would have died an early death, poor and exhausted. But this is not what happened.

Through a stroke of luck, and obsessive attention to footnotes, I stumbled across the life and work of Mabona. Over the span of four years I had the opportunity to gradually discover his writings, conduct interviews with him and elaborate a historical contextualisation of his life and publications. This book documents the fruit of this exploration and is the first study of any kind on this remarkable figure.

The book consists of two parts. Part 1 brings together two elements. On the one hand, there is the first-person account of his life that Mongameli Mabona so generously entrusted to me during two series of long interviews on 15 and 16 January 2016, and on 18 and 19 September 2018 (a list of these interviews is presented as an Addendum). These interviews were augmented by information given by his wife, Marta, and stimulating interventions in some of the interviews both by her, and their son, Themba. On the other hand, I embarked on a broad historical study to situate this extraordinary narrative. This work of contextualisation covers a very unlikely set of historical situations, as a sneak preview of the table of contents would reveal. By combining these two elements, I hope to offer a coherent and historically situated presentation of Mabona's account of his life. While the first part of the book includes accounts of Mabona's work in the wide sense of his divergent occupations, professions, and pursuits, Part 2 is devoted to his work in the narrower sense, namely to his complete writings. It was a daunting task to compile a complete list of his writings, and I remain haunted by the fear that I may have missed something. Nevertheless, the result is the very first examination of his entire body of writings. The objectives of this examination will be explained in the introduction to Part 2. The two parts of the book may be read separately, but they are intended to complement each other.

My first aim is to present a book that would be compelling to academics. It should be of value to those who study South African intellectual history (specifically philosophy, theology, and anthropology) and poetry, but also aspects of struggle history (the role of Christianity or of Black Consciousness). The book should also be relevant to scholars of African diaspora studies and indeed to anybody who takes an interest in *Présence Africaine* and the work of Alioune Diop. Finally, part of the discussion is so intertwined with events in Europe that it may also be of interest to some scholars of specialised areas of European history and intellectual life.

However, my second aim was to write this book in such a way that it would be as accessible as possible to the broader public. For this reason, I tried to keep the text relatively short. Where I engage with the development of Mabona as an author, the text is inevitably more specialised, but I hope that my decision to present the material by means of a broad review will give reasonable access to those readers who want it. I wrote the book in the conviction that many people, from very different situations in the world, may take an interest in it. Therefore the historical setting also serves to ensure that the divergent contexts discussed in the book become comprehensible to readers who are not acquainted with them. This is my rationale for including information or insights that may already be familiar to some readers.

Undertaking such a project in the absence of scholarly precedents is a perilous venture. I freely acknowledge that some avenues of exploration remain unexhausted. For this reason, the material had to be presented within a well-delimited framework. I avoided inflating the significance of the findings and qualified the conclusions. At the same time, the whole book implicitly reflects my conviction that Mabona's name should henceforth be familiar to scholars and students in the fields of academic study mentioned above. On the whole, I offer a wealth of fascinating and remarkable material, but refrain from prescribing to the reader how to assess it. That is for each reader to decide. The ambition of this study is rather to clear the terrain, to introduce its main protagonist and to give tools to others for further study. This is not the definitive work on Mabona. I hope, instead, that the book will be a useful first step to whatever else scholars may deem appropriate to do with this heritage. Indeed, in a spirit congenial to some of Mabona's writings, I call on my readers to consider this an invitation to take this exploration further, in directions that their concerns and competences will show them.

Perhaps the most pressing objective of this project was to have the book completed during Mabona's lifetime. At the time this manuscript goes to press, this is still possible.

I would like to thank to so many people who have helped me in this project. Among them are Rachel Mahlangu (University of Pretoria) and Stefan Derouck (KU Leuven) and their colleagues who helped me to obtain Mabona's writings. Aretha Roux produced a very accurate and useful transcription of the January 2016 interviews. Jos Lievens assisted me to work through Mabona's first doctoral dissertation by preparing a Dutch translation of its preface. I had the fortunate opportunity to work through Mabona's poems in the perceptive and erudite company of Pol Peeters. Idette Noomé shouldered the burden of editing the manuscript, as she has for many of my texts over many years. Mirjam Truwant and her colleagues at Leuven University Press worked through all the difficulties to accompany the manuscript to its publication.

Enormous gratitude is due to the Mabona family: Marta Mabona and Themba Mabona for their practical help and generous hospitality, Mongameli Mabona for patiently sharing his life narrative.

Finally, while working through the material that became this book, I was impressed all over again by the chance I have had in life to have parents who strove to instill the desire for fairness and justice in their children, even at a time when it was far from the evident thing to do. While I know that there must be shortcomings in this book, it is evident to me that without *these* parents, most of what I have written about here might simply have remained invisible to me.

Ernst Wolff
Leuven, October 2019

PART 1 - LIFE

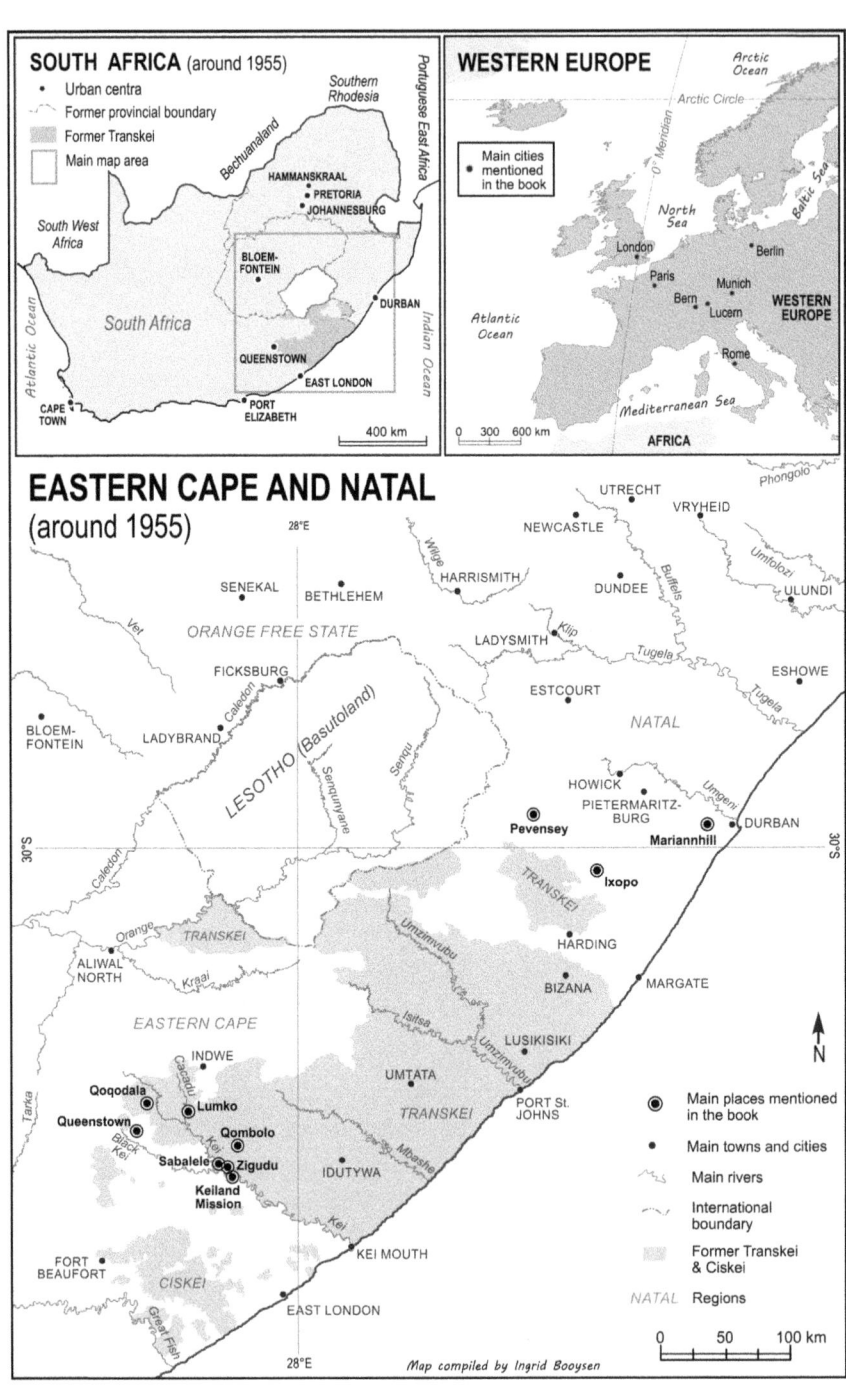

Qombolo, about 90 km to the east of Queenstown, in the south-eastern corner of South Africa, is where Mongameli Mabona was born. That was on 5 June 1929.

Like all other infants, he had no idea about the world which he entered, and only became slowly acquainted with it. But for us who want to look back at his life, a longer and broader view on events is required to understand the events. We need to know something of the historical construction of the world into which he was born and from which his life was to take its course. We also need to take note of this background, since it informed his later intellectual work too – as we will see in the second part of this book.

I pick up the narrative with a snapshot of traditional life in Xhosaland towards the middle of the eighteenth century.

CHAPTER 1

XHOSALAND: A HISTORY OF CONFRONTATIONS

1. A snapshot of Xhosa life in the mid eighteenth century

By the middle of the eighteenth century, there were various groups of Xhosa people who went about their daily concerns in the south-eastern part of southern Africa.[1] They lived in extended homesteads containing a number of families, and these patrilocal units were in turn part of larger lineage-based clans. Settlements were usually built close to a stream or tributary, and the people lived in round, beehive-shaped huts with thatched roofs, with low mud-dung plastered walls and floors.[2] The Xhosa, like their neighbours, relied heavily on the bounty of nature for their provisions, including food. For meat, they hunted. They also practised subsistence farming: sorghum was the staple, but they also cultivated maize,

---

[1] I use the term "Xhosaland" to designate the area occupied by Xhosa people during the whole period, in agreement with Mabona's own use: "In pre-colonial times the Xhosa speaking area stretched from Umzimkhulu to Rhamka (Gamtoas). This is the Xhosaland I am speaking of". Mongameli Mabona, *Diviners and prophets among the Xhosa* (1593 - 1856): A Study in Xhosa Cultural History. Münster: LIT, 2004, p. 431. Henceforth: DP. The exact demarcation of the area at each historical phase is not important. For the whole paragraph, see Reader's Digest, *Illustrated history of South Africa. The real story* (third edition), Cape Town: Reader's Digest Association South Africa, 1994, pp. 63–64; Les Switzer, *Power and resistance in an African society. The Ciskei Xhosa and the making of South Africa*. Madison: University of Wisconsin Press, 1993, pp. 24ff; and Jeffrey Peires, *The house of Phalo: A history of the Xhosa people in the days of their independence*, Berkeley and Los Angeles: University of California Press, 1981, Chapter 1.

[2] For a description of housing and related terminology, cf. DP, pp. 38–39.

millet, melons, beans, bananas, sugar cane, peas, and pumpkins.[3] Cattle was very significant in the provision of food (both for meat and milk); other livestock included poultry, goats, and sheep. When nature provided in abundance, life was abundant; conversely, changes of the season, times of scarcity, and drought made life hard. A number of safeguards helped them to absorb part of the shock of these vicissitudes: they stored grains, diversified their crops, provided each other with mutual support, and engaged in trade.

Much of daily life focused on providing for basic needs: farming and herding, constructing huts, working leather, etc. But beyond attending to their immediate needs, people were involved in a variety of activities, including mining iron and ochre and manufacturing spears and other tools which they could use to work, hunt, or fight. They worked ivory and made pottery. They also cultivated and enjoyed tobacco and *dagga*.

They traded cattle, copper, iron, and beads to create wealth, rather than as a means of subsistence. These goods offered a general means of exchange for goods and labour, functioning as a form of currency.[4] The goods were also exchanged as a form of speculation. Trade relations connected the Xhosa through various intermediaries with other peoples living farther to the north-east (the Hlubi) and the north-west (the Kwena), but also with neighbours closer by, such as the Mpondo. Trade included *dagga*, elephant tusks, and other valuables.

Accumulation of goods was fairly limited, with the notable exception of cattle, the kingpin of the Xhosa economy. Cattle was an essential medium of exchange in social relations (for instance, in payment of labour, in establishing marriage agreements between families, etc.). It also served as a symbol of authority. Different levels of wealth existed, but in Xhosa society these differences were limited. Regarding the social importance of cattle, Mabona would later write:

> Those of us who have seen the tailend of this cattle culture can only say that those who have not experienced or seen it can scarcely have an idea of what it was like and meant. Anybody who wants to understand the southeastern Bantu, though, must understand this background in all its implications.[5]

---

[3] Switzer, *Power and resistance*, p. 38, Hermann Giliomee, *The Afrikaners. Biography of a people*. Charlottesville: University of Virginia Press, 2004, p. 60.

[4] Cf. Peires, *The house of Phalo*, p. 95 and Chapter 7. True to my approach, I focus here on a particular moment in Xhosa history. In DP, Mabona has a section on the much older "Early Pre-Historic Trade and Migration Routes in Southern Africa" (DP, pp. 58–62).

[5] DP, p. 265.

Numerous aspects of routine life were subject to tradition and/or ritual, including, for instance, the formulae of respect, and more especially, the key events of life, such as coming of age, marriages, and deaths. Religious[6] practices were performed at the level of the homestead or clan, and were associated with the main features of life, such as agriculture and war. The distinction between religious and secular life was blurred, as unseen forces continually acted in ways impenetrable to human understanding and largely impervious to human influence.[7] There is no evidence of worship of a transcendent God; matters of good and evil were approached through the exemplars of the ancestors and through the mediation of traditional practitioners such as diviners.

Society was arranged primarily according to kinship relations, but ties could also be created through marriage. The chief, his counsellors, and the commoners formed the levels of social stratification.[8] Work and daily duties were divided according to social role expectations: men took charge of hunting and stock farming; women and children were responsible for agriculture and housekeeping. The homestead was the basic unit of production, and functioned and planned in relative autonomy – in agriculture, trade, and hunting – but collaborated with other homesteads and groups.[9]

The chiefs were responsible for the distribution of goods and trade, since they controlled land usage for agriculture, hunting, and dwelling; there was no private ownership of land. The chief was also the principal responsible for economic, religious, military, and judicial matters.[10] Together with his counsellors, the chief also arbitrated disputes and decided on appropriate strategies regarding defence, food security, and other general concerns. However, a chief – although this differed to some extent from ruler to ruler and in various historical phases – did not hold absolute power. There were kings, but their powers over their subordinates were limited. In effect, consolidated, centralised power depended on nodes of supportive power which relativised the centralised power. Similarly, the power of chiefs tended to be held in balance, mutually, or through the power relations in their clans.[11] The commoners granted the chief their respect

---

[6] Peires, *The house of Phalo*, Chapter 5. Mabona's own views will be summarised in Part 2, sections 7 and 9.
[7] Peires, *The house of Phalo*, p. 67.
[8] Switzer, *Power and resistance*, p. 34.
[9] Peires, *The house of Phalo*, p. 33.
[10] Cf. Peires, *The house of Phalo*, p. 31. Like land, cattle also belonged essentially to the chief, DP, p. 186.
[11] For details on the structures of authority in Xhosa society, cf. Peires, *The house of Phalo*, Chapter 3.

and obedience and made material contributions, and in this way participated in consolidating the chief's authority, but sometimes they refused to pay the imposed levies or fines, and they adopted various strategies to undermine the chief's authority and privileges. Sometimes, families split off from their chiefdom and moved away.[12] In turn, this obliged the chiefs to adopt what they considered appropriate counter-strategies. The internal dynamics of Xhosa society did not result only in decentralisation[13] – there were some chiefs who successfully consolidated their power, be it through force or by more peaceful means.

Factors such as the availability of grazing for cattle and the various internal power dynamics had an impact on the gradual migration of the Xhosa peoples towards the south-west,[14] intensifying their contact with the Khoisan people. The different groups of Khoi and San[15] had their own long history of settlement, intermingling, and strife, which I do not focus on here.[16] Those who came into contact with the Xhosa very often did for similar reasons of life and subsistence, which led to overlapping land use and competition. Intensified contact between the Xhosa and the Khoisan brought into play a range of interactions: on the one hand, cultural influence (especially notable in respect of language and religion); on the other, affected trade relations with the Khoisan. Sometimes matters became heated, causing tensions to flare up, and sometimes escalated into war. Nonetheless, over time, the Xhosa emerged as the more powerful group, leading to the incorporation of some Khoisan into Xhosa groups.

---

[12] Switzer, *Power and resistance*, pp. 34–35: "The Bantu-speaking chiefdoms of the eastern Cape never developed centralised states to the degree that the Zulu and Swazi did in the early nineteenth century, but the exact nature of the state and its role in these African societies have been the source of considerable controversy. According to social anthropologist David Hammond-Tooke, the Xhosa polity, for example, resembled a 'tribal cluster' of genealogically related but politically independent chiefdoms. Historian Jeff Peires, however, maintains the Xhosa polity was more like a segmentary state that had supplanted earlier, clan-based polities. Individual Xhosa political units may have been autonomous, but they were never independent of the paramount chief or of the genealogically related chiefdom. The paramount was the head of a discernible Xhosa 'nation' sharing a common language, royal lineage, and geographical origin. [...] Segmentation provided the crucial social mechanism for expansion in a genealogically related chiefdom like the Xhosa, but it never threatened the essential unity of the Xhosa people before the colonial era".

[13] Reader's Digest, *Illustrated history*, p. 64; Switzer, *Power and resistance*, p. 29.

[14] Switzer, *Power and resistance*, pp. 33–34.

[15] Cf. Switzer, *Power and resistance*, pp. 17–22.

[16] Later I will give an overview of Mabona's own views on the earliest history of Khoisan and Xhosa encounters – cf. Part 2, sections 7 and 9.

Lineage was a significant factor in Xhosa social structure, but the outer limits of Xhosa society were not determined on ethnic or geographical, but on political terms, in the sense that people such as Khoisan, survivors of shipwrecks along the coast, or renegade slaves were incorporated into Xhosa communities, provided that they accepted the ruling authorities (this is not to downplay the significant trauma which might be involved in such assimilation or to deny that the Khoi especially adopted various strategies to avoid such assimilation).[17]

To the north-east of the Xhosa lived the Thembu and Mpondo, whose social organisation and practices resembled those of the Xhosa. These groups too had to deal with the same dynamics of decentralisation and attempts to consolidate power. The groups interacted and interfered in each other's internal politics and sometimes intermarried.

2. Accelerated change: A typology of mounting conflict[18]

The snapshot above suggests how life in the south-eastern part of what is now South Africa developed over centuries, as people engaged with the complexities of everyday life and negotiated a wide variety of interrelations between groups. Then, during the last third of the eighteenth century, a group of migrant and settling Dutch farmers[19] were added to this mix, bringing with them the cultural heritage, ideas, ways of life, and the technical advantages of belonging to the sphere of influence of the Cape-based Dutch East India Company. They valued their autonomy, but remained dependent on the Cape for ammunition and various cultural goods, as well as symbolic goods, such as religious rituals.[20] They brought with them, first, the material and symbolic influence of the Cape and, then, after 1806, the administrative, political, and finally military power of the British Empire.[21]

---

[17] Peires, *The house of Phalo*, pp. 19, 23.
[18] For this section, see Leonard Thompson, *A history of South Africa* (revised fourth edition, by Lynn Berat), New Haven and London: Yale University Press, 2014, Chapter 2.
[19] The cultural complexities of this group are not of concern here.
[20] Switzer, *Power and resistance*, p. 48. For an overview of the relations between the Cape Colony and the *trekboere*, cf. Thompson, *A history of South Africa*, Chapter 2.
[21] "England's privileged position is obviously merely the consequence of the global dominance it has enjoyed since the French Revolution. The dynamism of its trade, and then of its industry; its demographic vitality, which was able to sustain strong overseas emigration; and last but

The Dutch considered themselves superior to both the Khoisan and the Xhosa. They based this perception on different appearances, presumed cultural superiority, and difference of religious conviction (even though they appear to have adhered selectively to recognisable tenets of Christian faith). Admittedly, their horses and firepower, as well as their ideas about private property and their desire to live without a state, were substantial factors of difference. But they had a lot in common with the Xhosa: most were not very literate, they sometimes wore similar clothing, used similar techniques for constructing housing, practised subsistence living, and relied on what nature provided for their survival. They shared a similar view of the social and economic significance of cattle, and their practical concerns regarding grazing were similar. The insistence of the Dutch farmers on individual land ownership contrasted with the communal view of the Xhosa, but neither of these groups saw land as a mere commodity as the British later did. Finally, the Dutch farmers' ideas about labour were closer to those of the Xhosa than to the capitalist wage-labour system introduced a century later. Perhaps even in their sense of superiority they were similar to the Xhosa, who, it seems, saw themselves as superior to the San (perhaps not even considering the San human[22]).[23] These similarities opened the way for an exchange of labour and trade. But, quite soon, another logical possibility took precedence: the overlapping interests of the Dutch and the Xhosa led to tension and then to mortal conflict. Disputes about land, grazing, cattle, and other livestock, aggravated by prejudices and other social or political frustrations, ended in killings.

The British, taken as a group, were an awkward combination of supremacist ideas and liberal egalitarian intuitions, of sheer military brutality and a desire for organising and order. They too were a source and later agents of conflict and ultimately war (from the first occupation of the Cape at the end of the century, 1795–1802, and later during the second occupation, from 1806 onwards). Whatever the differences and tensions between the Dutch and British may have been, the long-term outcome for those on the receiving end, the Khoisan and Xhosa, was quite similar (see discussion below).

However, this situation cannot be simply schematised as a stand-off between the Xhosa and a combined group of Europeans. Both the Dutch and the British

---

not least, its status as the leading maritime power, as much by the number of its merchant ships as by the superiority of its warships, enabled its leaders to impose their will and their decisions in most of the colonial conflicts". Jacques Frémeaux, *Les empires coloniaux. Une histoire-monde*. Paris: CNRS éditions, 2012, pp. 56–57. My translation.

[22] Peires, *The house of Phalo*, p. 138.
[23] Giliomee, *The Afrikaners*, p. 58; Switzer, *Power and resistance*, pp. 47–48, 85–86.

entered into alliances *and* conflicts with the Khoisan who, in turn, sometimes sided with some Xhosa groups, and sometimes sided against them. By and large, the Dutch were antagonistic to the British, with whom relations remained tense even though, at times, they pursued the same objectives. Sometimes agreements were made between the Xhosa and the Dutch, only to be complicated because of intra-group differences on either the Xhosa or the Dutch side. Once the Cape came under British rule, the Khoisan, Xhosa, and Dutch all equally wanted to get out from under it. Intermittent conflict arose and continued three quarters into the nineteenth century: a series of attacks and retaliations were followed by new agreements (real or treacherous) and new alliances (real or not). The British co-opted the help of other groups such as the Mfengu and Thembu in their relentless fight against the Xhosa, and internal dissension and conflict among the Xhosa were exploited by the new powers in the region.

This typological rendering of the tragic situation which emerged at the end of the eighteenth century should suffice to give an impression of the forces at play in the formation of the world that we focus on in this book. This fraught situation gradually led to the military and eventually total political dominance by the British in the south-eastern region.

Meanwhile, the cultural life described above either continued or was adapted to the new circumstances: people married, worked, traded, and devised plans to survive and prosper. The Xhosa, for instance, traded copper, obtained through mediation of the Khoisan, to the Thembu and the Mpondo people.[24] This is important: our attention falls mainly on the area farther to the east of this zone of conflict, but the conflict had knock-on effects upto this region. Similarly, the lifeworld of the Dutch and British changed because of other dramatic changes – both in the larger southern African region and in the world. I would now like to turn to these changes, which will take us from the eighteenth century to the formation of the unified South African state.

3. A changing region in a changing world

Bearing in mind these mounting conflicts, what were the general social and political trends that take us from the end of the eighteenth century to the formation of the Union of South Africa in 1910? Let us describe the general tendencies of

---

[24] Switzer, *Power and resistance*, p. 44.

the larger region and include some observations about the international situation of the region in this period.

3.1 Spread of Boers and British expansion

The biggest losers in this fray were undoubtedly the *Khoisan*, who were either assimilated into Xhosa groups or become labourers for the Dutch. Some survivors fled to the north. Freed slaves and their descendants, the descendants of mixed relations, and then also the Khoisan – a heterogeneous mix of people – were gradually administrated into a group named the Coloureds.[25] The Coloureds shared some social institutions, such as schools, with people of European descent. They also shared a language with the Dutch/Afrikaans speakers, and the Christian faith for those who were not Muslim, but their sociopolitical destiny was to be segregated gradually into a separate racial group, provided with their own institutions (or left without any).[26]

On the other side of the spectrum is the extension of the *British* colony, which imposed its law on the region and placed everything in the region under its regulation based in the Cape: labour relations, jurisprudence, language policies, religion, etc. An important element of British policy was the abolition of the slave trade, and then of slavery. Initially, the formal economy grew well.[27] However, as will be explained below (in §3.2), the general impact of the British on the entire territory was less positive.

The *Dutch* arrived at various compromises with their new circumstances. Under the British, they lost much of their autonomy; those who stayed on in the region were, however great their frustration may have become, mostly aligned with the British. But a significant minority fled north (with their Coloured labourers) in a series of attempts to realise the dream of independent and even stateless existence.[28] This in turn led to many confrontations with the existing

---

[25] Aspects of historical orientation to the "Coloureds" can be found in Mohamed Adhikari's *Not white enough, not black enough: Racial identity in the South African coloured community*. Athens: Ohio University Press, 2005.
[26] Cf. Thompson, *A history of South Africa*, pp. 65–66, 113.
[27] See Jeffrey Peires, "How the Eastern Cape lost its edge to the Western Cape: The political economy in the Eastern Cape on the eve of Union", in Greg Ruiters (ed.), *The fate of the Eastern Cape. History, politics and social policy*. Scottsville: UKZN Press, 2011, pp. 42–59.
[28] The complex assessment of the causes for this move need not detain us here. The most sympathetic reading of South African history from the point of view of the Afrikaners is that by Giliomee, *The Afrikaners*.

inhabitants of the respective regions these Dutch people entered. Here the temptation to revive old Frontier relations of domination with Africans proved to be irresistible.[29] This interaction ranged between agreements and treaties at one end of the spectrum to war and massacres at the other. A number of independent republics were set up (most significantly, the Orange Free State and the Zuid-Afrikaansche Republiek); however, these were soon in turn the target of the British empire. Although the state in each of these republics was initially unable to impose its authority and power over the local chiefdoms, the political organisation of the republics already laid the foundation for later relations with Africans. Despite the setback of themselves being colonised at the end of the South African War (1899–1902), the republics already anticipated the decisive role they – together with Dutch/Afrikaans-speaking people in the whole country – would play in shaping twentieth-century South Africa. Over this period the Afrikaans language emerged (although it also had earlier Cape slave origins). Gradually among Afrikaans people, the constructs of peoplehood, an identity, a language, a history, and a calling were generated.[30] This contributed to consolidate them, their ideals, and struggles, and laid the foundations for the later extension of these constructs into Afrikaner nationalism.

Whereas the descendants of the Dutch were eventually able to regain their social and political position in relative independence from the British at unification in 1910, the *Xhosa* and other African peoples in South Africa still had to wage a very long struggle for independence, until the end of the twentieth century and, indeed, beyond. However, in our period of interest, and more specifically the half-century from 1860 to 1910, according to Peires, the Eastern Cape region acquired its enduring features: the waning influence of the Cape liberal tradition; the destruction of a peasant economy, together with the rapid rise of migrant labour; and, finally, the inability of local elites to play their few remaining cards to the political and economic advantage of the people of the region.[31]

---

[29] Cf. Thompson, *A history of South Africa*, p. 103.
[30] Cf. Thompson, *A history of South Africa*, p. 135; Philip Bonner, "South African Society and Culture, 1910-1948", in Robert Ross, Anne Kelk Mager, and Bill Nasson (eds.), *The Cambridge history of South Africa. Volume 2*: 1885-1994. Cambridge: Cambridge University Press, pp. 254–318, here pp. 270–274.
[31] Peires, "How the Eastern Cape lost its edge...", p. 43.

3.2 British domination and its effects on Xhosaland and beyond

Irrespective of the details of the repeated wars in the region, the outcome was the subjugation of the Xhosa by the British, a fate that overcame all the African groups in what was to become South Africa. Their territory was gradually limited, then reduced; peoples were strategically divided and/or relocated and placed under new command or rule.[32] In Xhosaland and elsewhere in southern Africa, some Africans were still to enjoy some autonomy, but henceforth their "autonomy" was at best already framed by a system of foreign values, influences, and pressures. Initially, the Cape nominally endorsed non-racialism, so those African men who had the required property at their disposal enjoyed the franchise in the colony; however, this franchise was steadily eroded.[33]

The subjugating effects of direct armed confrontation aside, the authority of chiefs was diminished and "autonomy" increasingly meant the introduction of indirect rule, making chiefs responsible to the colonial authorities for the conduct of their tribespeople.[34] These authorities could intervene and interfere in Xhosa life with financial support from Britain with the ostensible justification of "civilising" the Africans, funding mission schools, and establishing some medical facilities for the Xhosa.[35] British rule gradually transformed the law and courts, administration and commerce, and exercised pressure in matters of education and religion.

The magnitude of these dramatic changes forced Xhosaland, and in similar ways most of the rest of the subcontinent, gradually to surrender its traditional ways "in the days of their independence",[36] to accept complex compromises, and end with a number of dysfunctionalities, never to turn back again. But this was only the start of many radical changes. Let us consider these changes over a long century from the perspective of Xhosaland.

---

[32] Switzer, Power and resistance, p. 61. For an overview, cf. Roger Southall, *South Africa's Transkei. The political economy of an 'independent' Bantustan*. London: Heinemann, 1982, pp. 60–67.
[33] Sheridan Johns and Gail Gerhart, *Protest and hope, 1882-1934*. Volume 1 of From *protest to challenge. A documentary history of African politics in South Africa, 1882-1990* (second edition), Pretoria: Jacana, 2014, p. 9; Mahmood Mamdani, *Citizen and subject. Contemporary Africa and the legacy of late colonialism*. Princeton: Princeton University Press, 1996, p. 69.
[34] Thompson, *A history of South Africa*, p. 98. Later, a form of "direct rule" through appointed headmen was instituted in the Transkei region (see Chapter 2, § 3, p. 46-47).
[35] Switzer, *Power and resistance*, p. 66.
[36] This is the subtitle of Peires's 1981 book *The house of Phalo*.

3.3 Changes from the Xhosaland perspective

Economy and labour

The south-western corner of Africa, the Cape, played a role in world trade for a long time, providing and buying commodities (agricultural) and labour (including slaves). However, this international role remained fairly limited, while local trade and trading with the interior slowly developed. Simultaneously, the Khoisan were progressively demoted from commercial partners to labourers – a fate later shared by the Africans of the Eastern Cape and then of the entire region.

Xhosa trade with the Dutch pre-dated settlement by the Dutch in the Eastern Cape by a long half-century. This trade then continued, fluctuating with the other contingencies of their interactions, and continued along similar paths with the British. From the nineteenth century onwards, items of English or European manufacture gradually entered these exchanges. From before the middle of the nineteenth century, the Xhosa sold agricultural produce to the British for export to North America.[37] Forms of trade with the Cape Colony were also internalised into inter-Xhosa practices. Paradoxically, while rising conflict started to close some commercial doors to the Xhosa, this conflict opened up possibilities for new partnerships and thus an expansion of existing trade relations.[38] This situation had diverse consequences. Some Xhosa people responded to the conditions by adapting to the new commercial forms and possibilities, which involved a shift to commercial agricultural production.[39] Some were able to consolidate a reasonable degree of autonomy on the basis of their ability to produce surplus goods, so, by the end of the nineteenth century, there were a substantial number of professional African farmers in the Eastern Cape.[40] However, many others had no or insufficient land, or could not manage to make the transition to the new form of production under demanding circumstances, and they became poorer and eventually destitute.[41] These conditions arose due to the variety of cultural artefacts that Dutch and British culture had to offer and, more significantly, the rise of world capitalism behind this offering.[42]

---

[37] Peires, *The house of Phalo*, p. 103.
[38] On the specific situation of the Xhosa, see the opening page of Peires's "How the Eastern Cape lost its edge…"
[39] Southall, *South Africa's Transkei*, pp. 68–69.
[40] Switzer, *Power and resistance*, p. 88.
[41] Southall, *South Africa's Transkei*, pp. 71–72.
[42] See, on the diverse origins of capitalism, also outside of Europe: Jürgen Kocka, *Geschichte des Kapitalismus*. Munich: Verlag C.H. Beck, 2017.

In traditional Xhosa culture, there was no labourer class (except if one wants to read the role of women in these societies as that of labourers[43]), but a working class formed as a consequence of the events outlined above. Xhosa people started working for Dutch farmers under circumstances ranging from forced labour by abducted Xhosa people, to a free exchange of labour for (modest) payment. As colonial power progressively expanded, newly settled British and Dutch farms also made use of workers – notably, without any symmetrical position existing regarding Xhosa land. Under certain circumstances throughout the two centuries to follow, some labourers would maintain a form of home in the Xhosa territory, while working for whites for most of the year, already putting into place the form of migrant work so typical of South African industries in the twentieth century. The phenomenon of landless, black labour tenants persists to this day.

Labour – particularly that provided by the Khoisan and Africans[44] – was subject to control and legislation from early on. Up to the beginning of the nineteenth century, African labour in the colony was prohibited, but the need for labourers in the expanding market overcame such regulation.[45] Finally, great numbers of Xhosa were allowed to enter the Cape Colony to be integrated into the workforce there. But here (as under other circumstances of colonisation, for example, in Zululand/Natal, where Africans were transformed by legislation into foreigners), the colonial power was never strong enough to overcome a contradiction that was constitutive of that power: it wanted to keep the Africans out, but the territory that was demarcated in this way could flourish economically only by drawing on the cheap labour which only those same Africans could provide. In brief, the homestead-based system of subsistence existence gradually made way for forms of labour and agriculture that offered at least some surplus production for markets. This was de facto a step in the direction of the integration of the labour force into a developing capital-based economy.[46]

Everyday life

Changes in economic relations and practices had an enormous impact beyond labour relations, to affect everyday life, as Switzer illustrates:

---

[43] Peires, *The house of Phalo*, pp. 103–104.
[44] The point here is that the different groups shared the same fate and, obviously, not to claim that Khoisan were not African.
[45] Switzer, *Power and resistance*, p. 84.
[46] Switzer, *Power and resistance*, pp. 86–88.

Currencies no longer favored were soon eliminated. The traders flooded the market with beads, for example, so they were worthless and could not be used by Africans in commercial transactions. Nevertheless, almost every traveller crossing the Fish River from the 1830s was in contact with Africans seeking to exchange whatever they had for European goods. The British-made Witney blanket, for example, supplanted the Xhosa rawhide kaross as a staple item of clothing in a single generation. Although numbers of traders were killed during the War of 1834-35 and frontier trade for some time thereafter slumped to below twenty thousand pounds a year, the Xhosa were now firmly in the colony's economic orbit. Women, for example, would spend less time in the gardens with the introduction of plow agriculture, and they gradually stopped making household utensils, clothing, or ornaments. European-made goods would supply the basic necessities, and among the Ciskei Xhosa at least most indigenous crafts were no longer being practiced by the 1880s.[47]

The practice of compelling slaves and labourers to carry passbooks when they moved pre-dates our snapshot period of the later eighteenth century (discussed in §1, above). Then, the dawn of industrial mining saw the systematic implementation of passes.[48] The other side of the successive pass systems is the enormous dislocations or "resettlements" that I refer to again later (see pp. 76 and 105).

The development of indirect rule (as described above, p. 28) turned the remnants of African settlement in rural areas into places of struggle for the heart of tradition. However, these struggles occurred in a framework of economic and political pressures which would make the interests of the colonial state weigh heavily on all parties.[49]

Religion

Although it is not possible to reconstruct in detail the historical development of Xhosa religion before the eighteenth century, it certainly incorporated some

---

[47] Switzer, *Power and resistance*, p. 85.
[48] Thompson, *A history of South Africa*, p. 121.
[49] Cf. Mamdani, *Citizen and subject*, p. 22.

elements of Khoisan religion.⁵⁰ Familiarity with Khoisan religious ideas, notably a stronger profile of a positive and a negative transcendent power than in traditional Xhosa religion, may have facilitated the subsequent adoption of Christian ideas of a God and a Devil by some Xhosa people.⁵¹ The idea of the creation of humankind has a parallel in Xhosa imagery that appears to be fairly readily reinforced by Christian imagery of creation. The Christian belief in resurrection was also well received in terms of Xhosa belief. These were of course tendencies and not the rule.

How Christian ideas came into circulation in this part of the world is a topic that we will return to later (see Chapter 2, §4). For now, it is important to note the effects of Christian missions.⁵² Whatever the intentions of each respective missionary or society may have been, the overall effect was never dissociated from the importation of Western culture and its paraphernalia. At the same time, the violence of colonial expansion repeatedly led to a rekindling of traditional views and opposition to Christianity, which came from the same world. The missions themselves were quite ambiguous: some mission stations became places of refuge, and missionaries did what they could to advance the legal and practical position of the Khoisan and Africans, but sometimes their ideas of conversion sat all too snugly with ideas about "true civilization" which helped to turn free humans into productive labourers.

---

50   Mabona's "long essay" (discussed in Part 2, §7) devotes a number of pages to the Khoisan-Xhosa relation in matters of religion, cf. "The interaction and development of different religions in the Eastern Cape in the late eighteenth and early nineteenth Centuries, with special reference to the first two Xhosa prophets", London, School of Oriental and African Studies, pp. 1–12.
51   Peires, *The house of Phalo*, p. 65.
52   Mabona articulated the context of religious change in the period under discussion in these dramatic terms: "We have witnessed how in the eighteenth century the massive confrontation with an alien race and an alien culture evoked radical reactions in Xhosa society. Pride of race and material greed on the part of the colonists were merely met with disdain and armed resistance by the Xhosa. But cultural aggression caused fear and consternation that gave rise to strange and abnormal syndromes of behaviour among the Xhosa. This spiritual crisis was deepened when the missionaries arrived in the Eastern Cape in 1816. Here was a massive and direct confrontation with an alien culture that caused in the Xhosa polity an acute crisis of identity. [...] One need only read the reports of the London Missionary Society and Basil Holt's 'Joseph Williams' to see what wave of religious frenzy and hysteria was raised in the first encounters of the Xhosa and other indigenous peoples of South Africa with missionary evangelisation" (DP, pp. 300–301). Marcel Dischl (*Transkei for Christ. A history of the Catholic Church in the Transkeian territories*. No place: no publisher, 1982, pp. 23–41) gives an overview of Protestant missions in his introduction to his history of Catholicism in the Transkei region.

Under these circumstances, some Christian ideas were adopted, but they were transformed to fit the traditional views and the personal insights of diviners and other people. This led to variants leaning more to the traditional and/or militant versions (cf. Nxele/Makhanda[53]) or more pacifist versions closer to the faith of the missionaries (cf. Ntsikana[54]). But in both cases, the relation between religious persuasion and political action was very close.[55]

African politics, anti-colonial resistance, and nationalism in Xhosaland

Xhosa responses to these events cannot be reduced to the military, cultural, and economic spheres. In the years before the Union, there were some protest movements (even if one omits outright military and other violent opposition), demonstrating a variety of orientations and convictions.

Movements that fought for equal franchise started to form in the Eastern Cape; for example, in 1882, there was the foundation of Imbumba Yama Nyama, a political organisation. In the 1880s, J.T. Jabavu started two newspapers for critical political journalism on concerns closer to Xhosaland and to the Cape.[56] New religious factions, such as Nehemiah Tile's Thembu Church and Mokone's Ethiopian Church (both established at the end of the nineteenth century), became vehicles for cultural politics and calls for autonomy. These instances represent opposing strategies: politics of liberal values or of African-centred values and modes of thinking.[57]

---

[53] See DP, pp. 301–303, 304.
[54] See DP, pp. 303–305.
[55] Cf. Peires, *The house of Phalo*, pp. 73–74.
[56] Johns and Gerhart, *Protest and hope*, pp. 7–8; critical of these people who had enjoyed a formal education in the mission schools, Simphiwe Hlatswhayo claims: "The elite disassociated themselves from any nationalistic movement such as the Ethiopianism movement or the Africa for Africans movement – even from the trade union movement". cf. *Education and independence. Education in South Africa, 1658-1988*, Westport and London: Greenwood Press, 2000, p. 41.
[57] Johns and Gerhart, *Protest and hope*, pp. 12, 14. "Counterposed to the hopes of those who clung to the promise of an inclusive Cape liberalism were those of an Ethiopian orientation. They argued that African self-preservation and advancement could best be realized through exclusively African organizations, acting with only minimal reference to white-defined standards of 'civilization'. This perspective was a forerunner of subsequent Africanist philosophies whose main thrust was to challenge white power through black unity and initiative rather than relying on cooperation with supportive whites. Neither position was completely exclusive of the other, but they were two distinct poles around which African politics would continue to revolve". (p. 14)

The first decade of the twentieth century demonstrated two other strategic options: the first option was armed protest against taxes, as was adopted in the Bambatha rebellion of 1906; the other option was to write petitions or compile resolutions, or even to lobby in London to air objections. The Bambatha rebellion was suppressed with military force; the non-violent option had no significant effect.[58] In these years, the Africans were not able to unify in order to set up a united front of resistance.

3.4 Changes from the broader South African perspective

Thus far, I have focused mostly on the Xhosa. However, their history has to be read against the bigger context of southern Africa. Leonhard Thompson writes that, by 1870, "[s]outhern Africa was occupied by numerous small agrarian societies, loosely linked by the dynamic forces of settler expansionism and merchant capitalism originating in northwestern Europe".[59] Despite these expansions, as a British colony, the Cape Colony remained tiny in proportion to the southern African region, compared to the settlement by people of European descent in North America at the same time.[60] The discovery of gold and diamonds and the subsequent mining and industrial revolution was to continue and amplify considerably the social dynamics preceding these events.[61]

The British consolidated their power over South Africa as a region[62] by military subjugation of the Boer republics – and with them, of course, the Africans and others who had progressively been forced by these republics to live in them – by the end of the South African War (1899–1902), but, in the long run, majority

---

[58] Johns and Gerhart, *Protest and hope*, pp. 16–20.
[59] Thompson, *A history of South Africa*, p. 107; and see overview, Thompson, *A history of South Africa*, pp. 107–109.
[60] Thompson, *A history of South Africa*, pp. 53, 108 (referring to the 1870s).
[61] Many historians see the discovery of gold and diamonds as a turning point in South Africa's history. By contrast, Peires, in "How the Eastern Cape lost its edge...", p. 43, argues that "[t]he great Nongqawuse cattle killing of 1856-7 marks the effective end of the frontier period in the EC – the period during which indigenous African people might reasonably have hoped to stop white expansion and preserve something of the political and economic integrity of the pre-colonial Xhosa way of life". I bear in mind both arguments.
[62] Not that there was simple harmony between what happened in the Cape Colony and British rule over the empire; cf. Thompson, *A history of South Africa*, p. 133. For the constitutional basis of such disagreement and the relevance thereof in practice see Peires, "How the Eastern Cape lost its edge...", p. 45.

sentiment was not pro-empire.[63] Whatever the different parties' interests, the Union of South Africa was formed in 1910. With some minor exceptions, all voters in the Union were white, and since the Dutch/Afrikaans-speaking section of voters was the biggest, they resurfaced at the beginning of the twentieth century as a major political power.

But let us look at some developments over this long century in more detail.

State form and administration

After 1806, the British imposed their laws, language, systems of administration, etc. to relativise or replace the Dutch ones. Whatever the particularities of British (and previously Dutch) governance, the way in which Africans were integrated into colonial rule displayed significant similarities to what had happened and was still to happen across its empire. The theoretical means I use to discuss this situation are taken from Mamdani's work on South Africa, which he claims applies to British colonies in Africa and sometimes further afield. Jacques Frémeaux, who studied colonialism as a global phenomenon, confirms the similarity of colonial practices everywhere. What he calls "legal dualism" consisted in granting indigenous peoples the nationality of the colonising power, without making them citizens; ironically, the colonising countries were democratic, and continued to claim to be so, while they did not extend the values of democracy to the colonised people.[64]

What Mamdani calls "regimes of differentiation"[65] were invented for contexts in which the native population was not exterminated, but rather remained by far the majority. This process consisted of two interdependent mechanisms. First, the state (or colony) was bifurcated, which entailed dividing the population in two: the "civilized" who were to be citizens in full right, and the "natives" who were destined to remain under the guardianship of the "civilized". Separate institutions were created for each. On paper, the "natives" were granted the freedom to continue traditional ways of life in designated rural areas. The colonial states then governed the "natives" indirectly by incorporating traditional leadership into the framework of the state (when it was not created from scratch): matters of family and community, customary law, and culture remained the preserves of the

---

[63] Thompson, *A history of South Africa*, p. 147. Hence Marc Ferro's ironic reference to the independence of settlers as the "highest stage of imperialism" (*Histoire des colonisations. Des conquêtes aux indépendances XIIIe-XXe siècle*. Paris: Seuil, pp. 326–334), referring to Rhodesia and South Africa, with a pun on Lenin.
[64] Frémeaux, *Les empires coloniaux*, pp. 264–265.
[65] Mamdani, *Citizen and subject*, p. 7.

traditional leadership, while the central government assumed power over people's rights and imposed "modern" (Western) law, the formal economy, international relations, etc. However, in reality, this "freedom" involved being subjected to displacements, the manipulation of traditional leadership forms, and overall framing by the "civilized" state. Furthermore, when indirectly ruled "natives" then had to sojourn inside the domain designated for the "citizens" (urban areas, but usually also large tracts of rural land), the "natives" were subject to laws of direct rule, the kingpin of which was their exclusion from all political rights.[66]

Such a bifurcated system requires a "justification" that ultimately depends on the "deliberate and conscious conflation of racial and cultural distinctions".[67] This is the core idea which would later subtend twentieth-century segregation and apartheid in South Africa. The specifics of the South African situation were not determined by the general logic of colonial governance, since this was shared with many other colonised regions. Rather, in my opinion, one has to add to this the interaction between the Afrikaans and English power blocks and then the specific intensification of the situation, established under British rule, through the apartheid laws after 1948, and all these factors must be understood in a context of uncommonly high levels of urbanisation, industrialisation, and wealth creation, coupled with extreme inequality.

Obviously, this advanced bifurcation could not be instituted overnight. After all, there were liberal and Christian forces and tendencies at work even in British law, to the point where equality before the law was a declared principle of law in the Colony. Still, this principle did not always match the practice and in the long run it was not upheld. Hence, Africans (but, in different ways, also Coloureds) became foreigners in the country of their birth. This was reflected in budgetary allocations and institutional arrangements. Africans were not, however, exempt from taxes.

Agriculture and mining

The nineteenth century saw a rapid transformation of the economic landscape. Wool production began (in the Eastern Cape by the mid nineteenth century),

---

[66] Mamdani, *Citizen and subject*, pp. 16–18, Chapters 3 to 5. However, the situation was often different in the Transkei – on the direct rule of that region, cf. Switzer, *Power and resistance*; Southall, *South Africa's Transkei*, p. 88.

[67] Martin Legassick, "British hegemony and the origins of segregation in South Africa, 1901-14", in William Beinart and Saul Dubow (eds.), *Segregation and apartheid in twentieth-century South Africa*. London and New York: Routledge, 1995, pp. 43–56, here p. 50 (referring to the period after the 1899–1902 war).

followed by ostrich farming and sugar cane plantations.⁶⁸ To advance the sugar industry, workers were imported from India, most of whom would stay on and become a permanent part of South African society, contributing to the region's social diversity.

It is only with slight exaggeration that Hart and Padayachee claim that, by the last three decades of the nineteenth century, "[t]he great mining houses *were* South African capitalism at this time".⁶⁹ Mining was practised in the southern African region long before European people arrived. However, the discovery of very large deposits of diamonds (1867) and gold (1886) in the interior accelerated changes in South Africa, not only regarding mining, but virtually every aspect of life, with a wide ripple effect – in different ways in different sections of society. This enormous change could happen not only because of the quality and diversity of deposits, but also because of the advanced science and technology, coupled with financing and markets, for which the connection with the world financial capital at the time, London, was a boon.⁷⁰ Initially, mining required solid financing, but it soon generated a lot of money and became independent. However, two additional factors were needed to help mining flourish. The first was predictable coordination of business with the state. One of the reasons for Britain's casting

---

68   Switzer, *Power and resistance*, pp. 83–84; Stanley Trapido, "Imperialism, settler identities, and colonial capitalism: the hundred-year origins of the 1899 South African war", in Robert Ross, Anne Kelk Mager, and Bill Nasson (eds.), *The Cambridge history of South Africa*. Volume 2: 1885-1994. Cambridge: Cambridge University Press, pp. 66–101, here pp. 71–72.

69   Keith Hart and Vishnu Padayachee, "A history of South African capitalism in national and global perspective", in *Transformation: Critical Perspectives on Southern Africa* 81/82, 2013, pp. 55–85, here p. 63. See further: "South Africa did not develop a staple export comparable to Australian wool and Canadian timber. All this changed with the discovery of diamonds at Kimberley in 1868 and of gold in the Rand around the same time. Suddenly from the 1870s South Africa became a major exporter of precious minerals. For three decades from the 1880s, South Africa participated fully in a globalisation process driven by imperial rivalry and haute finance (Polanyi 1944), with Britain at the centre of both", Hart and Padayachee, "A history of South African capitalism…", p. 62. They comment, furthermore, that "Charles Feinstein (2005) depicts South Africa as being trapped until now between its origin as an imperialist export enclave and an aspiration to become a fully modern industrial economy which has been frustrated by continuing reliance on cheap black labour. The two poles of this story are export enclave development and 'national capitalism', the attempt to harness economic growth for the benefit of all citizens. South Africa has seen two such attempts, the first launched between the wars for the benefits of Whites only (led by Afrikaners); this culminated in the apartheid regime installed after the Second World War. The second is the ANC government's drive to develop a genuinely inclusive national economy with the result that we have already indicated" (p. 60).

70   Cf. Trapido, "Imperialism, settler identities, and colonial capitalism…", p. 74.

its imperial net over the Dutch or "Boer" republics was that they were (or would become) an obstacle to this end.[71] Another reason was the fact that mining required cheap, reliable labour. For this, Africans (from the larger subcontinent), but also imported Chinese labour and some Dutch/Afrikaans people and other urban residents, were coerced into different levels of low-paid labour.

For millions of African men, this meant working most of the year in areas where they had no title to settle, or they were restricted to specific areas; they only returned home on holidays, and the women and the elderly had to maintain the continuity of the family. Everyday life at and around the mines was structured according to a more systematic instrumentalisation of racist relations dating from a previous era.[72] It may be noted that during the first decades, the greater industrial system also resulted in the emergence of some wealthy African farmers who provided food for the mines, and a considerable number of so-called poor whites who struggled to make a living in the new towns.[73]

From the point of view of infrastructure, the economic boost made possible the formation of a banking sector, and considerable extensions to the transport system, particularly the railroads. Postal and telegraph services[74] were also developed in response to greater urbanisation and industrialisation.

Education

During this period, sometimes more liberally inclined administrations provided education for some African children. However, broad-based schooling was not part of the agenda, even though some Western-styled education for Africans, provided almost exclusively by missions well into the twentieth century, was introduced and maintained. The curriculum transmitted Western cultural values; in fact, the political powers counted on this and subsidised mission education for this reason.[75] Unsurprisingly, the main purpose of mission-led education was to transmit Christianity, and the primary objective of teaching was to facilitate evangelisation; consequently, universalism and non-racialism were often part of the educational ethos.[76] Some of those educated through this

---

[71]   Trapido, "Imperialism, settler identities, and colonial capitalism...", pp. 86–87 (Trapido's entire chapter deals with the causes for the war); Hart and Padayachee, "A history of South African capitalism...", p. 64.
[72]   Cf. Thompson, *A history of South Africa*, pp. 112, 121.
[73]   Thompson, *A history of South Africa*, pp. 111–112, 132.
[74]   Thompson, *A history of South Africa*, p. 6.
[75]   Hlatshwayo, *Education and independence*, p. 31–32.
[76]   Hlatshwayo, *Education and independence*, p. 30.

system were integrated (to different degrees) in colonial society; often they came into conflict (or experienced tensions) with the remaining traditional authority of chiefs, or simply with traditional ideas and values as such.[77] Differences also arose between the older generation and the views of "urbanised" migrant labourers.[78]

The ambiguity of the missions played out in other ways too. Missionaries had an interest in local languages and started working on recording a linguistics of the Bantu languages. The Bible was translated into Tswana, Xhosa, and Southern Sotho by 1855.[79] The missionaries also started studying (sometimes representing and sometimes misrepresenting) Africans from an anthropological point of view,[80] making their work serviceable to invading administrators, but also archiving cultural heritage.

---

[77] Thompson, *A history of South Africa*, p. 113; Hlatshwayo, *Education and independence*, pp. 40–41, 45.

[78] Norman Etherington, Patrick Harries, and Bernard Mbenga, "From colonial hegemonies to imperial conquest, 1840-1880", in Carolyn Hamilton, Robert John Ross, and Bernard K. Mbenga (eds.), *The Cambridge history of South Africa, Volume 1: From early times to 1885*, New York: Cambridge University Press, 2010, pp. 319–391, here p. 319.

[79] For the history of the Bible translation into Xhosa, see Dischl, *Transkei for Christ*, pp. 38–39. It has now become quite common to refer, in English, to South African languages by using the word by which they are designated in those languages. Accordingly, I should have referred to Setswana, isiXhosa, and Sepedi. In this book, I do not follow this practice, simply because, for the sake of symmetry, I would then have to do the same for European languages – Deutsch, Nederlands, Français, etc. – which would be too awkward.

[80] Etherington, Harries, and Mbenga, "From colonial hegemonies...", 328–329.

CHAPTER 2

(DIS)UNION: THE WORLD OF MABONA'S YOUTH (1910 TO THE MID 1950s)

Although his childhood was spent in Xhosaland (the territory of the Transkei, as one should start calling it, following the historical developments to be recounted), the Union of South Africa, formed in 1910, was the backdrop of Mabona's entire youth and young adult life. I will start by situating the new country in an international perspective, then I will describe some of the major developments during the first four decades of its existence and gradually zoom in again on the situation in the Transkei region where our protagonist was born.

1. International and Union politics

With unification in 1910, the Union of South Africa was created as a self-governing dominion of the British Empire, so it remained a more or less willing member of an alliance of semi-autonomous communities under the British monarch.[1] The question of its borders had not been settled definitively, since the question of whether some neighbouring states and territories were to be incorporated within its borders[2] had not yet been resolved. Also, for some time to

---

[1] Thompson, *A history of South Africa*, p. 160.
[2] Bill Freund, "South Africa: The Union Years, 1910-1948. Political and economic foundations", in Robert Ross, Anne Kelk Mager, and Bill Nasson (eds.), *The Cambridge history of South Africa. Volume 2: 1885-1994*. Cambridge: Cambridge University Press, pp. 211–253, here pp. 244–245.

come, internal and external politics had to deal with the complex considerations of determining the Union's strategic belonging to, or resistance against, the British Empire and possible alliances or conflicts with the rising power that was Germany.

Internal politics was dominated by two issues: the relation between the former enemies, the Boers/Afrikaners and English-speaking people, who shared power among themselves, and the relations between this unlikely pairing and the other inhabitants of the country.

The first issue focused on such issues as class relations, national symbols and the relation to Britain. Afrikaners still felt the after-effects of the devastating South African War (coupled with the worst drought in ages), and had to address the development of so-called "white poverty"[3] and difficulties in adapting to urbanisation. On top of this, they were in competition with cheap black labour. But, through tough struggles, the white labourers succeeded in guaranteeing that they held positions involving semi-skilled work.[4] The issue of making the Union officially bilingual (English and Dutch, then Afrikaans) was therefore no trivial matter: apart from the symbolic value of recognition, it effectively opened the civil service (and subsequently private positions) to Afrikaans-speaking people. At the time, nobody in power dreamt of elevating any African language to the same level – creating yet another barrier to prosperity for the speakers of these languages.[5]

At the time, Afrikaners were the majority electorate and they succeeded in making this count. As a group, their material fate improved (but never to the level enjoyed by their English compatriots); nevertheless, this did not prevent many from enduring significant poverty, associated, amongst other things, with the 1929 depression.[6] Afrikaner politics ensured that Afrikaner interests and ideals remained on the stage of formal politics. Meanwhile, numerous organisations were founded to promote the interests of Afrikaners in an array of social domains.[7] Particularly from the 1930s, a specific form of Afrikaner Nationalism formed, out of which the National Party victory of 1948 would grow.

Afrikaner interests sometimes overlapped with those of the English-speaking population: for some, the overlap was the relation to British power (which led to South Africa's support for Britain in the Second World War); for many, it was

---

[3] Cf. Bonner, "South African Society and Culture...", pp. 259–263.
[4] Thompson, *A history of South Africa*, pp. 159–160; Southall, *South Africa's Transkei*, p. 31.
[5] Freund, "South Africa: The Union Years...", p. 213.
[6] Freund, "South Africa: The Union Years...", p. 227.
[7] Freund, "South Africa: The Union Years...", p. 231.

economic interests; for the overriding majority, it meant the consolidation of white power over black autonomy.[8]

The second issue, "race relations" as it came to be called, concerned the Coloureds and Asians/Indians, but primarily revolved around blacks (my use of these terms, henceforth, has to be understood as reflecting the historical classifications). Whatever remnants of representation remained for these groups (particularly in the Western Cape) were destined to be eliminated in the decades after the formation of the Union. The Union was designed for white domination of black people, as in other similar places shaped by British colonial influence, albeit in different ways, such as in the United States and Australia.

Legislation was passed to separate groups, maintaining social inequality where they interacted. The essence of these laws concerned land ownership, the establishment of areas for black settlement, the regulation of movement and settlement, the regulation of labour, and variants of all these categories to be applied to "Coloureds" and "Indians".[9] These laws of segregation were developed later in apartheid legislation in the strict sense after 1948. The underlying idea of "separation" should be used circumspectly.[10] One should not be hasty to typify these laws of unequal privilege and segregation as mechanisms of exclusion, since excluded people cannot contribute their labour to the economy and cannot be subject to taxes.[11] Manuel Castells has demonstrated how marginalisation is also a form of inclusion,[12] and this is the point here: the "non-whites" were integrated into the economic and state system of the Union of South Africa, but this was overwhelmingly at their expense and in order to make them productive for the Union's economy.

Focusing on land, successive laws restricted black ownership to just under, then just over, ten per cent of the country's land surface. In both cases, this is roughly similar to the division of land in Southern Rhodesia, but considerably lower than the situation in France's North African colonies.[13] In these black-

---

[8] Freund, "South Africa: The Union Years...", p. 234.
[9] Freund, "South Africa: The Union Years...", p. 235, also summarised by Elikia M'Bokolo, "Les pratiques de l'aparthéid", in Marc Ferro (ed.), *Le livre noir du colonialisme. XVIe – XXIe siècle: de l'extermination à la repentance*. Fayard/Pluriel: Paris, 2010, pp. 627–639.
[10] See also my comment on the contradiction of colonial power above (pp. 30) and the similar irony at work in apartheid (p. 105).
[11] On taxes, see, for example, Bonner, "South African Society and Culture...", p. 284.
[12] Manuel Castells, "The rise of the fourth world: informational capitalism, poverty, and social exclusion", in *End of millennium*, Oxford: Blackwell, 1998, Chapter 2. The fact that his argument is based on more recent events does not invalidate this insight.
[13] According to Frémeaux, *Les empires coloniaux*, pp. 147–148.

owned areas they enjoyed limited autonomy and could practise subsistence farming, under conditions instated before the Union (see Chapter 1, pp. 29-30). The flip side of this is that the majority of black men had to migrate to wage-earning work for their livelihoods. The consequence is that they lived for most or all of the year in white-owned territories as foreign labourers – where no land ownership was possible for them.[14] From the point of view of their employers and of the state, this movement of labourers had to be regulated carefully.

2. The economy

Despite recurrent recessions,[15] especially the Great Depression of 1929, which started with the Wall Street Crash in the United States and cascaded to the rest of the world, and its aftermath, which lasted well into the 1930s, the country enjoyed slow but uneven economic growth. Mining (primarily gold, but also diamonds and later coal) was ahead of the other sectors of the country (agriculture, infrastructure, commerce) and was to serve as the driver to develop other sectors of an otherwise largely undeveloped country.[16] Initiatives which had proven successful earlier, such as the production of ostrich feathers and wool, ran into difficulties, but the textile industry took off.[17] Generally, the South African economy resembled that of other colonial territories in consisting to a very large degree of the exportation of primary materials and foodstuffs. Nevertheless, important groups with a local base were established, such as De Beers and Anglo American in the mining sector or Standard Bank and Barclays Bank.[18]

The state subsequently succeeded in establishing significant institutions: the national electricity provider (ESCOM), a state-owned steel industry (ISCOR), the Reserve Bank, the South African Broadcasting Corporation (SABC), and the Council for Scientific and Industrial Research (CSIR).[19] All date from the middle of this period. Communications infrastructure was set up, and a transport network was developed (e.g. tarred roads and railways). Later in this period, in

---

[14] Southall, *South Africa's Transkei*, pp. 24–26.
[15] Bonner, "South African Society and Culture...", p. 260.
[16] Freund, "South Africa: The Union Years...", p. 211.
[17] Freund, "South Africa: The Union Years...", p. 221.
[18] Frémeaux, *Les empires coloniaux*, pp. 153–157; Hart and Padayachee, "A history of South African capitalism...", p. 68f.
[19] Freund, "South Africa: The Union Years...", p. 248.

the 1940s, the state also augmented its social spending (notably in its systems of school feeding, pension, and disability) on all population groups, but as can be expected, without changing the discriminating structure of distribution.[20]

More generally, labour laws steadily increased income rights and possibilities for white workers, while excluding most black people from these advantages. The same holds for housing, schooling, and access to medical services. Coloureds and Indians did marginally better than black people, having a few more social privileges, and in general earning a bit more too. Initially, Coloureds enjoyed more rights in the Western Cape than Africans; Indians faced fewer obstacles to enter business.[21]

Urbanisation increased steadily. Although urbanisation among Africans was less advanced than in the other population groups, by the end of the Second World War, they outnumbered other groups in the cities. Subsequent developments would gradually see the dismantling of racially mixed slums in the cities in favour of a typical urban development pattern in South Africa, where "locations", "informal settlements", and other residences of black people were located several kilometres away from the residents' places of work in the (separate) white and more affluent towns, cities, and suburbs.[22] Together with the reserves, this pattern of differential settlement was based on a legal order, and resulted in a racial differentiation of lifestyles that patently resembles the world described by Fanon at the beginning of the *Wretched of the earth*.

3. Separation – reserves – labour

The reserves were places of severe constraint. Generally, they were overpopulated and badly managed, and services were scarce. Wide-ranging poverty prevailed.[23] The situation increasingly deteriorated, making life hard and making it almost impossible to sustain any income-generating activity.[24] The population grew,

---

[20] Freund, "South Africa: The Union Years...", p. 241.
[21] Thompson, *A history of South Africa*, p. 171.
[22] Cf. Thompson, *A history of South Africa*, p. 170; Bonner, "South African Society and Culture...", p. 261.
[23] Southall, *South Africa's Transkei*, pp. 80–81.
[24] Freund's assessment on this point (in "South Africa: The Union Years...", p. 221) seems a bit more positive in general and reflects less deterioration than in Thompson, *A history of South Africa*. However, the overall picture remains bleak.

amongst other things because farm labourers were expelled to the reserves; at the same time, unequal trading conditions made it increasingly difficult to maintain the existing commercial agriculture in the reserves.[25] Bonner describes the Transkei region as reaching more or less subsistence-level self-sufficiency.[26]

In some cases, as in the Ciskei, the system of traditional leadership suffered a loss of legitimacy and vitality under the pressures of migration and the interference of the administration.[27] However, this does not mean that the traditional system of chiefs overall was dead or was reduced to a complete object of manipulation by powerful authorities from the outside. In other places, such as the Transkei, chieftaincy remained an object of contestation, depending on the region, the kind of chief in question, and the needs of the people. What remained of traditional life was as much an instrument people could use to advance their own interests as it was an object of de- or re-tribalization in the service of external political or economic interests. The point is that despite extreme constraints, local populations in the reserves were not mere passive objects, nor was the form of traditional culture static.[28]

The general model of indirect rule imposed on the reserves has to be qualified in the case of the Transkei in this era. When historians describe this situation rather as one of direct rule, they have in mind the fact that the region was administrated by a team of (white) regional magistrates under a Chief Magistrate. Overseeing tasks was delegated to appointed non-traditional headmen, rather

---

[25] Southall, *South Africa's Transkei*, pp. 74–75, 82–84.
[26] Bonner, "South African Society and Culture...", p. 280.
[27] Cf. Jeffrey Peires, "Ethnicity and Pseudo-ethnicity in the Ciskei", in William Beinart and Saul Dubow (eds.), *Segregation and apartheid in twentieth-century South Africa*, London and New York: Routledge, 1995, pp. 256–284. My focus here is only on the first four decades of the Union.
[28] This point is argued by William Beinart, "Chieftaincy and the concept of articulation: South Africa circa 1900-1950", in William Beinart and Saul Dubow (eds.), *Segregation and apartheid in twentieth-century South Africa*, London and New York: Routledge, 1995, pp. 176–188. Bonner (in "South African Society and Culture...", p. 275) summarises the major trends: "Nevertheless, some broader patterns or traditions are discernible beyond the chaos. The best known of these are the Transkei model of direct personal administration by white magistrates, sidelining chiefs and using appointed headmen, and the system of indirect rule through chiefs granted civil jurisdiction, which prevailed in Zululand and Natal. A much more diffuse Transvaal model ruled through chiefs and not headmen but was then reworked in each locality through the whims and idiosyncrasies of individual sub-native commissioners. The Orange Free State's one tiny reserve area had no tradition at all and was left largely to administer itself".

than to traditional chiefs.[29] The functions of the magistrates ranged from tax collection and dispute arbitration to the management of agriculture and promotion of political stability. Headmen took charge of tasks such as allocating territory, arbitrating civil disputes, and dealing with matters of private life through customary law.[30]

This system was designed to undermine the authority of the chiefs. Yet, an unintended consequence was that the chiefs, sidelined by the magistrates and headmen, were less compromised through involvement with the adversary and could thus retain "backstage" authority and influence – unable, however, to oppose the erosion of the chieftaincy in the long run.[31] However, in the late 1920s, when government opposition to remnants of traditional government had been successful, and a need for stricter control over reserve populations was identified, legislation was passed to reinvigorate tradition. In effect, this meant introducing measures for greater standardisation of customary law, according to its new legal status and power. This meant that the Transkei was effectively "retribalized", and this process was guided by the Natal model of indirect governance. Hence, the whole process was subject to what is called "the Shaka fallacy" – essentialising traditional culture to a particular preconceived patriarchal and authoritarian

---

[29] Southall, *South Africa's Transkei*, pp. 88–89. Mamdani also recognises the initial establishment of direct rule in the Transkei (CS, p. 66). He qualifies the subsequent system of administration through magistrates and headmen in the same region as "a form of rule that would closely approximate French-style indirect rule" (CS, p. 86).

[30] Switzer, *Power and resistance*, p. 95; Bonner, "South African Society and Culture…", p. 275. It seems that Mabona intended his generalisation to apply to all eras of Xhosa cultural life when he explained: "Most of the law among the Xhosa-speaking peoples is customary law. There is and has been in practice very little legislation. If any reference is made to some form of legislation, it will be in terms of *umthetho wale nkundla* ['the law of this court'], whereas the paterfamilias will speak in terms of *umthetho walo mzi* ['the law of this household']. Thus the guardians of legal customs are inkosi ['the chief'] and his amaphakathi ['councillors'] and *izibonda* ['local headmen'] at the national or tribal level, and abaninimzi ['the heads of homesteads'] at the family level. The role of diviners in the purely legal machinery is very indirect and the ancestors constitute really only the ultimate sanction in the public sphere" (DP, p. 251).

[31] Southall, *South Africa's Transkei*, p. 89. Bonner, "South African Society and Culture…", p. 275. Mamdani's insistence on noting the manipulation of tradition by colonial powers has to be situated in a larger economy of tradition creation – European and African – even to the point of Africans Europeanising and Europeans Africanising in the same practice, see Terence Ranger, "The invention of tradition in colonial Africa", in Eric Hobsbawm and Terence Ranger, *The invention of tradition*, Cambridge: Cambridge University Press, 1983, pp. 211–262, here p. 226.

view of it.³² Since such engineering is designed to undermine people's ability to adapt to changing circumstances, Taiwo calls it social freezing, or socio-cryonics.³³

According to the new dispensation, a council, representing mainly the reserve's upper class, existed alongside the administrative order. In principle, it deliberated on non-political matters; in practice, it made pronouncements on political issues, but it remained conservative and had no real powers.³⁴ In 1955, the council system was replaced by a Territorial Administration, which promoted the re-establishment of the chieftaincy at the expense of the headman system. Headmen were subsequently subordinated to the chiefs, but were still incorporated into the Bantu Authorities system.³⁵ The chiefs, in turn, had to negotiate their intermediary role between the population and the white state, the responsibilities of their office and the temptation to take advantage of a position of relative privilege and power. Thus the strategy of indirect rule was deployed.³⁶

The large-scale migration of men to the cities, which implied that more than half of working men were absent from the Transkei, had a significant knock-on effect, as women, children, and the elderly had to maintain subsistence farming.³⁷ Work opportunities existed outside the homestead, in commerce, in domestic service, in industries, or on farms where many of the people resided in any case, living, as Thompson observes, under circumstances fluctuating between paternalism and exploitation.³⁸ At the same time, the mines flourished, drawing on an ever-widening web of labourers from the reserves – the Transkei provided a third of all labourers in mines³⁹ – but also from other southern African countries. In 1936, when Mongameli Mabona was school-going age, a quarter of the male population, more than half of the work-aged men, were absent from the Transkei

---

32 Bonner, "South African Society and Culture...", pp. 275–283; Southall, *South Africa's Transkei*, pp. 104–105 (for Transkei). This fallacy is to be contrasted with a more anthropologically sound view provided by Terblanche, discussed in Mamdani, *Citizen and subject*, p. 45.
33 Olufemi Taiwo, *How colonialism preempted modernity in Africa*, Bloomington: Indiana University Press, 2010.
34 Southall, *South Africa's Transkei*, pp. 90–95.
35 Southall, *South Africa's Transkei*, pp. 97–98. For details, Southall, *South Africa's Transkei*, pp. 104–106.
36 Southall, *South Africa's Transkei*, p. 114.
37 Bonner, "South African Society and Culture...", p. 293; Southall, *South Africa's Transkei*, p. 77 (whose statistics refer to the mid 1930s).
38 Thompson, *A history of South Africa*, pp. 164–166. See also Bonner's depiction of paternalism as "involving some measure of quasi-kinship between farmer patriarch and labour tenant families" ("South African Society and Culture...", p. 285).
39 Southall, *South Africa's Transkei*, p. 78 (again referring to the 1930s).

most of the year.⁴⁰ These migrant workers, for whom the reserves were still something of a "home", lived most of their lives in a decidedly different urban or industrial world. At the same time, these conditions formed the backdrop for notable class differences within the Transkei, based primarily on differences of land and livestock ownership.⁴¹ Only a few found jobs were in the homeland itself, mostly as employees of the state, teachers, or members of the clergy.⁴²

4. Transkei: Culture, religion, education

In both the Transkei and Ciskei, two distinctive cultural strategies emerged: "red", traditionalist, leaning towards being anti-modern; versus "school", leaning towards Christianity, often with formal education. These strategies were reflected in people's dress, food, housing, and lifestyle choices. However, these approaches were not mutually exclusive, but rather denote tendencies on a spectrum.⁴³

Numerous cultural shifts took place under the influence of experiences in the cities, changing circumstances in the rural areas and negotiation between them, based on migratory labour: traditional forms of authority were challenged here; new dances were introduced there. New forms of sport (such as cricket) coexisted with old forms of sport (such as stick fighting).

New religious movements were formed, either exclusively home-grown, with messages of repentance and ethical reform (for example, the movement led by Nontetha Nkwenkwe) or with some institutional church influence or ideas from Marcus Garvey from North America (for example, those led by Enoch Mgijima and Wellington Buthelezi).⁴⁴

---

⁴⁰ Southall, *South Africa's Transkei*, p. 77. Absence of men from home in Transkei rose, roughly, from a quarter in 1910 to half in 1950 (much lower than Zululand's over 80%), cf. Bonner, "South African Society and Culture...", pp. 280, 255. Many men of Mabona's parents' generation would already have embarked on migration work in the mines.
⁴¹ Southall, *South Africa's Transkei*, pp. 85–86.
⁴² Southall, *South Africa's Transkei*, p. 88.
⁴³ Bonner, "South African Society and Culture...", pp. 278–279; Switzer, *Power and resistance*, pp. 10–11.
⁴⁴ Bonner, "South African Society and Culture...", p. 280; Hlatshwayo, *Education and independence*, p. 45.

In this era, the expanding Christian missions played an increasingly important role in the unfolding of South African history in general, and in the Transkei in particular. Mass conversion to Christianity started only at the end of the nineteenth century, and then African Christians also produced their own strains of conviction and expression, notably in Zionism. The established churches, through their missions, were to play a significant role in practical matters: they constructed institutions such as residences and hospitals, and continued the study of local languages.[45] Arguably, their most significant influence remained in the field of education.

Formal education of black children was not widespread. Where there was any such education, the overriding majority of school-going black children were in mission schools.[46] The South African Native College (later Fort Hare University), founded in 1916, had strong mission ties, and was the only resident institution for tertiary education for black students in South Africa (it also received many students from other African countries) until the end of the 1950s.

> Out of oral historical traditions and the spoken word emerged a historiography written by Xhosa scholars in Xhosa (notably by Samuel Mqhayi and J.H. Soga). Their work appeared in the first Xhosa newspapers in the mid nineteenth century.[47] The beginnings of Xhosa newspapers are as synonymous with J.T. Jabavo as Christian spirituality is with Tiyo Soga. The printing of Xhosa texts was initially supported by missionary infrastructure (notably the Lovedale Press), before being ironically undermined for some time by the same infrastructure. As these examples show, the mission institutions helped form the tiny non-traditional African elite. From their circles came many of the black opponents to the segregated state.

It is also worth noting the establishment of institutions to provide medical care by several mission societies in a region where public facilities were sorely lacking.[48]

---

[45] Richard Elphick, "Mission Christianity and interwar liberalism", in Jeffrey Butler, Richard Elphick, and David Welsh (eds.), *Democratic liberalism in South Africa. Its history and prospect*, Johannesburg and Cape Town: David Philip, 1987, pp. 64–80, here. 69.

[46] Elphick, "Mission Christianity...", p. 69, citing statistics from 1928. See also Thompson, *A history of South Africa*, pp. 172–173.

[47] Peires, *The house of Phalo*, pp. 171–179.

[48] Dischl, *Transkei for Christ*, p. 40 catalogues these institutions.

5. Resistance nationally and in the Transkei

The critical voices (of different degrees of distance and audibility) derived their justification from four main sources: liberalism, Marxism, the missions, and the lived experiences of black people. Each either had international networks or strove to establish them. From the variegated forms of resistance, two may be selected to illustrate these divergent approaches.

The South African Native National Congress, later the African National Congress, like other early protest movements,[49] benefited from leadership that had received formal education, often in mission institutions. This enabled the leaders to articulate their claims in the language of liberal values, which they claimed for the whole population.[50] Typically, their strategy consisted of pursuing constitutional reform through strategic lobbying[51] and some labour action. They also sent delegations to London and participated in other international forums to express and promote their causes.[52] In the same vein, a regrouping of people of similar political fate occurred. A number of "non-European" conferences were held from the late 1920 onwards to facilitate consultation between racially segregated groups.[53] One can read the young Mandela's grave reservations about the efficiency of these and other subsequent peaceful means of resistance in his speech from the dock during the Rivonia Trial.[54]

The Industrial and Commercial Workers Union (ICU) was the first national trade union for black members.[55] It was started in Cape Town and became a reasonably sized, more radical movement. Besides championing labour rights on farms and industries, it also opposed the successive pass laws. Compared to the aforementioned movements, its ideas were more pronouncedly Africanist and its agenda for land reform was more radical.[56]

---

[49] Cf. Bonner, "*South African Society and Culture...*", pp. 294–306.
[50] Thompson, *A history of South Africa*, p. 174.
[51] Thompson, *A history of South Africa*, p. 175.
[52] Johns and Gerhart, *Protest and hope*, pp. 44–45.
[53] Johns and Gerhart, *Protest and hope*, pp. 63–66.
[54] Nelson Mandela, "The Rivonia trail", in *No easy walk to freedom*, Heinemann: Essex, [1965]1990, pp. 162–189, here pp. 165–169.
[55] Johns and Gerhart, *Protest and hope*, p. 69.
[56] Thompson, *A history of South Africa*, p. 176; Johns and Gerhart, Protest and hope, pp. 74–75.

Regarding the ANC, ICU, and Communist Party in the 1930s, Johns and Gerhart conclude that they "fell into disarray, undermined by their own internal disputes and harassed by government authorities".[57] Later, from the 1940s onwards, labour movements grew stronger again, but faced the combined resistance of industry and government. A similar fate befell the ANC, which gathered momentum again in the 1940s. It is also worth mentioning that Ghandi's first experiments with passive resistance[58] had an important impact on the way people thought about resistance.

Focusing more specifically on the Transkei region, there were recurrent incidents of protest and resistance. Three examples suffice to illustrate this point. More than once, movements of passive resistance arose as a response to increased taxation to fund the "dipping" of livestock during outbreaks of the rinderpest (1897 and 1912–1913).[59] In the early 1920s, Christian women led boycotts against shops.[60] Finally, Mgijima's Israelites millenarian group, stationed at Bulhoek, refused to evacuate public land and attempted to protect themselves with rudimentary arms. They were ejected by the police and many were killed in what is now known as the Bulhoek Massacre of 24 May 1921.[61]

Lastly, one should not forget the resistance to injustice by individuals, within the limits of their abilities and insight, in their everyday actions.

---

[57] Johns and Gerhart, *Protest and hope*, p. 69.
[58] Johns and Gerhart, *Protest and hope*, pp. 29–32; Robert Deliège, *Gandhi*, Paris: Presses Universitaires de France, 1999.
[59] Southall, *South Africa's Transkei*, pp. 95–96.
[60] Southall, *South Africa's Transkei*, pp. 96–97.
[61] Johns and Gerhart, *Protest and hope*, pp. 50–51.

CHAPTER 3

ENTER MONGAMELI

I have now sketched the historical and sociopolitical context of a life started in 1929. This should help give an impression of how the broader sociopolitical circumstances in which Mongameli Mabona's youth was to take place came to be. All of this suggests that Mabona belonged to his time and place, and that is indeed correct. However, on his own admission, during his youth, most of the politics passed him by. Furthermore, when we look more closely at his life, it soon becomes clear that his life narrative breaks in significant ways from the destiny that we might expect the historical conditions to have carved out for him.[1]

---

1   People respond in quite diverse ways to the general life circumstances. Reflecting on the situation in the reserves, Thompson maps this diversity as follows: Following the white conquest, new cleavages meshed with old in the African societies. One can distinguish four main tendencies. [Here Thompson has an endnote: 'Here I have adapted William Beinart and Colin Budny's analysis in "Introduction: 'Away in the locations,'" *Hidden Struggles* 11-12'.] The African masses were largely concerned with their immediate situation, whether they resided in the reserves, on white farms, or in towns or were migrant laborers moving between the reserves and the white areas. Their grievances were specific, and with a few exceptions, they held fast to traditional African values. Whatever their situation, they relied heavily on their extensive kinship networks. Poor or incapacitated people received food and shelter from relatives. African women were especially resilient in the responsibilities that were thrust on them. ¶ Second, the chiefs and headmen more or less reluctantly, and more or less skilfully, adapted to the loss of their autonomy and to their ambiguous roles in the white state. Third, a small, relatively prosperous educated elite monopolized the salaried jobs – high school teachers, ministers in the mission churches, official interpreters. They tended to accept the premise of liberal ideology, with its distinction between barbarism and civilization, and to see themselves as the modernizers of African society. Finally, many people had a little education, but failed to get or to hold salaried jobs. They were particularly frustrated, alienated from traditional society but excluded from the benefits of modernization. Many joined independent churches and espoused an Africanist ideology, with modern as well as traditional elements. (Thompson, *A history of South Africa*, pp. 173–174). Cf. Bonner,

1. Birth and first years

On 5 June 1929, Mongameli Mabona was born at his "grandmother's place" in Qombolo,[2] as the second child of Nohni Frances Qhoboshijane and Joseph Gideon Mabona.[3] His paternal grandfather, who was a councillor to the chief at Tsolo,[4] gave both grandchildren their names. He called the elder brother Sigidi, which means "a million", to wish the child great wealth (the grandfather himself owned a lot of cattle). In addition, he received Benedict as a baptismal name. The younger of the siblings he named Mongameli, that is, "ruler", hoping that one day he would become a chief. Mongameli was baptised Anthony Dominic (hence the frequent reference to him in his and other's publications as Anthony or Antoine or Domenico Mabona). His mother had a different vision of her sons' future: she thought that Sigidi would become a teacher and Mongameli a priest. But his father shared this anecdote with him only decades later, the day he was consecrated as deacon. Sigidi later studied law, but died young (around 1955) of tuberculosis.

In the first two chapters, I plainly set Mongameli Mabona's life in the context of the history of the Xhosa people. Indeed, he self-identifies as Xhosa. However, when he is asked about his origins, he identifies as Sotho: he is a Gambo (incorrectly associated or identified by his contemporaries with the "Fingos"). And he had a distant Scottish great-grandmother.[5]

"South African Society and Culture…", p. 275, cited above: "In consequence, local voices and practices filled in the silences and gaps in the empty vessel of segregation, so that life in the segregated reserves was bewilderingly diverse. Even in the twenty-six districts of the Transkei, there was so much variation as to render it difficult to extract any generalisation. ¶ Nevertheless, some broader patterns or traditions are discernible beyond the chaos. The best known of these are the Transkei model of direct personal administration by white magistrates, sidelining chiefs and using appointed headmen, and the system of indirect rule through chiefs granted civil jurisdiction, which prevailed in Zululand and Natal".

[2] For all that follows, cf. Interview 1.
[3] The names are written according to the spelling confirmed by Marta Mabona in correspondence on 10 January 2019. In "Jugend Mongameli", the Mabona family spells the names "Quoboshiane" and "Guideon". DP, "Gratitude" cites the family name of the uncle "Qhoboshiyane" (as below).
[4] Remarks in DP, p. 216 give the impression that Mabona was not spontaneously identified as a person of royal lineage.
[5] Interview 7, 2:40".

Since his mother died when he was only a year old, he has no recollection of her. In fact, after her death, he confused her with an aunt. His relatives wanted to spare the toddler's feelings, so they refrained from speaking about his mother, with the result that he knows very little about her. She seems to have been a teacher at Nqolosa and Camama; in fact, she must have been one of the first African teachers,[6] at least from that region. He outlines his father's biography as follows: "My father Joseph Guideon became a teacher in Blythswood and Buntingville. Later he went to Cape Town for work at the Dominican nuns and was baptised as a Roman Catholic Christian. [...] As a Catholic he visited Kailand Mission, where he met my mother, who was teaching in the school of Camama".[7] I will say more about his father below.

After the death of his mother, the young Mongameli lived with his maternal grandparents. His upbringing was undertaken by one of his uncles, Babana Qhoboshiyane, his mother's youngest brother, who was about eighteen years old at the time. It is to him that Mabona addresses an emotional word of thanks in the "Gratitude" section which opens the 2004 publication of his thesis, *Diviners and prophets*. In the same passage, he also remembers with gratitude his maternal grandmother, Nohanjelwa Qhoboshiyane (née Tshangana), who looked after him when, at the age of two years, he fell seriously ill and no "school" treatment could be found for him. He describes her as a medicine woman (her husband was also a healer[8]); her treatment, administered over several months, consisted of herbal infusions. She certainly left a profound impression on her grandchild. *Diviners and prophets* includes a number of his childhood memories of her – he retrospectively assigned her the role of an anthropological "instructor": she taught him a story about the origin of their people (DP, p. 127), a praise song (DP, p. 140), and illustrated a point of Xhosa language, as in the name given to him (DP, p. 262), uNototi, the man of small tins (the reason for this name is not given). He goes so far as to claim that "she could have been the crucial driving motive in my choice of the theme of this work" (DP, "Gratitude"). Elsewhere, Mabona describes her as a rich woman, or at least as having inherited wealth, as she owned goats, sheep, and cattle. He recollects that when he was young she owned eighty head of cattle. It was at this grandmother's home that Mabona was born and spent his first years.

---

6   "Jugend Mongameli".
7   "Jugend Mongameli".
8   "Jugend Mongameli", correspondence with Marta Mabona (10 January 2019).

2. Early childhood in Qombolo

Thanks to his recollection of his childhood memories as one of the sources for his anthropological studies, we have some material we can use to evoke this world. (I will later also mention rare film material which provides at least some visual record of this world – see p. 63.) Thus we get an impression of people's interactions with their environment.

We learn about people and weather:

> Oncoming tornadoes or storms can be heard miles away in Southern Africa. In my young days, whenever this terrible sound was heard, in the uncanny silence which precedes such storms one would hear also people starting to shout at the top of their voices, they would come out of the huts with their red blankets in their hands and stand in the *inkundla* and wave their blankets vigorously in the north-east direction saying '*Eeeemboooo, woyaaa woyaaa*' (To Emboland, go that way, go that way[9]). They would repeat these shouts and their gestures of shooing away, till the storm either arrived and forced them into the huts or passed them by. The *inkundla* position was thought to give the people the authority and power of the ancestors. The storms generally arrive when the *ikhaba* (the new plants) are said to *ukukhephuza* (to grow towards maturity) just before they produce florescence. The shooing away ceremony (*ukuhesha*) is directed to the lord of storms, chief *Namba*, lord of the corn – sorghum in this case – and of all wealth. He is supposed to be coming to claim the corn and is with this ceremony being sent about his business to his own kingdom of *Embo* whence sorghum is supposed to have originated in the first place.
>
> On the other hand, when the fields were visited with locusts and all the methods generally used to get rid of them had failed, a group of young girls of puberty age and a bit over would be carefully selected and sent for days to go naked around the fields singing: '*woyaaa, woya, woyaaa; sivela kwa Khama, mbo, mbo; sivela kwa Khama, mbo, mbo*' (go away, go away, do go away; we are from Khama land, Embo, Embo, we are from Khama land, Embo, Embo). (DP, p. 197)

---

[9] Translations in parentheses are original to Mabona's text in DP.

Where there are locusts, there are other insects too: "Whenever we saw a green mantis as children we would gather around it and say '*ngci ngci mntan'ezulu uz'usicelele ingubo kuyihlo*' (please, child of heaven, pray your father to give us a blanket)." (DP, p. 181).

And plants:

> Even today in Xhosaland, if one sees a euphorbia or a pair of euphorbias growing in an old kraal site, one can be sure they were planted on the birth of twins. Besides a small verse and the basic drum rhythm, one thing we were carefully taught as pre-school children by the old people was how to draw a euphorbia tree on the sand or just in the dust. I do not think there is any eight-year old Xhosa child who cannot do that. We were not told why we had to do that but we knew that the drawing represented *umhlontlo* (the euphorbia). (DP, pp. 217–218)

In fact, he adds, these are "the three things which were carefully taught us as children, namely: to draw the tree of twins (*umhlontlo*), the basic drum rhythm, and the little verse I shall presently set down" (DP, p. 269, extensive details pp. 269–270).

And there are animals:

> There is a small frog with reddish patches on its skin which loves to repair under a clump of soil in a ploughed field when it is raining. People hoeing the fields after the rains quite often turn this little creature up. I still remember the awe with which it was regarded and it was called *inkosazana* (the princess). Its other name was *Nochebeyi* (the lake dweller). In the old days the person who turned *Nochebeyi* up would immediately shout for everybody around to hear: *akuhlakulwa kuvel'inkosazana* (there should be no hoeing, the princess has appeared). This word would be passed from field to field and in a whole *isithili* people would down tools for the day. (DP, p. 275)

We also learn about the children's games:

> As young children we had a game which we loved because we were 'frogmarched' – affectionately and face upward – and swung gently from side to side by the others who were the while singing 'Thelele mvubu' (Thelele hippopotamus). There was frequent demand for this game, though we didn't know the meaning of the word 'Thelele'. We understood the term mvubu as meaning hippo, though we couldn't

> fathom what the connection might be between our action of swinging and a hippo. We were thrilled, though, to imagine that we were swinging this big fierce animal from deep pools of which we were afraid. (DP, p. 263, an explanation of the elements that were not understood by the children in this anecdote is offered on the same page.)

Mabona remembers myths from childhood (DP, p. 199), but he also recollects ritual oblivion:

> As children we had heard mention now and then of *amaZimba* – as humans, not cereals[10] – and we had some vague idea of vast numbers of fierce fighting men. But, when we put questions, the answer was laconic: '*akuthethwa ngalo nto*' (that's no matter to speak about). Thus, even black African historians, not much aware of the ethnographic barriers blocking their perspective, have missed a clear view of this vast conflict between Africans and foreigners on the East Coast towards the end of the 16th Century. (DP, p. 132)

Although the autobiographical anecdotes in *Diviners and Prophets* serve to give substance to Mabona's study on Xhosa culture, there are a few recollections that also reflect the cohabitation of traditional Xhosa culture and Christianity – the "red" and "school" aspects of his ambient world (see again p. 49). This is reflected in the following anecdote:

> As a young boy I used to see a very old man who might have been a model of traditional piety. He was blind and always needed a young boy to lead him wherever he went. At every few steps he would say *Camagu, hobe* (Dove, have mercy), and when asked how he got blind, he would reply that he was blinded by *inkwenkwezi* (a star/lightning). Even grown-ups no more knew or remembered that the dove was *Sifubasibanzi*'s messenger and intermediary or that the word *inkwenkwezi* also meant lightning. So, this old man, always dressed in traditional costume, with his snow-white hair and star-struck eyes lifted to the skies as he said '*Camagu, hobe*' became a cherished object of fear and fascination. My father was a teacher and this old man used to come quite often to have his letters dictated and we children would scamper off in fear and dread of we knew not what whenever he came in reciting his unending

---

[10] "*Amazimba*" can also mean "sorghum", cf. DP, p. 124.

ejaculatory prayer which we would hear even during pauses in his talk or dictation. (DP, pp. 184–185)

The same is echoed in contestation of traditional ornament: "When missionaries or teachers in the name of [C]hristianity, broke these ritual necklaces – *ubulunga* – there used to be incredible scenes of almost hysterical rage on the part of the parents and weeping and distress on the part of the pupils. I was, at the time, absolutely nonplussed at such reactions" (DP, p. 183). Or again in funeral practices:

> When I was young, some traditionalists[11] still did not want to have their dead buried in a coffin but wanted *ukungcwaba ngala ndlela yakudala* (to bury them in the old way) with an alcove for the corpse to be put in a contracted or foetal posture. Such burials were spoken of in hush-hush terms by *amagqoboka* (Christians), but they still existed. I have myself seen one where the side-chamber was used to put the corpse stretched out and in front of the side-chamber a mat of the deceased was hung like a curtain so that the soil would not directly fall on the corpse. There were also some grave goods: some tobacco, a pipe, a spoon and I don't now remember what else. (DP, p. 252)

One may understand the whole following passage to refer to Mabona's personal experience in his youth:

> It is clear that the colour red is the royal colour in the Xhosa colour scheme. The diviner, on the other hand is called '*umntu omhlophe*' (the white person). A diviner will generally dress in white, at least his/her beads around the head, the neck, the wrists and ankles will all be white. In my youth, when someone died in the family, the traditionalists put away their red blankets and donned white. Initiates into manhood are also daubed white and so were also recently delivered women. A traditionalist who was renowned for her knowledge once told me that the white colour was used to mark people who were supposed not to attend public gatherings and to be seen from far by others so that they could take necessary precautions. I asked what these precautions were against, and she answered that such people had in their blood something

---

11 Cf. also "I have attended many funerals conducted by traditionalists where I heard an equivalent formula used in general: '*Uye emboniselweni z'usikhangele*' (you have gone to the highest point, watch over us)" (DP, p. 318).

> which could constitute a danger for others. On pressing her further, she gave the name of this something as *umgcalagcala*. I had known the use of this word only in connection with the bad temper of persons e.g. *lo mntu ulugcalagcala namhlanje* (this person is in a bilious aggressive temper today); or of animal e.g. *le nja ilugcalagcala* (this dog is very vicious). On the other hand a circumcision expert told me that he had to daub the initiates with *ifutha/ingceke* (a liquid emulsion of white clay) because it draws out *ifithi yobukhwenkwe* (boyhood distemper). (DP, p. 196)

Some time in his youth, he also learned about the training of diviners – he writes:

> Herbal medicines in the form of baths, infusions and smoking are used to achieve deep slumber at night and thus facilitate communication with the ancestors in sleep. During the day herbs are used again to help *ingqondo* to focus attention in seedless concentration. In such concentration, promoted and enhanced by the practice of *ukuphehla ibekile*, one is not allowed *ukuthetha ngentliziyo* (to speak with the heart). In my young years I used to watch diviner novices at this exercise as my home was not far from a master diviner's place. If we got up early enough we could also hear their daily predawn chorus which is called *ukutsholoza kwabakhwetha beghirha* (the predawn novice's melody). [...] This was the school of Nkebe Tyhalibongo, a master diviner of the Mfene (baboon) clan, one of the best known *amagqirha* among the Ndungwana (Diya) section of the Thembu tribe at that time. (DP, p. 350)

Whereas these recountings testify to Mabona's earliest initiation into the ambient culture, tensions and all, he was soon at the age at which the first social distinctions became operative. Speaking about the traditional game of stick-fighting,[12] he explains why he was never good at it. One learns how to stick-fight while herding cattle with other boys. But Mabona missed out on this part of his socialisation because he was responsible for looking after his stepmother's children and taking over some of her chores, and he was going to school when others were herding cattle. So let us turn to our protagonist's school days.

---

[12] Interview 1.

3. Life in Zigudu – Catholic background (1)

It seems that the main motivation for Mabona's father, Joseph Gideon Mabona, to take his two boys from Qombolo to Sabalele, where he was a teacher, was to ensure that his children would be close enough to a school to be able to attend regularly. Mabona senior had only two years of college training, so (probably due to changing legislation, requiring the third year) he had to leave the Sabalele school, a government school, and moved to Zigudu after only a year and a half. At the same time, Mabona's father, who converted to Christianity fairly late in life,[13] assumed duties as a catechist in Zigudu. Here he worked until the end of his life, and was respected by the people of the region. The exact chronology of these events is not clear, but it seems that the young Mongameli started school at the normal age, seven, in Zigudu,[14] so he grew up close to the school and to the church.

Christianity was to become a major dimension of Mongameli Mabona's life. His boyhood was, as we have seen, that of a Xhosa lad in the Transkei. However, he was also born into another history, that of the Roman Catholic Church. This fact played a central role in how his later youth was spent and in the course his life would take until the mid 1970s.[15]

Although Catholic initiatives in the southern African subregion, notably in Mozambique, date from the sixteenth century, Catholics were prohibited (first by the Calvinist-oriented Cape authorities, then by the new British authorities) to establish missions in the Cape Colony until 1820.[16] This is one of the reasons that Catholicism initially lagged behind Protestant churches in South Africa. In Xhosaland, Catholic missionaries were latecomers compared to the Wesleyans, Methodists, Anglicans, and others.[17] Consequently, Catholic institutions of education are also younger than those established by other Christian denominations.

---

[13] Interview 6, 55".
[14] In interview 7, 5", he suggests that he already started school in Sabalele and that his father was his first teacher.
[15] I explain some of the intricate developments in Catholic administration to provide a frame for understanding Mabona's different moves and to situate his early work in an intelligible framework.
[16] Dischl, *Transkei for Christ*, p. 44.
[17] Dischl, *Transkei for Christ*, pp. 18–37.

From the earlier history of Catholicism in South Africa, only two related facts are pertinent here. First, the spread and planning of the implantation of the Catholic Church were undertaken in consultation with, and with deference to, Rome, in particular the Congregation for the Propagation of Faith, the *Congregatio de propaganda fide*. This institution will be relevant later (see pp. 68-69 and 80-81). Second, the difficulties in managing this implantation resulted in a wide range of religious orders from different western countries coming to the south-eastern regions of South Africa.

Two centres of missionary implantation are of particular importance to Mongameli Mabona's life. In Mariannhill, to the east of Durban in Zululand (now part of the Durban metropolis), Trappist monks founded a mission in the 1880s.[18] This is far from the region where Mabona grew up, especially considering the terrain and modes of transport then available. However, by the end of the nineteenth century, Franciscan brothers and Dominican sisters had arrived in Xhosaland and started a mission station and farms on the western bank of the Kei river.[19] The Keilands farms are about 40 km to the south-west of Qombolo and less than 6 km south of Zigudu, where an outpost of the Keilands mission was established and Jesuits founded a school which opened its doors in 1900.[20] In 1908, this post and the school were taken over by the Trappists[21] from

---

[18] Dischl, *Transkei for Christ*, pp. 51–52.
[19] Dischl, *Transkei for Christ*, p. 51.
[20] Dischl, *Transkei for Christ*, p. 124.
[21] Dischl mentions internal Catholic criticism against Trappist missions in South Africa even in the early years: "Another serious criticism was levelled at the Trappist method of education. The original method of Abbot Pfanner to combine book learning with manual labour was accepted and admired, but as the years went on the point of higher education was sorely lacking. Lourdes had in 1922 still only a Primary School while it should have had a High School and Industrial Training Centre. The consequences of this neglect of high education were grave; there were no Catholic people with degrees while there were about 60 among Protestant Blacks. The Catholic Church had only two Teacher Training Colleges for black teachers – (Mariazell since 1909 and Mariannhill since 1915). There was not a single black Catholic nurse and among the 56 members of the Bunga there was not one Catholic. While Protestant Blacks edited newspapers like IMVO, ILANGA, UMTETELI and others, there were neither black Catholic editors nor such organisations of any kind. The Protestant missions produced officials, clerks, medical doctors, nurses, lawyers and public leaders, while such people were absent in the Catholic field" (Dischl, *Transkei for Christ*, p. 130). We will see that Mabona was critical of the education he received, even decades later.

Mariannhill.[22] Soon afterwards, the school received government subsidy.[23] In 1910 the Trappists opened a school at Sabalele,[24] and gradually a whole network of other schools in the south-western region of the Transkei followed.[25] For many years, the Keilands mission station and its network depended on the Dominican sisters for "schools and charitable work".[26]

It is in this milieu that Mabona's father began to work as a catechist. He built a house for himself and his two sons in Zigudu, and at some point he remarried. As a catechist, he had to meet people to teach them the Catholic faith and respond to their questions. This was probably often done at outstations of the missions (at Sabalele, Nqolosa, Camama, and elsewhere) at least four times a week, but sometimes daily. He must have worked closely with Fr. Peter Graeff[27] and probably, from 1948, with Fr. Stephen Phako.[28] Mabona could not say whether his father engaged in any specific attempts to Africanise expressions of Catholic faith. Sometime during the 1930s, the Pallottine Missions made a silent film (one hour and forty minutes long, black-and-white, silent) on life at the mission station. The storyline is fictional, but there are glimpses of the world in which Mabona grew up. The film is entitled "Maboni im Land der Abakhweta",[29] using an adapted version of his father's name, and his father also acted in the film. At this stage it may seem irrelevant to emphasise Joseph Gideon Mabona's profession, but the significance of this point will become clear later.

Mabona remembers seeing people departing to work on the mines and seeing them return again. During the time when he was still in Qombolo, one of his grandfathers probably migrated to work as a miner. As a child in Zigudu, he was intrigued by this other world into which people disappeared and wanted to know more about the mines. He also knew a man who worked in the sugar plantations.[30]

---

[22] Dischl, *Transkei for Christ*, pp. 95–96. They started another station at Cwele to the east of Mthatha before the end of the nineteenth century, but it was short-lived, Dischl, *Transkei for Christ*, pp. 56–57.
[23] Dischl, *Transkei for Christ*, p. 125.
[24] Dischl, *Transkei for Christ*, p. 125.
[25] "At the end of 1929, Keilands conducted schools at Saliwa, Nciba, Zigudu, Sabalele, Matakane, and Nonqute, Dischl, *Transkei for Christ*, p. 285.
[26] Dischl, *Transkei for Christ*, p. 287.
[27] Interview 1.
[28] Dischl, *Transkei for Christ*, p. 287.
[29] This name is cited in Dischl, *Transkei for Christ*, p. 286; the digitalised version generously sent to me by Mabona's son-in-law, Raymond Ochsenbein, starts without a name.
[30] Interview 7, 1:47".

Meanwhile, the young Mongameli started to attend primary school. He continued at Zigudu until Standard 4 (i.e. the sixth school year). He later reported that, from his third year in school, he started to learn German from the missionaries (we know that at least one nun taught at his school), but he did not advance far with German in his childhood. At some stage in those years, Fr. Graeff already started to teach him Latin.

It is possible that the following incident occurred around the end of his time in Zigudu – it opens a window on the cultural cross-currents that he was likely confronted with regularly:

> The moon, the sun and everything else is supposed to have come from a cavern that is thought to be at the horizon between sea and sky [...]. I was once brought very sharply up against this idea. I was then about eleven or twelve years old – and happened to get into a conversation with two boys much older than myself – seventeen or eighteen by my estimate. They had done very little schooling and did not have a high idea of school education. Because they were so much older, I called them 'Buti' (elder brother) – even today this is the epithet I put in front of their names. One was called Ngangabekho Ndikolo and is still living at the time of writing and the other was called Qakatyana Saula who later became a diviner, and unfortunately died last year (1991) shortly before I visited home after twenty years of exile. I had wanted to see him for reasons connected with this writing and more.
>
> The two young men – boys in Xhosa because they had not yet undergone circumcision – said with obvious disdain, 'What, do they say in your school, happens to the stars during the day as we do not see them?' 'The sun is too bright in the day for the stars to be seen. Nothing has happened to them. They have just disappeared', I said promptly. 'Have they told you how you can make them visible?', was their next question. 'So I can see them? I should see stars in broad daylight? That is impossible', I said. 'Throw a stone into this shallow water without disturbing the sand at the bottom.' I did so and created bubbles. I had not known that the reflection of a bubble is in the form of a star, so I believed I was really seeing stars at the bottom of the water. But the two young men added that the sky too was down there, as I could see. But I said, 'No, that is merely the reflection of the sky and also of the stars. My reflection is also in the water, but I am not in the water. You want to confuse me.' 'You are confused. Where do you think the sky is?',

they asked. I thought they were teasing, but replied politely as it was demanded of me by custom, 'It is up there and all above us.'

But they said, 'It is also down there, very far down, as far down as you saw in the water.' I said, 'No, But' Ngangabekho and But' Qakatyana, you also know that that was only a reflection (*umfanekiso*).' They asked me again, 'Do you then mean to say, *kwedini* (boy), that the sky and the earth are not together?' This was said as if earth and sky were man and wife. I said, 'It is clear to see that the sky is far above and the earth is far below.' They then changed tack and said, 'Look at the horizon. The borderline of the sky and the borderline of the earth are together (*imbambe yezulu nembambe yomhlaba zihlangene*)'. Put in this context, I seemed to be seeing this fact for the first time, though I would surely have observed it all the time. I was no more so sure of myself and my 'school knowledge', so I became the inquirer, 'How then is it that here the sky is far above us?' '*Hay!, kwedini* (no, boy) *akukho kuba phantsi akukho kuba phezulu; kuya ngokuba umi phi. Ingqondo iyaguquleleka. Ingqondo iyaphenduleleka* (there is no up and down; it depends where you stand. The mind is turned round. The mind is turned the other way round).' I was in real confusion and did not say anything further. I had great respect for my two elder brothers and I knew I could gain much from their company. (DP, pp. 212–213)[31]

This anecdote illustrates in vivid detail how the differences between "red" and school" would have been part of the ambient social reality of Mabona's childhood. In fact, looking back, he considers the difference to have been simply the question of who had attended formal school and who not (the "red" referred to a dominant colour of traditional clothing). Likewise, his "grandmother had converted and become 'school'". Perhaps oversimplifying his position, he states categorically: "I was never red".[32]

---

[31] Perhaps from the same time: DP, p. 261, "One time, on the road near Cathcart I pointed out a stand of *imiphanga* (bread trees) which are sometimes mistakenly called *amasundu* (palms). I made the same mistake, but one of the older boys was more knowledgeable and said these trees were *imiphanga* and not *amasundu*, moreover he went on to say that he had heard that in the old days people were able to make beer from palms. My question then was: could they make real *utywala* (beer) from palms? He said, 'Yes, but it was not called *utywala* but *iphombe*.' Much later I met this term in ethnographic descriptions of east Africa. It does not exist anymore in Xhosa culture and has virtually disappeared from the Xhosa lexicon".

[32] Interview 7, 1:36".

Joseph Gideon Mabona did not discuss the politics of the day with his children. Not because he was ignorant of events, but he rather wanted to practise an impartiality that would be compatible with his devotion to his work as a catechist. Still, the young Mongameli was aware of political differences related to ethnic representation, issues around cattle dipping, and the price of maize. Missionaries served as relays of news, both in Zigudu and later at the seminaries. Radios and newspapers were quite rare (but not absent), so the local shopkeepers were important disseminators of news. Considering his childhood in general, Mabona recalls that people were not very informed about colonial politics or the Second World War. However, he recalls the internment in Pretoria of some of the German missionaries. Graeff, because he had been in the country for longer than five years by 1940, would not have been interned.[33]

But it was not necessary to follow current news to be disturbed by the most patent political reality: "the fact that we were ruled by white people and not by black people was always strange and this is always something which people fought against. Yes, they didn't like it. No the people who ruled us, the white people, not black people, why? Why are we not ruled by black people?"[34] People questioned details of the law. Or why they had to pay doctors. They questioned whether the regulations regarding the dipping cattle were motivated exclusively by the government's concern for animal health.

At the same time, people "looked at the missions as something quite different from the government. They were quarrelling with the government".[35] The mission station seems to have taken a very central place in the life of people in that region. Mabona confirms this:

> People depended on the mission very much. And... there's another thing, there was Father Peter there. He was looking very much after the people. He looked especially for the children who were coming up standard 6, standard 7 and he helped them to go to the, to the college, Mariazell.[36]

Mabona describes Peter Graeff as particularly eager to advance the formal education of the children: he encouraged parents to send their children to Mariazell, to the point that some parents started to avoid him to escape his urging.

---

[33] See details throughout Dischl, *Transkei* for Christ.
[34] Interview 1.
[35] Interview 1.
[36] Interview 1. The mission at Mariazell, 220 km north of Zigudu, just south of Lesotho, had a boarding school and a Catholic teacher-training college.

It seems that he may even have lent money to some families or found other means to support parents to send their children to secondary school.[37]

Already in Standard 3 (the fifth school year), Mabona told his priest – I assume the same Fr. Graeff – that he wanted to become a priest. To appreciate the consequences of this early decision, we need to look at the mechanics of the Catholic Church administration at the time, in the bigger region.

4. Ixopo – Catholic background (2)

In the meantime, a number of changes in ecclesiastical administration took place – changes that mark out the chessboard on which Mongameli Mabona's activities in the Catholic church were to play out until the 1960s. Without this background, the relation of the Transkei Catholics to the Church administration is unintelligible. First, in 1909 the Trappists of Mariannhill were re-institutionalised as the Congregation of the Missionaries of Mariannhill (CMM).[38] Second, throughout the 1920s the southern part of Natal and the whole of the Transkei formed one Vicariate under the Mariannhill Fathers.[39] Third, this Vicariate was then split, so that, during the 1930s, the central and southern parts of Transkei fell under the bishop of Mthata (then Umtata).[40] Fourth, around 1930, the Keilands mission station, falling just outside of the Transkei, came under the administration of the Pallottine missionaries based in Queenstown.[41] Fifth, shortly after the Second World War, it was decided to incorporate the southern part of the Transkei region (which until then fell within the ecclesiastical administrative region of Umtata) into the diocese of Queenstown; this was finalised in 1952 under Bishop Rosenthal.[42] This meant that the whole region of Mabona's youth,

---

[37] Interview 1.
[38] Dischl, *Transkei for Christ*, p. 94.
[39] Dischl, *Transkei for Christ*, p. 133.
[40] Dischl, *Transkei for Christ*, p. 134.
[41] After the First World War, German missionaries were expelled from former German colonies. Eventually, in 1926, one of these groups, the Pallottine missionaries, originally based in Cameroon, were made responsible for the Queenstown diocese (Dischl, *Transkei for Christ*, p. 133). "The outstations Zigudu and Saliwa, just across the river, were still visited by the Keilands missionaries. This situation was legalised in February 1933 when the Propaganda fixed a new boundary between the Queenstown and Umtata mission territory, attaching these Transkeian outstations of Keilands to Queenstown." Dischl, *Transkei for Christ*, pp. 149–150.
[42] Dischl, *Transkei for Christ*, pp. 190-191, 282.

the region to which he would revert once he was ordained, henceforth fell under Queenstown.

The Trappists who founded Mariannhill, like the Pallottines who later took over in Queenstown, came from German-speaking countries and continued to receive co-workers from these countries – hence the predominance of German-speaking members of the clergy in this history.

The first vicar apostolic appointed by *Propaganda Fide* to the Mariannhill congregation, Bishop Fleischer, already made Africanisation of the church in the territories of the Transkei a priority.[43] This was a concern, since at that stage, with a few exceptions, all clergy were still white, and the black parishioners remained a small minority.[44] This concern was kept on the agenda of Joseph Grueter, who took over as vicar apostolic in 1941 and then as bishop of Umtata. Apparently, Bishop Grueter wanted to promote "indigenous vocation" and for this reason he requested missionaries to identify talented boys to be sent to the Minor Seminary in Ixopo. Dischl reports that from 1941 to 1968, sixty-five boys from the Transkei region were sent there and their studies were financially supported. However, only a few of them became priests in the end.[45] This was precisely the rare path followed by Mongameli Mabona. This is why a twelve-year-old boy from Zigudu would be sent 450 kilometres away to start his secondary school education in Ixopo.

In order to appreciate what this path entailed, we need to explain what the name Ixopo (and, thereafter, Pevensey) stand for in the world of South African Catholicism.

---

[43] Dischl, *Transkei for Christ*, p. 135; Philippe Denis, *The Dominican Friars in Southern Africa. A social history* (1577-1990), Leiden, Boston, and Cologne: Brill, 1998, p. 203.

[44] Dischl, *Transkei for Christ*, pp. 137–138. The statistics of personnel at Keilands in 1927 indicates this: "Fr Albert Schweiger, one Brother, six Dominican Sisters, six black teachers in ten schools, 270 Catholics". Dischl, *Transkei for Christ*, p. 147.

[45] Curiously, although Dischl could catalogue six such cases, Mabona is not among them (Dischl, *Transkei for Christ*, p. 190). This may be accounted for if one assumes that Mabona was sent to Ixopo and Pevensey by the prefect of Umtata, but upon returning to his home region, this region fell under Queenstown. This supposition is partially confirmed by the fact that Mabona was ordained by Bishop Rosenthal of Queenswood. (It would also mean that the six catalogued cases were either all from the later Umtata diocese, or were ordained before the split.) Lastly, if Dischl's list is used as an indication of Xhosa priests, and assuming that there were not too many people in a similar position to that of Mabona, then we may make the informed guess that Mabona may have been, after Canisius Moleko (1948) and Alois Hliso (1950) (cf. Dischl, *Transkei for Christ*, p. 283), the third Xhosa Catholic priest.

One could trace this story back, as Philippe Denis does, to the foundation of *Propaganda Fide*, when it was declared that the missions had to train indigenous clergymen.[46] At numerous stages, the popes reaffirmed the importance of this task for the church, notably through a number of encyclicals in the 1920s. This also involved recognition of the local believers in the sense that they were to receive an education on an equal level to their European brethren and sisters, which is not a negligible issue. Furthermore, this new impetus entailed a move towards the indigenisation of the Church, in the sense that traditional cultures were to be respected as far as the Church authorities deemed them compatible with the main aim: the propagation of the Catholic faith. This training of local clergy was to be undertaken under the auspices of *Propaganda Fide*.[47] In reality, the equality expressed in these encyclicals did not always materialise and, as we will see later, this was to become the object of arguably Mongameli Mabona's most celebrated act.[48]

As a direct consequence of this mixture of desiderata, new seminaries were founded to take charge of this training. Hence, in 1925, about a hundred kilometres to the south-west of Durban, a clerical seminary was founded at Ixopo, and it became known as the Mariathal Latin school, and later, St. Mary's minor seminary.[49] Initially, a number of European students with a vocation for mission work in South Africa received training there too.[50] However, while black students were trained either at Ixopo or at Roma in Lesotho (in both cases only in small numbers), other South African students had to go overseas for their training.[51]

---

[46] Denis, *The Dominican Friars*, p. 203: "Since its foundation in 1622 and with renewed vigour during the pontificate of Leo XIII, the Congregation for the Propagation of the Faith had made it clear that indigenous clergy should be trained in all Catholic missions".
[47] On all of this, see George Mukuka, "The establishment of the Indigenous Catholic Clergy in South Africa: 1919-1957", *Studia Historiae Ecclesiasticae* XXXIV/1, 2008, pp. 305–334, here pp. 306–310.
[48] Cf. Chapter 5, §5.4, (pp. 126-127) on the *Black Priests' Manifesto*.
[49] George Sombe Mukuka, *The other side of the story. The silent experience of the black clergy in the Catholic Church in South Africa* (1898-1976), Pietermaritzburg: Cluster Publications, 2008, pp. 134–135; Denis, *The Dominican Friars*, p. 203. One of the members of the team who finally decided to establish the school at Ixopo was Father Schweiger from Keilands – thus establishing the link between the western Transkei and Ixopo. Dischl, *Transkei for Christ*, p. 137.
[50] Dischl, *Transkei for Christ*, p. 139.
[51] Denis, *The Dominican Friars*, p. 127.

Mabona probably arrived in Ixopo in 1942. In his class, there would have been Zulu- and Xhosa-speaking children.[52] Of the practical life at the seminary in Ixopo, not much is known. Initially, Latin, English, arithmetic, history, and geography were taught, in addition to religion and Church history.[53] It seems likely that Mabona would have had, among others, Fr. Marcel Dischl (the author of the reference book on the Catholic Church in the Transkei) and Fr. William Storch as teachers.[54] We also know that he had contact with Fr. Paul Ngobese, a person whom he held in great esteem.[55] Normally, Mabona should have attended junior seminary for six years, but seeing that his Latin was already quite advanced (remember, he had already started learning it in Zigudu), he skipped the first class and so he matriculated in 1948.

The major subject taught at Ixopo was Latin,[56] but the teaching was poor; in fact, Mabona spent some of his free time to advance his studies by himself. He remembered that geography and history were also taught.[57] But he remembers more being dissatisfied with the quality of schooling there and writing many letters of complaint to the bishop. Other pupils did the same. Their education was considered to lag far behind what they perceived the quality of education in the rest of South Africa to be. The teachers seem to have been insufficiently trained themselves. However, Mabona mentions that things changed towards the end of his schooling. These changes had a lot to do with the arrival of Fr. Francis Schimlek in Mabona's matriculation year. Schimlek was qualified as a teacher and taught English. Mabona describes him as a devoted teacher who did his best to bring his two students up to matriculation level. In the "Acknowledgment"

---

[52] In the long run, training Xhosa students in the Zulu area of Ixopo proved unsatisfactory, and later a minor seminary was started in Mthatha in 1972. Cf. Dischl, *Transkei for Christ*, p. 190.
[53] Mukuka, *The other side*, pp. 135–136.
[54] Dischl, *Transkei for Christ*, pp. 199, 233.
[55] Cf. DP, p. 177: "Father Paul Ngobese, F. F. J., who was a man of outstanding intellect and character, told me in the early forties [...]". "Jugend Mongameli": "The African priest Fr. Paulus Ngobese had great influence on me through his holiness. I often went to visit him".
[56] Michael Lambert's, "The classics and black South African identities", in *The classics and South African identities*, London: Bristol Classical Press, 2011, pp. 91–124, is a fascinating study on the politics of education. It includes references to D.D.T. Jabavu's lecturing Latin at the University of Fort Hare (p. 99) and the role of Classics in the said debates about equality of education (e.g. pp. 101–106). However, he has more the study of Greco-Roman culture and literature in mind, and the study of Latin in the context of seminary education is hardly mentioned.
[57] "Father Oscar, an African priest from Marianhill, was very good in teaching biology. Prof. Nass with an enormous knowledge in physics and maths, was unfortunately very poor in his teaching. So I had to study on my own for these subjects." "Jugend Mongameli".

section of his biography of Father Bernard Huss, Schimlek thanks, amongst others, "Frater Anthony Mabona for collecting information on the work of Father Barnard Huss".[58] A year after this book was published, Schimlek wrote another, *Medicine versus Witchcraft* (Mariannhill, 1950), to which Mabona would devote a good deal of discussion, much later, in *Diviners and prophets*.[59]

In the end, Mabona's only classmate, Ferdinand Sebekoa, abandoned matriculation during the final examination and went back home to the Free State. Mabona describes his own matriculation examination as an exhausting ordeal. He passed with a third-class matriculation (in the state exam), but even that was better than he had expected.

Not much information could be gathered about Mabona's life outside of the seminary at this time. Yet, the following account from his anthropological work reflects this phase of his life:

> As boys we used to challenge each other: *kawuhlale ungacingi okwexeshana* (just stop thinking for some time). The challenger would look the other boy in the face and watch his eyes. If the eyes failed to come to rest but betrayed restlessness, the challenger would say: 'Oh, you will never be able as *inkwenkwe endala* (a grown up boy) *ukuphehla* a girl.' By about the age of eighteen one was supposed to be able *ukuphehla ibekile* for casting a spell on the girl he was courting and make her 'come' to him. This 'coming to him' mostly consisted of her going to fetch water from the fountain or common watering place at an unseasonable moment when there would be nobody else around. As I have already indicated, the fountain or the watering-place was a favourite tryst for young lovers. Young men before circumcision have more carefree ways and easier access to girls. It was therefore only in extreme cases that boys would resort to the practice of *ukuphehla* a girl. For some time after circumcision, though, the young men were supposed to disappear into some area of invisibility in society and avoid the public view. They engaged ritually in intensive personal decontamination through daily *ukugaba* (ritual vomiting) and the observance of social avoidances. They also avoided *umlaza* (ritual contamination) through the daily bath – often with *intelezi* (herbal admixture) - and developed psychic strength by frequent *ukuphehla ibekile*. The latter practice could be used also for negative purposes. It was,

---

[58] Francis Schimlek, *Against the stream. Life of Father Bernard Huss, C.M.M. The social apostle of the Bantu*. Mariannhill Natal: Mariannhill Mission Press, 1949, p. 3.
[59] Cf. DP, pp. 334–338.

therefore considered a dire threat if somebody said: *Ndiyakukuphehlela* (I will *phehla* for you) i.e. I will cast a spell on you by means of *ukuphehla*.[60]

After the holidays he was to resume his studies at Pevensey.

5. Pevensey – Catholic background (3)

In the 1940s, the senior section of the seminary became independent and then relocated to Pevensey. Black priests were trained at this institution, which was named St. Peter's Major[61] Seminary. It is here that Mabona continued his training for the next five or six years.[62] Thirty-nine priests had been ordained there by 1957;[63] and in 1958 the enrolment was twenty-one students, giving a sense of the size of the institution.[64] Mukuka, following David Moetapele, claims that the academic quality of the institution left much to be desired. Six or seven priests served as lecturers,[65] and they were not necessarily equipped for this task.

However, elsewhere, Mukuka acknowledges that "[i]n the early 1950s more trained staff was channelled to the Seminary, for example, Henry Karlen, DTh., Pirmin Klaunzler, PhD., and Thomas Respondek PhD".[66] Karlen taught moral theology; Klaunzler taught philosophy.[67] Dischl confirms both views when he relates that, in 1951, the later bishop Henry Karlen "was sent to South Africa because the Major Seminary at Pevensey in Natal was in dire need of qualified teachers. From 1952 until November 1957 he taught Moral Theology and Canon Law".[68] These individuals would have lectured Mabona.[69] Standards were raised when the Dominicans took over the institution in 1957, but Mabona had

---

[60] DP, p. 345.
[61] St. Peters started functioning as a major seminary in January 1946. Denis, *The Dominican Friars*, p. 219.
[62] It was not possible to determine this with certainty.
[63] Mukuka, *The other side*, p. 155.
[64] Denis, *The Dominican Friars*, p. 221.
[65] Denis, *The Dominican Friars*, p. 221.
[66] Mukuka, *The other side*, p. 155.
[67] Mukuka, *The other side*, p. 150.
[68] Dischl, *Transkei for Christ*, p. 192.
[69] I have not been able to confirm this. The only other lecturer at St. Peter's at the time Mabona attended that I was able to identify is the Trappist missionary Fr. Fleischer, mentioned earlier, cf. Dischl, *Transkei for Christ*, p. 332.

already left a number of years before.⁷⁰ The new director was Oswin Magrath, whom I mention here because Mabona was to work with him later in the 1960s. In the meantime, a training facility for white students, St. John Vianney, was opened in Pretoria in 1951, and the students of the two institutions had occasional meetings. At the end of the decade, St. Peter's seminary relocated to Hammanskraal, some 50 kilometres to the north of Pretoria.⁷¹

Apart from the poor academic quality of the institution at Pevensey, there seem to have been other problems too. Mukuka describes the conditions as follows:

> When the seminarians were trained by the CMMs, the situation was really deplorable. The food was bad. The students saw that the rector – who used to dine with them – ate different, better food. This soon became a point of tension between the staff and the students. [...] the students were provided with textbooks from which to learn, but were not allowed to use the library.⁷²

He points out that the students' questioning of the institution was not merely spurred by the day-to-day life at the seminary, but also echoed the broader national political contestation of the rising apartheid state.⁷³

It is not clear how great Mabona's exposure to politics was at the time. We know that he read, at least occasionally, the Zulu-dominant newspaper, *UmAfrika*, founded by the Mariannhill mission.⁷⁴ The newspaper's regional and ecclesiastic situation did not prevent it from covering "Africa-wide news and, in some cases,

---

⁷⁰   Mukuka, *The other side*, pp. 149–150.
⁷¹   Denis, *The Dominican Friars*, p. 222.
⁷²   Mukuka, *The other side*, p. 151.
⁷³   Mukuka, *The other side*, pp. 152–153.
⁷⁴   Cf. DP, p. 212. The Contemporary Cultural Studies Unit team (of the former University of Natal), describes the newspaper's early orientation as follows: "The origins of *UmAfrika* reveal that Mariannhill missionaries were amongst the pioneers in developing an understanding of what black South Africans wanted to read at the turn of the century. Both *Izindaba zaBantu* (Bantu Topics), which ran from 1910 to 1929, and its successor combined secular with non-secular news. *Izindaba zaBantu* started as a bi-monthly, becoming a weekly in 1923. Responding to a period of unrest, *Izindaba's* name was changed to *UmAfrika* in 1929 because the Mission feared that Izindaba would be incorrectly perceived to be the voice of the government's then Department of Native Affairs. Although it does not appear to have been acknowledged as such, this name change was probably UmAfrika's first political statement: it successfully distanced itself from links with the state and avoided alienating its 2,000 strong readership", "Community and the Progressive Press: A Case Study in Finding Our Way", *Journal of Communication Inquiry* 12/1, 1988, pp. 26–44, here p. 30.

world news".[75] This may have been the channel through which Mabona and his peers learned about the rise of Nkrumah in Ghana (before Independence in 1957). Mabona thinks that he may have learned from Nkrumah's freedom movement through newspapers that were brought to the seminary, implying the possibility that papers other than *UmAfrika* were available. Furthermore, he recalls his hearing about Nkrumah as rather exceptional – he and his fellows otherwise did not have much information about what was happening in other African countries.

But back to the academic work. Training at St. Peter's probably essentially covered philosophy (two years) and theology (four years). According to his own account, Mabona was not very interested in the specificity of Catholic theology, compared to that of other Christian theologies. Nor was he particularly attracted to Catholic philosophy or the interpretations of Aristotle and Aquinas that he would have encountered in the curriculum. In general, Mabona had an ambivalent relation to the subjects studied at the seminary. On the one hand, he admits that it was difficult for him to concentrate on philosophy and theology and he attributes this simply to his not believing in what he was taught.[76] On the other hand, he seems to have gathered material for his own parallel curriculum, "always doing something else". He remembers that Réginald Garrigou-Lagrange[77] figured as an important figure in the philosophy and theology of the seminary, whereas he wanted to know about Martin Heidegger and Gabriel Marcel, or Jean-Paul Sartre and Maurice Merleau-Ponty, and theologians such as Henri De Lubac and Yves Congar.

"Not believing" in the philosophy and theology he was taught thus meant more a rejection of the way he was taught than of the disciplines as such – as he has also confirmed, stating: "I didn't want to limit myself with this theology or this philosophy. [...] for me, the question was what is philosophy today, what does philosophy say today, what does theology say today? That was the most important".[78]

Having completed his studies successfully, Mongameli Mabona was ordained in December 1954, but not before a personal catastrophe: both his father and his brother died during the year or two before his ordination. The medical cause of

---

75   CCSU, "Community and the Progressive Press...", p. 31.
76   These are all his expressions.
77   In fact, Mabona couldn't get his name and tried "Garrigou" – Réginald Garrigou-Lagrange is the only person whose name could possibly fit with his description: "he was known to be the *the* Catholic theologian, *the* Catholic philosopher", Interview 3.
78   Interview 3.

death for his brother was given as tuberculosis; Mabona ascribed it to the severe psychological distress that the dawn of apartheid had on his brother.

6. Early priesthood

Because of the changes in Catholic church administration (described above) Mabona's ordination took place in Queenstown, and Bishop Rosenthal probably officiated. Dischl describes Rosenthal as having a "great interest in indigenous vocations" and adds that it was "a red letter day for him and for Keilands Mission when the Apostolic Delegate Lucas ordained the two brothers Stephen and Michael Phako on 8 December 1946".[79] A decade after his ordination, Mabona, who had known Rosenthal since his childhood,[80] described him in these words: "The Most Reverend and famous Johannes Rosenthal, S.A.C., Bishop of the diocese of Queenstown, where I am incardinated, has long won the admiration of the whole Xhosa people for his goodness and his great expertise in administrative matters".[81] A very enterprising man, Rosenthal initiated the expansion of the system of missions, and the construction of schools, churches, and medical facilities. The cathedral of Queenstown was one of his projects, as was the establishment of Glen Gray Hospital.[82] The late 1950s saw the foundation of the Catechetical Institute of Lumko (to which we will return in Chapter 5, §5.1).

After his ordination, Mabona worked under the Queenstown diocese and started fieldwork at Qoqodala, which was located 10 km north of the town. During this time, he also assisted Fr. Nicolas Soucy at the mission of Cofimvaba.[83] Marta Mabona suspected that he may have been involved in Africanising the church in Thaba Maria and McKay's Nek (40 km to the east of Qoqodala). This was indeed part of Rosenthal's broader project of Africanising[84] the local church. Subsequent enquiry has established that Mabona was not directly involved in the

---

[79] Dischl, *Transkei for Christ*, p. 283.
[80] "Jugend Mongameli".
[81] Mabona, *De statu catechistarum*, pp. VI-VII. "Totius Xosarum gentis admirationem et propter bonitatem et propter gnavam in rebus gerendis sollertiam iamdiu sibi conciliavit Reverendissimus et illustrissimus Dominus Joannes Rosenthal, S.A.C., Episcopus dioceseos Queenstownensis, cui incardinatus inservio."
[82] According to http://dioceseofqueenstown.mariannhillmedia.org/history/ (last accessed 3 June 2019).
[83] Dischl, *Transkei for Christ*, p. 293; according to him, between 1955–1957.
[84] Or "indigenisation" as it was apparently called then – Interview 6, 1:36".

design of the famous rondavel-style church building at McKay's Nek. However, he did participate in general discussions with the bishop on how to design and furnish church buildings for Xhosa people.[85]

Mabona had to preach a lot and found it exhausting. This is how he describes his approach: "I didn't preach in the way of teaching people. My sermon was more in explaining to the people, you know, what the faith is; how, why we are given this, [...] not to say we should do this – I avoided that".[86] But he also had time and opportunity to deepen his acquaintance with everyday practices and institutions around him, as is shown in the following reflection:

> When, as a Major Seminarian and as a priest I attended discussions at the courts of chiefs among the Zulu and among my own people, the debates became so subtle and were expressed with such symbolism that I was glad that I was not taking an active part so that I would not have to answer any questions, because, thought I knew all the words and expressions used, yet I was entirely lost as to sense and meaning.[87]

Whatever one makes of this episode, one does not get the impression that the theological studies and priestly work led to his complete alienation from the ambient culture.

In the meantime, South Africa had made the great 1948 transition. Mabona was to witness the first years of the Nationalist government as a priest. He declares: "When apartheid came, it hit us terribly". He mentions forced removals, the expropriation of agricultural land, the disruption of existing farming activities, violent, even fatal, conflict with police, and the disorientation and disruption of people's lives.[88]

Later, we will return directly to the increasingly forceful establishment of the apartheid state. But first, we need to look at a most extraordinary turn of events.

---

[85] Interview 6, 1:17"; Dischl, *Transkei for Christ*, pp. 296-297: "The missionary supervising the construction of this truly African church was Fr A. Skottnik, who also engaged in other undertakings. With the help of other missionaries and African people, he compiled a new catechism, and issued it as a well-illustrated ringbook [...] McKay's Nek became a well known 'Diocesan Centre for Literature in Xhosa'".
[86] Interview 2.
[87] Mabona, "African mentality in a world frame", p. 4.
[88] Interview 1.

CHAPTER 4

ITALY

Mongameli Mabona was working as priest at Qoqodala when, one day, something life-changing happened:

> And then, what happened was, after three or four years in the field, the apostolic delegate, who was at that time Damiano[1] [...] came down to say to me 'you should go to Rome'. He did not even ask me whether I wanted to go or not. He simply said 'You should go to Rome. People have tried to talk to you that you should go to Rome and you think you are not ready or something, I don't know. Do you think that you are wiser than all these people? Now, I give you an order, go to Rome! Prepare and go. Prepare and when you're prepared, come to me.' So, I prepared and went to Pretoria where he was and then he said: 'now next thing, he said, you take a plane and you go to Rome.' You know, that's how I went to Rome.[2]

To be sure, he was not the only African from South Africa to be sent to Rome to complete his studies. The first four Zulu priests (ordained between 1898 and 1907) received training from missionaries in South Africa before being directed to Rome.[3] However, my impression is that these first four were the exception rather than the rule.

---

[1] Celestine Joseph Damiano (1911–1976), who was born in New York, was the Apostolic Delegate for South Africa from 1952 to 1960. https://web.archive.org/web/20111008183418/http://www.blessedjohn23.org/camdens_bishops.html (last accessed 29 September 2019).
[2] Interview 3.
[3] Denis, *The Dominican Friars*, p. 203; Dischl, *Transkei for Christ*, p. 136.

1. Italian society after World War II

When Mabona arrived in Italy, that country had barely had a decade to rebuild itself from the disorder left behind by Fascism and the Second World War. By the middle of the 1950s, Italy could still be described as largely underdeveloped, with "oases of modernity" in the car, steel, and chemical industries concentrated in the north.[4] On average, Italians had a much lower standard of living than their European neighbours.[5] Few houses had amenities or electricity, and illiteracy was high. The disposable income of people in the south was about half that of their northern compatriots. In fact, poverty, unemployment, and landlessness characterised social life in the south.[6]

Dramatic socio-economic changes were to change this picture over the decade (the mid 50s to mid 60s) during which Mabona was in the country. This Italian "miracle" saw enormous industrialisation, a booming economy, and a rapid increase in personal wealth.[7] American funding[8] and the possibilities opened by Italy's membership of the European Economic Community played no mean role in these changes, but the availability of cheap new sources of energy (gas and oil) helped too. Finally, as can be expected, the abundant availability of cheap labour was indispensable to this "miracle".[9]

However, the north-south divide remained and even increased. The continued concentration of wealth in the north and the difficulties of a transition from a predominantly agrarian society to an industrialised one in the south remained major factors that shaped Italy's sociopolitical landscape of the time. Major politics of agrarian reform and land redistribution were implemented,[10] but this was a limited success. Where it was inadequate, it could be considered a factor contributing to the increasing urbanisation during that time.[11] Furthermore,

---

[4] Christopher Duggan, *A concise history of Italy*, Cambridge: Cambridge University Press, 1994, pp. 261–262.
[5] Sergio Romano, *Histoire de l'Italie du Risorgiomento à nos jours*, Paris: Seuil, 1977, p. 244; Duggan, *A concise history of Italy*, p. 262.
[6] Romano, *Histoire de l'Italie*, p. 244.
[7] For the statistical figures, see Romano, *Histoire de l'Italie*, pp. 239–244; for a detailed discussion, see Martin Clark, *Modern Italy 1871-1995* (second edition), London and New York: Longman, 1996, pp. 348–353.
[8] Romano, *Histoire de l'Italie*, p. 238.
[9] Duggan, *A concise history of Italy*, p. 263; Clark, *Modern Italy*, p. 350.
[10] Duggan, *A concise history of Italy*, pp. 256–259; Clark, *Modern Italy*, pp. 354–357.
[11] Duggan, *A concise history of Italy*, p. 261.

combined with industrialisation, it created the impetus for enormous intra-Italian migration[12] and international emigration.[13]

Urbanisation led to sociopolitical tensions, but also to developments away from the traditional lifestyle.[14] New products of industry infiltrated people's everyday lives – a notable example is the shifting prevalence from the 1950s to the 1970s from the use of bicycles to scooters and, later, cars.[15] Increased availability of appliances such as vacuum cleaners, refrigerators, and washing machines enabled many women to move from home-centred lives to professional careers, while opening homes for professional cleaning, etc.[16] Regional traditional culture and dialects became less prominent.[17] Despite a steady decline in church attendance, there was still high formal support for the Church, much of which was motivated by cultural or political considerations. But there was a strong trend towards gradual secularisation.[18]

There is general agreement that the social fibre of life in Italy at that time worked on patronage ("state clientelism"[19]). This was subtended by remnants of the "traditional feudal ethos of the [s]outh",[20] but this was not limited to the south. Another contributing factor was the Christian emphasis on the value of the family, which could easily be extended from close relatives to more remote relatives and friends at the expense of state-mediated relations and obligations.[21] Clark describes this as "a curious mixture of faction networks and a quest for efficiency, of financing party politics and a genuine concern for welfare, of jobs for supporters and moral crusade".[22] Whether one calls this corruption or *sottogoverno* does not change the outcome much: aside from the everyday politics of patronage in institutions, state bureaucracy grew excessively.

---

[12] Duggan, *A concise history of Italy*, p. 264; Gaia Giuliani and Cristina Lombardi-Diop, *Bianco e nero. Storia dell'identità razziale degli italiani*, Florence: Mondadori Education, 2013, p. 107.
[13] Romano, *Histoire de l'Italie*, p. 244.
[14] Duggan, *A concise history of Italy*, p. 265.
[15] Clark, *Modern Italy*, p. 368.
[16] Cf. Giuliani and Lombardi-Diop, *Bianco e nero*, p. 101.
[17] Clark, *Modern Italy*, p. 369.
[18] Clark, *Modern Italy*, pp. 370–371.
[19] Duggan, *A concise history of Italy*, p. 260.
[20] Duggan, *A concise history of Italy*, p. 260.
[21] Duggan, *A concise history of Italy*, p. 260.
[22] Clark, *Modern Italy*, p. 335.

In politics, the Christian Democrats consolidated their power in the 1940s, but from the 1950s, they had to rely on coalitions to retain power.[23] The post-Stalin revelations and Soviet politics of the 1950s put the formerly strong Italian Communist Party under severe pressure, and the Italian Socialist Party moved to the centre, which soon facilitated its entry into government in coalition with the Christian Democrats.[24] However, this did not mean that the sociopolitical system depended any less on patronage.[25]

2. Everyday life in Rome

It is difficult to say how a priest from South Africa would fit into this picture. In a sense, coming from a distant world, he did not fit in – he was neither particularly welcomed, nor aggressively ostracised. It seems that Italy's short-lived colonial history reflected racial categories back in the Italian peninsula.[26] There is also reason to believe that some of the Fascist ideology of eugenics survived in popular prejudices.[27] However, it is not easy to imagine how significant a role this would have played in interpersonal exchanges in post-war Rome, where African immigrants were still quite rare. At the same time, Mabona's position as a Catholic, and more importantly as an ordained priest, would have enabled him to score some social points.[28] According to his own recollection, only very few black people were to be seen in the city and his impression was that the Italians did not feel awkward about contact with Africans (I take this to mean that he did not experience encounters with Italian strangers as typically humiliating).

However, one may suppose that he soon noticed that his confreres were not all welcomed in Rome in the same way: those who fell administratively directly under the Vatican (those from Europe and North and South America) mostly studied at the Gregorian University and were housed by it; those who came from the newer mission fields of Asia and Africa fell under the authority of *Propaganda Fide* even in Rome, and studied at the Urbaniana, the Pontifical Urban University,

---

[23] Clark, *Modern Italy*, pp. 327–329.
[24] Romano, *Histoire de l'Italie*, p. 246.
[25] Clark, *Modern Italy*, pp. 333–334.
[26] Giuliani and Lombardi-Diop, *Bianco e nero*, pp. 99, 117.
[27] Giuliani and Lombardi-Diop, *Bianco e nero*, p. 126.
[28] See, for instance, the opportunity to contribute to public debate (under §4, pp. 86-87).

and were housed by it. However, it is worth mentioning that Damiano, who sent Mabona to Rome, was himself an alumnus of the Urbaniana.[29] Mabona and his fellow students could not have missed the differences in prestige, even course material, and patterns of socialisation. While Mabona confirms this pattern, he also mentions exceptions, for example, of African students studying at the Gregorian University.[30] The Jesuit lecturers at the Gregoriana were reputed to be better than those at the Urbaniana. To Mabona's recollection, the lecturers at the Urbaniana were mostly Dominicans, lecturers from other orders, and secular priests. Furthermore, he remembers the reputation of the Gregoriana as the institution with better students and he recalls being mocked by students from the Gregoriana on the basis of the supposed inferiority to students from the Urbaniana.

It has not been possible to find out much about Mabona's life in Rome as a student. He probably received accommodation and financial support from the Pontifical Society of St. Peter Apostle.[31] This accommodation would have included meals. However, in practice, this also meant that his private life was framed by that of the institution and that he would not have had many opportunities to pursue a private life outside the institution. He remembers that there were a good number of African students, for instance, from Ghana, the Congo, and Tanzania, but none from South Africa other than himself. Since the student body was comprised of people from Asia, Africa, and Europe, the institution's solution to facilitate communication was to expect students to communicate in Latin among themselves when they were together, for example, in the dining room. This practice was later changed, and besides, the authorities at the college spoke to the students in Italian. Mabona recounts that many students were proficient in Latin (citing the Chinese students as a prime example), but many students struggled to follow when the professors lectured in Latin. He says he "enjoyed it", adding that he "always liked Latin", and he remembers professors expressing surprise at his level of proficiency. He also sang in a conservatory choir.

This leads us to three major experiences of Mabona's life in Rome: his studies, the Second Congress of black writers and artists, and preparations for the Second Vatican Council.

---

[29] https://web.archive.org/web/20111008183418/http://www.blessedjohn23.org/camdens_bishops.html
[30] Interview 6, 35".
[31] Mabona, *De statu catechistarum*, p. VI; Interview 6, 31".

3. Mabona, the student and researcher

It seems likely[32] that he received a bursary from *Propaganda Fide*, which had directed him to study at the Urbaniana. However, he points out that he sometimes also attended lectures at the Gregoriana.[33] It is probable that he had to do some course work (exegesis, dogmatics, moral philosophy, and spirituality) and that he wrote a first paper, probably in Canon Law, since this had to serve as preparation for his thesis.[34]

It was his own choice to stay on in Rome and to start a doctorate in theology.[35] The introduction to his thesis provides us with valuable information about this aspect of his life.[36] He preferred to specialise in canon law. His decision was motivated, on the one hand, by the fact that he found the other theological disciplines too speculative.[37] Besides, the other theological disciplines seemed more suitable as a preparation for teaching, which Mabona at that stage did not imagine would be his future.[38] On the other hand, he anticipated that a solid background in canon law would help him to deal with the practical problems that might arise from his priestly duties at the missions. But the field of canon law offers a wide range of possible themes. The first sentence of the introduction to the thesis justifies his choice in a scholarly way: while there were already many works on catechism, he identified a lacuna in studies on the catechist.[39] I was at first perplexed by this choice of theme, but then came to suspect that it was linked to his father's work. Mabona confirms this.[40] Without stating explicitly what the exact motivations were that led him to choose the theme, in this respect, he

---

[32] The information in this paragraph was provided to me by Jan Dumon.
[33] Interview 3.
[34] Mabona thinks for some reason he was exempt from this (Interview 6, 36"). However, the French version of his 1962 article (i.e. before the completion of his doctorate), "Éléments de culture africaine", introduces him as "Antoine Mabona: Originaire du Cap, Afrique du Sud. Licencié en Droit canon" (p. 150). The English version does not give this information (p. 114).
[35] However, he did so with agreement from his bishop, Rosenthal, and the "bishop of Rome", cf. Mabona, *De statu catechistarum*, p. VII.
[36] I thank Jos Lievens for preparing a Dutch translation of this introduction for me.
[37] Interview 3.
[38] Interview 6, 46". In the interview, the example of the "everyday" utility of this discipline was in "hearing cases", e.g. marriages (between people of different religious persuasions). For preaching, seminary theology sufficed.
[39] Mabona, *De statu catechistarum*, p. I.
[40] Interview 6, 53".

cites his own background and that of the "people [he] lived with". Most were not Christian and had "nothing to do with the Catholic Church". His grandfather (paternal, if I follow correctly) was not a Christian, and his father converted only in his adult life. On his mother's side, his grandmother was a convert. Christian faith remained something new. This social context instilled "something that is deep within" him, as he describes it. He identifies this "something" as traditional Xhosa culture, which remained with him, even though he was Catholic from his childhood on. At the same time, he recognises that Catholicism had also "grown into his background". Thus, in his childhood, people coupled traditional practices with Catholic ceremonies and, in a way, he did something similar in his life in general.

Much of his research was carried out in libraries. However, he had the opportunity to consult with specialists at different institutions.[41] At the Ludwig Maximilians University in Munich, he consulted with Klaus Mörsdorf and Michael Schmaus.[42] The family of Ludwig Späth received him there and Mabona thanks them as his friends. From the interviews, it seems he may have made several such visits to Munich.[43] In Brussels, Mabona was received by Fr. Georges Delcuve, S.J. of the Lumen Vitae Institute. Finally, Canon Brien, director of the Institut supérieur de Pastorale catéchétique, and P. Honoret, director of the Service de l'Institution religieuse, were his interlocutors in Paris.

---

[41] Mabona, *De statu catechistarum*, p. V.
[42] They acted as his "consultants" (Interview 7, 8"). Michael Schmaus (1897–1993), was professor of systematic and medieval theology, first in Münster from 1933, then in Munich from 1946 until his retirement in 1965. He is the author of many authoritative studies, including *Katholische Dogmatik* (5 volumes) and *Der Glaube der Kirche* (6 volumes) and many works of historical investigations. Cf. Leo Kardinal Scheffczyk, "Schmaus, Michael" in *Neue Deutsche Biographie* 23, 2007, pp. 123–124. Klaus Mörsdorf (1909–1989), from 1946 until retirement in the 1980s, was professor of canon law in Munich. Considered one of the leading authorities of this discipline in Germany at the time, he published a number of authoritative studies, among which updated versions of Eduard Eichmann's *Lehrbuch des Kirchenrechts auf Grund des Codex Iuris Canonici*. Mörsdorf was also co-founder and for years co-editor of the *Münchener Theologische Studien*. Cf. Winfried Aymans, "Mörsdorf, Klaus", in *Neue Deutsche Biographie* 17, 1994, p. 683f. Both Schmaus and Mörsdorf served as advisors at the Second Vatican Council during the last part of Mabona's period in Rome. Cf. Karin Nußbaum, "Klaus Mörsdorf und Michael Schmaus als Konzilsberater des Münchener Erzbischofs Kardinal Julius Döpfner auf dem Zweiten Vatikanischen Konzil. Eine Untersuchung aufgrund des Konzilsnachlasses Kardinal Döpfners", *Münchener Theologische Zeitschrift* 55, 2004, pp. 132–150.
[43] Cf. Interview 3.

Cyrillus Papali of the Order of Carmel Discalced (born in Cochin, Kerala, India, in 1902) acted as his supervisor for the study.[44] Mabona indicates that Papali was professor of catechetics; I observed that it is elsewhere claimed that he was appointed as professor of missiology and tasked to teach Hinduism.[45] His bibliography does indeed contain a substantial list of publications on Hinduism.

Mabona praises Papali and his other lecturers in theology, but he reserves a special mention of Fr. Emilio Springhetti, S.J., because of their friendship and because of his admiration for him.[46] Springhetti taught Latin in Rome for many years and published numerous books. For two years, Mabona studied with him at the Schola Superior Litterarum Latinarum at the Gregorian University.

The title of the thesis, then, is *De statu catechistarum in ecclesia* ('On the position of the catechists in the Church'). Commenting on the fact that he wrote it in Latin,[47] Mabona remarked:

> I was the only one who wrote my thesis in Latin because we were allowed to write in English and in our own mother-tongue, whatever it was, though of course there... if I had written this thing in Xhosa, they would not have understood.[48]

I think, strictly speaking, this still left English as a viable option. Perhaps Latin was just easier... As far as my research has been able to establish at the time of my writing this biography, Mabona is the only living South African with a doctorate written in Latin to his name.

Looking back at his university experience as a whole, Mabona comments as follows: "All I can say is that I felt in Rome that I was really... advancing intellectually [...] especially at the *Propaganda*, at the University". In fact, in his assessment, Urbaniana was a good university to the point of his being "excited" when he thinks back to it.[49]

---

[44] Confirmed in Interview 7, 7".

[45] "Cyril Bernard Papali", *Wikipedia, The Free Encyclopedia*, https://en.wikipedia.org/wiki/Cyril_Bernard_Papali (last accessed 1 June 2019) – there are reasons to question the accuracy of this article.

[46] Mabona, *De statu catechistarum*, p. VI: "Nostrae amicitiae causa et admirationis sensu permotus hic eum speciatim nominare volo. Ceteros quoque Professores in hac insigni Universitate amicos gratiis abundantissimis prosequor."

[47] Jos Lievens, who helped me by translating the Introduction of the thesis, commented on Mabona's "Ciceronian Latin" (correspondence 1 July 2018); Mabona described it as "church Latin".

[48] Interview 3.

[49] Interview 3.

And what did he finally think of his abrupt call to go to Rome? We read the following in the Introduction to his thesis:

> The Most Reverend and famous Celestinus Damianus, who was once the Apostolic Delegate for southern Africa, encouraged me most to go to Rome to continue my studies there. Words are not enough to express my gratitude to him. This very passionate shepherd will therefore know that my heart will always be very grateful to him.[50]

Pure compliance with formal rhetoric? Perhaps not – if one takes into consideration the whole scope of experiences he had in Rome, of which more will follow.

4. Further intellectual work

Mongameli Mabona's intellectual work as apprentice theologian was not restricted to research for his thesis. At some stage in the late 1950s, he started to collaborate with students of the African Association of St. Augustine. The annual review of this Association was named *Lux*, and Mabona was the editor of the journal for some years. His very first publications appeared in this review: "Africa's true position and destiny" and "African mentality in a world frame" (both appeared in the 1958–1959 edition). In this issue, he is also indicated as the president of the Association.

It is probable that Mabona participated in the 1963 All African Students Conference in London.[51] A radio broadcast reported on the event on 17 April 1963 as follows:

---

[50] Mabona, *De statu catechistarum*, p. VI: "Ut Romam, studia ulterius persequendi causa, adirem mihi auctor praecipuus fuit Reverendissimus et illustrissimus Dominus Celestinus Damianus, Africae meridionalis quondam Apostolicus Delegatus, cui quantum gratitudinis debeam haud dictu facile est. Noverit ergo ardentissimus ille pastor gratissimum erga eum meum animum semper mansurum esse."

[51] My claim is based on Joseph Boakye Danquah's "Letter to the editor", *Ghanaian Times*, 6 May 1963, as republished with a prefatory note as "The 'force' of Ghanaism", in Joseph Boakye Danquah, *The Ghanaian establishment. Its constitution, its detentions, its traditions, its justice and statecraft and its heritage of Ghanaism*, Accra: Ghana Universities Press, 1997, pp. 183–185. I say "probable", because the author refers to "Mr. Anthony B. Mabona" (Mabona's second initial is D.), who was a student in Italy at the time.

Some 200 delegates attended the opening today of the second pan-African congress of African students in Europe and in the United States to discuss African unity. The conference was organized by four African associations in Europe and the United States: The Committee of African Organizations of Britain, the Federation of Students from Black Africa and France, the Union of African students in Europe, and the Union of African students in America. Among those seated on the platform were the Ghana High Commissioner in London, Kwezi Armah, Congo Leopoldville chargé d'affaires Thomas Kanza, and the Yogoslav ambassador, Mr. Prica.[52]

Mabona's presentation at the conference was published in the *Ghanaian Times*[53] and was hailed by the journal's editor as a "revolutionary address on African culture and World Revolution".[54] Following Danquah's reading, the presentation dealt with the "traditional European mentality" and the African view of the universe as a "system of forces". Mabona advocated a personalist-realist view on reality and an approach to African unity in all dimensions of human existence (for instance, cultural unity and unity with the whole world).

Of a completely different nature is his participation in the conference on "The use of audio-visual equipment for education in Africa", held in Milan on 26 and 27 April 1962.[55] A collection of papers was selected from this event for publication in *Africa: Rivista trimestrale di studi e documentazione dell'Istituto italiano per l'Africa e l'Oriente*. The introduction to this collection of papers describes the event in the following terms (my translation):

> On 26 and 27 April, the First International Congress on the Use of Audiovisual Media for Education and Vocational Training in Africa was held in Milan, in the halls of MIFED. The congress was the initiative of the MIFED [Mercato Internazionale del Film e del Documentario] and

---

[52] "African student parley opens in London", broadcast from Monrovia Liberia on the ELWA Radio Station, as cited by the Foreign Broadcast Information Service (USA), *Daily Report, Foreign Radio Broadcasts* 75, 1963, p. 11.

[53] To date I have not been able to get a copy of this.

[54] Danquah, "The 'force' of Ghanaism", p. 183.

[55] Alhaji Isa Kaita, Jean Christophe Mackpayen, Sy Mamadou, Mohamed Said Samantar, Doudou Gueye, E. E. Esua, Godwin Paul Doe, F. Lukusa, Gian Luigi Pezza, Camillo Bonanni, and Antonio Mabona: "Impiego degli audiovisivi per l'educazione in Africa", in *Africa: Rivista trimestrale di studi e documentazione dell'Istituto italiano per l'Africa e l'Oriente* 17/4, July–August 1962, pp. 179–198, here pp. 197–198.

of the International Committee for the Development of Educational and Cultural Activities in Africa (CIDAECA). It was attended, by delegates and observers from the Governments of 21 African countries and numerous specialized Italian, European and international organizations. In four intense working sessions, problems, projects and experiences were exposed and discussed and some practical conclusions were drawn which, on the one hand commit CIDAECA to carry out certain actions, which are currently underway, on the other hand urge MIFED to convene a second conference as soon as possible (as will be effectively convened in April), in which the Italian and world industry that is interested in the production of audiovisual media is also called to participate. The complex problems of education and professional training in Africa and of the possibilities and methods of use of audiovisual media were the subject of interesting contributions from the speeches and presentations delivered at the conference last April, of which we give a selection.

Mabona's contribution, of which an extract was published, revolves around the untapped human and economic potential of the African continent. He emphasises the need for mass education based on intercontinental collaboration in a spirit of shared humanism. He acknowledges the role that radio and cinema could play. Incidentally, he probably gave the presentation in Italian – his years in Rome enabled him to acquire a significant proficiency in Italian to the point that he recalls once being asked if he came from Libya, and another time someone exclaiming not knowing that there were black Italians.[56]

These three examples of work beyond his theological research open a window to another significant part of his life in Italy. For, as significant as it was for him to study in Rome and to overcome the enormous obstacles to complete his doctorate, Mabona was also exposed to an entirely different (but not unrelated) set of influences. The exact order in which events unfolded is not clear, but the fact that they took place is of central importance for the life and work of Mabona.

---

[56]   Interview 6, 29".

5. Second Congress of Black Writers and Artists: Alioune Diop and *Présence Africaine*

It just so happened that the Second Congress of Black Writers and Artists took place in Rome in 1959 when Mabona lived there. To appreciate why this could be such a significant experience for him, we have to take a step back by speaking about its organiser: Alioune Diop.

Diop[57] was born in 1910 in Saint-Louis, Sénégal, where he grew up. After his initial studies at the University of Algiers, he advanced his education in Paris. There, he joined approximately five thousand peers from Africa (of whom, in 1940, only about a hundred were students), the Antilles, and Guyanne (most of whom were, like Diop, French citizens at that time).[58] This proved to be an extraordinary milieu for networking between people of African descent – as much for Diop as for many of his fellow students – Senghor, Césaire, Rabemananjara, Damas, and others. But Diop also made the acquaintance of many French peers: Camus (whom he knew from Algiers), Gide, Breton, Griaule, Picasso, Sartre, Mounier, Leiris, Balandier, and others. Many of these people would support his work throughout his life.

Diop thus took part in the growth of the intellectual climate that saw the emergence of *négritude*. At the same time, he built close ties with Fr. Maydieu and other Christians and converted to Catholicism.[59] From associates such as Sartre, Mounier, and Maydieu, he learned about the value and potential of intellectual journals, such as *Les temps modernes*, *Esprit*, and *La vie intellectuelle*. Additionally, in formal and informal ways, Diop continued to make connections with younger students – including Cheikh Anta Diop and Abdoulaye Wade – as a mentor.[60] Soon after the war, he also married and started a family.

The apparent disparate statements of the last paragraph represent the most important lines of development of his life narrative; these dimensions often converged in a number of highly significant events, some of which extended

---

[57] Unless indicated otherwise, all information is derived from Philippe Verdin's biography: *Alioune Diop, le Socrate noir*, preface by d'Abd Al Malik, Paris: Lethielleux, 2010.

[58] Verdin, *Alioune Diop*, pp. 50, 129.

[59] On religious conviction among intellectuals for the African diaspora in France, cf. Abdoulaye Gueye, "De la religion chez les intellectuels africains en France. L'odyssée d'un référent identitaire", *Cahiers d'études africaines* 162/2, 2001, pp. 267–291.

[60] Verdin, *Alioune Diop*, p. 100.

over decades, related to his promotion of African culture. Culture should be understood here in the broadest sense, to include (but not to be reduced to) politics, intellectual life, the arts, etc. The general orientation of Diop's work, at least in the late 1940s, can be summarised in the following theses:

> The originality of African civilization, the need for cultural exchanges between the two continents [Africa and Europe, including the African diaspora], the veiled criticism of exploitative colonialism and the mediocrity of settlers, the appeal to the forces of the mind, the concern for the regeneration of Europe and the original development of Africa.[61]

This also corresponds with the foundation of the journal *Présence Africaine*, which he launched with the support of many of his associates, named above. The first edition appeared at the end of 1947. From the beginning, it contained contributions on a wide variety of themes on African culture, dialogue with Europe, and also poetry and literature. In practice, *Présence Africaine* extended its publication activities to include books by Africans and/or on African issues. The first book published by Diop was a re-edition of an obscure tome formerly published by Lovania Press in Elizabethville, under the name *La philosophie bantoue* by Placide Tempels.[62] The combined effect of publishing influential works, plus work from the *négritude* movement (e.g. a second publication of Césaire's *Discourse on colonialism*) and later the entire oeuvre of Cheikh Anta Diop, was to establish the reputation of *Présence Africaine*. In a sense, the names of Césaire and Anta Diop symbolically represent two dimensions of the mission of *Présence Africaine* as a publisher: the advancement of African literature and arts,[63] and the desire to make scientific contributions, in particular in historiography.[64] These two dimensions overlap, insofar as they both are also forms of politics pursued by other means.

Excursion: The journal *Présence Africaine*

But before we return to the life work of Alioune Diop, it is necessary to zoom in on the journal he founded. What is of interest here is the general ideological

---

[61] Verdin, *Alioune Diop*, p. 149.
[62] Verdin, *Alioune Diop*, pp. 147, 199–208
[63] On literature in *Présence Africaine*, cf. Marc-Vincent Howlett and Romuald Fonkoua, "La maison Présence Africaine", *Gradhiva* 10/2, 2009, pp. 106–133, here pp. 121–130.
[64] On historiography in *Présence Africaine* (especially Anta Diop and Joseph Ki-Zerbo), cf. Howlett and Fonkoua, "La maison Présence Africaine" 115-121.

orientation from which the journal started and the first changes this orientation underwent in response to world events. The journal *Présence Africaine* aimed to ensure greater recognition of African culture and to be a space in which African culture could find public expression. Gradually, this cultural agenda espoused the bigger aim of African independence. Diop was convinced that the best way for a journal to contribute to these objectives was to create a forum for the plurality of voices and views; that is to say, the journal had to refrain as much as possible from imposing its own ideology and to allow encounters between Africans and Europeans, between people of the most divergent persuasions, to express the full scale of their correspondence and disagreements. Clearly, such an enterprise still presupposed a view. Diop wanted to celebrate African history and transmit knowledge of its cultures, but this was always linked to contemporary creation, study, and political engagement. This is not a nostalgic culturalism, but a view of Africa as "the place of a history in the making".[65] As much as the history of defeat, deprivation, and exploitation remained part of present reality, the project was to assume this present in creative and reflective engagement with the modern world.[66]

But this general orientation of the journal was more than a mere direction. One could identify the substance of this orientation in two steps. First, while the journal had to be representative of diversity and contestation, Diop believed in the constructive outcomes of such oppositions. This conviction was based on his own humanism, as Hewlett and Fonkoua explain:

> In the name of a humanist vision of history, Alioune Diop has taken up the challenge to think both Senghor's 'civilisational' universalism and Césaire's political radicality. Two universalisms confronted each other: one 'ecumenical' ('the civilization of the universal') and the other more oriented towards an approach largely inspired by Marxism.[67]

Second, this approximation of the journal's ideology can be unpacked by a more historical view of its gradual change. According to Salah Hassan, a significant shift in general (cultural)political orientation can be observed over the first decade of the journal's editions. Hence the initial plural orientation to liberal

---

[65] Howlett and Fonkoua, "La maison Présence Africaine" 108.
[66] Cf. Howlett and Fonkoua, "La maison Présence Africaine", p. 112. The whole *Présence Africaine* 2010/1–2 (N° 181-182) is devoted to the work and heritage of Alioune Diop; it contains the contributions to the International Symposium Alioune Diop, the Man and his Work Facing Modern Challenges.
[67] Howlett and Fonkoua, "La maison Présence Africaine", p. 112.

humanism, communism, and Pan-Africanism gradually changed into a marked predominance of Pan-Africanism, notably from 1955:[68]

> In 1947, liberal humanism, based on the projection of a universal civilization and informed by European philosophical and ethnographic modes of thought, dominated the journal's editorial line. The inaugural issue of 1947 testifies unequivocally to the hegemony of these cultural values. The appearance of the new series marked the shift in power relations within *Présence Africaine* resulting from the emergence outside the journal of newly hegemonic sources of cultural legitimation on the periphery: political Pan-Africanism, nation-statism, African socialism, and nonalignment. The shift is apparent not only in the stated anticolonialism and antiracism of the new editorial collective in 1955, but also in a reorganization of the division of intellectual labor and the political engagement of the literary contributions, confirming the decisive – although not uncontested – triumph of Pan-African forces associated with the journal.[69]

This change in ideological orientation can be attributed to an appropriation of the Bandung Conference (April 1955), the beginning of the Algerian uprising, and the spread of the effects of the "Cold War" to the colonies as a fairly late response of radicalisation to these events.[70] The net effect was a tendency to leave the more optimistic view of an African reconciliation within a universal humanism, for a more articulate contestation of geopolitical inequalities, exploitation, etc. "Tendency", because this change is not to be construed as a break, but rather as a shift in general emphasis.[71]

This description of the journal's orientation is of great significance for us, since, with its continuities and shifts, it maps the objectives and ambitions for which the journal stood, but also the different stances that were taken up in it. In

---

[68] Cf. Salah D. Hassan, "Inaugural Issues: The Cultural Politics of the Early 'Présence Africaine', 1947-55", *Research in African Literatures* 30/2, 1999, pp. 194–221, here p. 194.
[69] Hassan, "Inaugural Issues...", pp. 194–195.
[70] Cf. Hassan, "Inaugural Issues...", p. 198.
[71] Mudimbe's qualified endorsement of Hassan's analysis emphasises the importance of noticing the later emphasis present in earlier editions, just like the earlier emphasis remained present in the later (Valentin Mudimbe, "'À la naissance de *Présence Africaine*: La nuit de foi pourtant'. Lettre à Éric Van Grasdorff", *Rue Descartes* 83/4, 2014, pp. 117–136). The volume, *The surreptitious speech. Présence Africaine and the politics of otherness 1947 – 1987*, Chicago: Chicago University Press, 1992, edited by Mudimbe, remains an invaluable collection of studies on *Présence Africaine*.

short, it sketches a milieu of intellectual and artistic work with which the student Mongameli Mabona was to be confronted and in which he was going to be taken up, as we will see later.

But the importance of his years in Rome for Mabona's life is premised on still another dimension of the journal's project. It intended not only to publish ideas that could in turn be sharpened through debate, but also to contribute to the circulation and exchange of ideas beyond the immediate circle of intellectuals. Its ambition was also a broader one of sensitisation and education. This objective had an impact on the medium of expression. At its inception, the journal was French, but sometimes articles were published in English too. Then, from 1960, a complete English edition was published.[72] This is in keeping with the journal's policy of African unification and the broad dissemination of ideas. However, if I interpret the evidence correctly, this was to have a significant consequence, in that authors who wrote in English could gain much easier access to publication and their essays would be translated. To this point too, we will soon return (see p. 97).

* * *

After this detour on the journal *Présence Africaine*, we can now resume the discussion of Alioune Diop's work and the events surrounding it.

It has been noted that many of the contributors to the journal and books printed by this publisher were penned by African expatriates.[73] This fact reflects a larger phenomenon of the growing dynamism of African intellectual, artistic, and cultural life as concentrated in the former colonial powers (the same can be said for some political movements[74]). Diop certainly used the networks and institutional platforms available to him to establish and institute means by which to further African cultural politics as he understood it. This is most eloquently demonstrated by the first and second Congress for Black Writers and Artists, held respectively in Paris (1956) and Rome (1959).

Unfolding the logic of his cultural politics, but also in response to the Afro-Asian Conference in Bandung (April 1955),[75] Diop, with collaborators from

---

[72] Information received from KU Leuven librarian Stefan Derouck on 5 October 2018.
[73] Cf. Verdin, *Alioune Diop*, p. 170.
[74] Cf. Saïd Bouamama, *Figures de la révolution africaine. De Kenyatta à Sankara*, Paris: Découverte, 2014, pp. 28–36.
[75] Cf. Howlett and Fonkoua, "La maison Présence Africaine", p. 110.

Africa, the Antilles, the United States, and the people around him, organised the first Congress for Black Writers and Artists that took place in Paris at the Sorbonne in 1956. It brought together an impressive line-up of writers, intellectuals, and artists from Africa and the African diaspora, both anglophone and francophone. Among them was one South African-born artist and musician: Gerard Sekoto. Other notables were Mercer Cook, Richard Wright, R.P. Bisanthe, Jacques Rabemananjara, Aimé Césaire, Frantz Fanon, Édouard Glissant, Boubou Hama, Mamadou Dia, Cheikh Anta Diop, Leopold Sedar Senghor, Abdoulaye Wade, and Amadou Hampâté Bâ.[76] Unexpected tensions emerged during the Congress: the views of many of the Africans and the Afro-Americans diverged, and there was political friction among participants (partially due to outside intervention). But overall, the Congress was an enormous success. It confirmed the importance of Pan-African intellectual and artistic collaboration, and forcefully reaffirmed the condemnation of racism and colonialism. As a contribution to coordinate the different aspirations of Africans, Antilleans, and Afro-Americans, and as collective cultural and intellectual self-affirmation, the Paris Congress was a historical event of the highest international importance.

The presentations of the Congress were published in *Présence Africaine* in an English and a French volume[77] and were widely disseminated. The success of the Congress and the subsequent standing that its organiser enjoyed facilitated the establishment an institution that could channel and augment the momentum created by the Congress. In the very same year, 1956, Alioune Diop founded the Société africaine de culture (SAC[78]), following to some extent the model of the Société européenne de la culture, in which he had participated for a number of years. The objectives of the SAC would be furthered by conferences and other meetings, on themes such as underdevelopment, religion, women in Africa, African cinema, and apartheid.[79] Of all of its activities, only one is of concern for our purposes.

Without this background, it is hard to grasp the significance of the Congress that Mabona happened to be able to attend in Rome, where it took place from

---

[76] According to the list provided by the UNESCO website for the fiftieth anniversary of the conference: http://portal.unesco.org/fr/ev.php-URL_ID=34700&URL_DO=DO_TOPIC&URL_SECTION=201.html (last accessed 8 November 2018).

[77] The English version is 1959/1–2 (N° XXIV-XXV) and the French one is 1959/4–5 (N° XXVII-XXVIII).

[78] A critical view on the SAC is offered by Frantz Fanon, *Les damnés de la terre*, Paris: La Découverte, 2002, pp. 204–206.

[79] Verdin, *Alioune Diop*, p. 274.

26 March to 1 April 1959. Its theme was "Unity and responsibility of/for the black African culture".[80]

In the three years separating the two conferences, the geopolitical climate had changed considerably. For francophone Africa, the 1958 Constitution of the French Union opened the difficult path to the end of the French imperial project and to the different national situations from which participants spoke. Sékou Touré, who defiantly rejected the Constitution, and by 1959 was the head of state of an independent Guinea, gave a presentation in absentia.[81] Franz Fanon also participated while he was allied to the *Front de libération nationale* (FLN) in the Algerian war of independence which was being waged at that time. Another participant, Senghor, who would become the first president of independent Senegal in 1960, supported the Constitution, for a variety of pragmatic and principled reasons. Furthermore, while some delegates wanted to remain true to the geopolitical alternative of the non-aligned movement, others openly stated their loyalty to communism. The question of unity, figuring in the conference theme, was highly topical.

At the same time, whereas the first Congress relied very strongly on private initiative, the second took place in Rome at the invitation of (amongst others) the Italian government and the mayor of Rome, and enjoyed support and financial aid from UNESCO. They thus enjoyed the moral support of the Italian head of state and the Pope.[82]

I could not ascertain whom Mabona met at the conference or confirm which sessions he may have attended. He may have met compatriots Sekoto and Mphahlele. At the conference he may have attended presentations reflected in the two volumes of proceedings – I select those whose themes were subsequently echoed in his own later work:[83]

• From the first volume:
— Cheick Anta Diop, "African cultural unity (I)" (pp. 66–72);
— Aimé Césaire, "The man of culture and his responsibilities" (pp. 125–132);

---

[80] "Unité et responsabilité de la culture négro-africaine", cf. Etienne Lock, *Identité africaine et Catholicisme: problématique de la rencontre de deux notions à travers l'itinéraire d'Alioune Diop (1956-1995)*. Doctoral dissertation in history. Université Charles-de-Gaulle – Lille-III, 2014, here p. 112.
[81] Cf. also Lock, *Identité africaine*, 113.
[82] Verdin, *Alioune Diop*, pp. 286–287; Lock, *Identité africaine*, p. 115f.
[83] Following the conference, proceedings were published in two volumes of *Présence Africaine* in 1959. The principle behind the distribution of articles, sometimes translated, into a French and an English volume is not clear to me.

- Robert Sastre, "Theology and African culture" (pp. 142–152);
- Es'kia Mphahlele, "Negro culture in a multi-racial society in Africa" (pp. 221–227);
- Léopold Senghor, "Constructive elements of a civilization of African Negro inspiration" (pp. 262–294); and finally
- Pope John XXIII's response at the "Audience granted by His Holiness to The Society of African Culture" (pp. 469 à 470)[84]

- From the second volume:
    - Taita Towet, "The role of an African philosopher" ("Le rôle d'un philosophe africain", pp. 108–128);
    - John Mbiti, "Christianity and indigenous religions in Kenya" ("Christianisme et religions indigènes au Kenya", pp. 129–153);
    - Vincent Mulago, "Theology and its responsibilities" ("La théologie et ses responsabilités", pp. 188–205); and
    - Gerard Sekoto, "Responsibility and solidarity in African culture" ("La responsabilité et la solidarité dans la culture africaine", pp. 263–267).[85]

Not in the conference proceedings is the paper "Culture and nation" ("Culture et nation")[86] read by Fanon, subsequently published as "Fondements réciproques de la culture nationale et des luttes de Liberation" (the second half of Chapter IV of *Les damnés de la terre*).[87]

Finally, having access to these editions of *Présence Africaine*, Mabona would have been gladdened and encouraged by the motion condemning

> notably in Algeria, Kenya, Nyassaland, the Congo, Angola and Rhodesia, and particularly in the Union of South Africa, violence in the most diverse forms and segregation in its most intolerable aspects, continue to be exercised against the peoples, in violation of the fundamental right of peoples to dispose of themselves, and of the fundamental rights of the individual, threatening to disunite the natural and human elements which are indispensable to the flourishing of culture.[88]

---

[84] *Présence Africaine* 1959/1–2 (N° XXIV-XXV) Second Congress of Negro Writers and Artists.
[85] *Présence Africaine* 1959/4–5 (N° XXVII-XXVIII) Deuxième congrès des écrivains et artistes noirs (Rome: 26 March–1 April 1959).
[86] Cf. Alice Cherki, "Préface à l'édition de 2002", in Fanon, *Les damnés,* pp. 5–15, here p. 9.
[87] Frantz Fanon, "Mutual foundations for national culture and liberation struggle", in *The wretched of the earth*, New York: Grove Press, 2004, pp. 170–180.
[88] "Motions", *Présence Africaine* 1959/1 (N° XXIV-XXV), pp. 461–463, citation 463.

This is in line with the continued engagement for the South African cause, by both *Présence Africaine* and the SAC.

Major recurrent themes throughout the conference proceedings are interdisciplinary study, the unity of African culture globally, the possible coordination of promoting African culture and (Catholic) theology, the critique of all forms of oppression and exploitation, and some tendencies to human universalism, but with cultural pluralism and the embrace of African culture, without sacrificing modernity or progress.[89] Moreover, the significance of the Congress for philosophy can be measured by a reflection by Jean Kinyongo:

> It was only in 1959 that the expression African philosophy, already used in 1958 by Janheinz Jahn in his famous book Muntu, was definitively adopted. The resolution of the Subcommittee on Philosophy at the 2nd Congress of Black Writers and Artists – the first true charter of African philosophy – emphasises the name African philosophy, which thus became part of current practice and usage.[90]

The opportunity to attend this conference would leave an enormous impression on the student Mongameli Mabona. In fact, one can trace this impact in his publications from right after the event. However, one may, with equal confidence, claim that the most significant encounter for Mabona was with the person of Alioune Diop, his welcoming personality, his indefatigable work for the cause of African culture, and perhaps also his faith. In any case, it is about him that Mabona exclaimed: "I was *very* close to that man".[91]

Henceforth, Diop and *Présence Africaine* were to be a major point of orientation in his work: "[...] whenever I had holidays I went to France to work with him".[92] But it is not clear when exactly this happened. Only two periods appear to be plausible: 1959–1963 (the time between their first encounter and Mabona's leaving Rome) and 1972–1980 (between Mabona's arrival in London and Diop's death). On the basis of Mabona's contributions to *Présence Africaine* publications, I assume that the two men were in relatively frequent contact during the first period; from the "Gratitude" section in *Diviners and prophets*, we know

---

[89] On the difference of orientation between the two congresses, cf. Lylian Kesteloot, "1956 – 1959. D'un congrès à l'autre", *Présence Africaine* 2007/1 (N° 175-176-177), pp. 125–129.
[90] Jean Kinyongo, "La philosophie africaine et son histoire", *Les Études philosophiques* (Philosophies africaines) 4, 1982, pp. 407–418, here p. 413. My translation.
[91] Interview 3.
[92] Interview 3.

that they already met in London early on during the second period and several times after that in Paris.

Diop prompted Mabona to work on the relation between the European thought he was exposed to at university and African thought, for instance, on African philosophical terms.[93] Mabona remembers that some Africans with whom he had contact at that time were afraid that *Présence Africaine* would "take things too far" and explore directions that the Church would not approve of (and that they should instead bow to church authority). However, Mabona dismisses the view that the journal's work had this implication.[94] Diop's objective, and Mabona's too, was finding forms of thinking in agreement with traditional expression.

The first tangible outcome of this encounter is a series of publications submitted by Mabona to *Présence Africaine*. The first of these was a republication of the article "Towards an African philosophy", initially the third and last of his contributions to *Lux* (namely in the 1959 edition). Except for the short contribution to "Impiego degli audiovisivi per l'educazione in Africa" (cited above), all of Mabona's remaining publications of the 1960s were presented in *Présence Africaine*:

— five articles, including "Towards an African philosophy", all of which appeared in both French and English;
— one chapter, "The depths of African philosophy", published in *Personnalité africaine et catholicisme* and drawn from his book manuscript (see below pp. 100-101); and
— eight poems (the first in 1965,[95] the others in 1970).

Later, in 1996, a series of his texts were again published by *Présence Africaine*:
— three on South African liberation history;
— two short interviews; and
— two short reviews on South African literature.

One cannot miss that already, formally, the array of contributions correspond with the range of objectives of *Présence Africaine*: intellectual, scientific, and artistic.

But the influence goes deeper than this, because during his time as a doctoral student, Mabona also completed a book manuscript entitled *The outlines of*

---

[93] Interview 6, 1:12".
[94] In fact, according to the interview, up to the present, Mabona considers the question of the relation between the Church and tradition to remain unresolved.
[95] This poem, "The sea", was also published in *New Coin* in the same year.

African philosophy in 1962.[96] He wrote the book in one year and intended it as a sketch; he wanted to see whether people would be interested in it (and indeed, to raise interest in it), before resuming the task of writing African philosophy. However, the feedback of his first readers was discouraging: the argument of the book required a much deeper competence in mathematics and physics, which Mabona readily concedes he did not have. Thus the book remained unpublished. However, part of its content is reflected in the chapter "The depths of African philosophy", evoked above. Years later, he would still comment on it: "In 1962 I wrote a manuscript of 155 pages based on a model of the three-step motion I have described in connection with the concept of *Ithuba*. The title of the script was rather wistful: The Outlines of African Philosophy".[97]

Thus, on the surface, we find a young priest studying theology and researching for his doctorate, and all indications are that he took this seriously. At the same time, we have the bulk of the second strand of his intellectual work produced in this time. However, he did not see any contradiction between this work and this new endeavour of philosophy.[98] This mutual accommodation was facilitated by his view of philosophy as an inborn human ability, a kind of reasoning, rather than something one learns (in the first place) at school.

A second outcome of Mabona's encounter with Diop had less spectacular results. To present this, we have to turn to another major event of the time: the Second Vatican Council.

6. Preparing for Vatican II

It just so happened that one of the most important events in the long history of the Catholic Church took place in Rome while Mongameli Mabona lived there: the Second Vatican Council. The Pope who received a delegation from the SAC at the Vatican during the Second Congress of Black Writers and Artists,[99] John XXIII, initiated Vatican II. Preparations for the Council started in different

---

[96] Interview 6, 15:10".
[97] DP, p. 400.
[98] Interview 6, 1:05".
[99] Cf. Pope John XXIII's response at the "Audience granted by His Holiness to The Society of African Culture", published as "His holiness replies", in *Présence Africaine* XXIV-XXV/1, 1959, pp. 469–470.

forms, basically from after his inauguration in 1958, but the formal preparations began in mid 1960, after advice was gathered from Catholic theologians from all over the world.[100] The Council itself was to start in October 1962 and to last until the end of 1965 (even though John XXIII died mid 1963).[101] One would expect that these events would make an impression on a Catholic priest working in Rome at that time. And this is indeed true for Mabona, but not for the most obvious reasons. Quite the contrary: the Council itself was of much less significance to him than a part of the preparatory work in which he was involved. To appreciate this fact, one has to know the initiatives of one lay member of the Catholic Church, Alioune Diop.[102]

During the preparatory phase preceding Vatican II, an opportunity was given to the Catholic members to express their views on the important themes to be discussed during the Council. The African Catholic churches eagerly responded to this invitation. But independently from the Church structures, Diop mobilised the SAC to prepare a submission too. More precisely, he initiated a broad consultation with African Catholics to study this question. He was assisted particularly by the Cameroonian Jesuit Meinrad Hebga.[103]

The consultation was launched through an open letter, "De la contribution de la personnalité africaine à la vitalité du catholicisme" ("On the contribution of African personhood to the vitality of Catholicism"), dated February 1962. Consolidating contributions and other initiatives, including a study meeting (26–27 May 1962), a working document "Les questions considérées comme particulièrement importantes et urgentes" ("Questions considered to be

---

[100] Cf. Jean Mpisi, *Le Cardinal Malula et Jean-Paul II. Dialogue difficile entre l'église "africaine" et le saint-siège*, Paris: L'Harmattan, 2005, p. 80.

[101] On the international political context and political consequences of Vatican II, cf. Paolo Borruso, "Catholic Italy and post-colonial Africa: the new subjects of an informal commitment in the 1960s", *Cahiers de la Méditerranée* 88, 2014, pp. 99–111. On the chronology, see Mpisi, *Le Cardinal Malula*, p. 77.

[102] "This is how the incarnation of theology calls that of the Catholic Church; and it is understandable that the Congress [of black writers and artists] of Rome thus reaffirmed the inescapable reality of an African Catholic Church, making Alioune Diop, who was its inspirer and organiser, an important figure in the advent of a Christianity transformed in accordance with the aspirations of Africans. His role is therefore truly foundational, because the process of the 1959 Rome Congress will almost unceasingly feed into the discourse on the Catholic Church in post-colonial Africa." Lock, *Identité africaine*, p. 123 (my translation).

[103] For more on the background and organisation of SAC in view of its contribution to the council, cf. Mpisi, *Le Cardinal Malula*, pp. 97–99.

particularly important and urgent") was issued in June 1962.[104] The justification for the SAC's initiative to get involved in the pre-conciliar discussions resides in its own mission, namely "to seek, formulate, and defend the African presence in the Universal culture: Art, history, literature, philosophy, etc...".[105] Hence the SAC considers it an obligation "to reflect on culture through religious life"[106] and in this case very specifically the life of African Catholics. Hence the call on all African Catholics to contribute to a collective reflection in the service of

the gradual consideration, in the very fabric of Catholic life, of the categories and values of our civilizations, the emergence of new African experiences and concepts on man, religious sensitivity, piety, holiness, the invention of African institutions (born of our situation, our trials, our initiatives and the fervour of our faith).[107]

This is the spirit in which the SAC then offered a working document[108] in which the following themes were adressed: spirituality, liturgy, theology, ecumenism, the laity, and social problems (including issues such as family, education, economics, dowry [*dot*], and polygamy).

I have indicated that this initiative was presented as continuous with the mission of the SAC. But the continuity stretches further back: one can read in these documents an explicit continuation of thought from the second Congress of Black Writers and Artists, in particular its subcommission for theology.[109] Also, this continuity stretched into the future: in direct continuation of the spirit of the open letter "On the contribution of African personhood to the vitality of Catholicism", a volume of studies was prepared and published early on during Vatican II, under the title *Personnalité africaine et catholicisme* ("African personhood and catholicism").

The idea was not simply to collect a number of suggestions for the Council, rather

---

[104] Both of these can now be consulted in Tharcisse Tshibangu, *Le concile Vatican II et l'église Africaine. Mise en œuvre du concile dans l'église d'Afrique (1960 - 2010)*, Limete: Epiphanie, 2012, pp. 19–20 (for the letter); 21–28 (for the working document). Historical background: Mpisi, *Le Cardinal Malula*, p. 98.

[105] Cited in Tshibangu, *Le concile Vatican II*, p. 19.

[106] Cited in Tshibangu, *Le concile Vatican II*, p. 19.

[107] Cited in Tshibangu, *Le concile Vatican II*, p. 20.

[108] Republished in Tshibangu, *Le concile Vatican II*, pp. 21–28.

[109] Cf. its declaration in *Présence Africaine* and in Tshiba Tshibangu, *Le concile Vatican II*, pp. 20, 24 respectively. This is confirmed by Tshibangu, *Le concile Vatican II*, p. 83.

> We thought it was our duty to express our point of view, after having been silent and passive for centuries. Africans and Christians, proud of both backgrounds [*appartenance*], we want to speak out loud and clear, with the freedom of the children of God[110]

as Meinrad Hebga wrote in the introduction to the book. Interestingly, he also explains how the contributions were obtained: "Our Secretariat in Paris has sent more than two thousand letters, leaflets and circulars to hundreds of bishops, priests and laity of both sexes, requesting articles, advice and suggestions".[111] To his own admission, the response was disappointing, however, one person who did respond was Mabona. His is the only English chapter in the book, which contains articles by authors such as Ela, Lufuluabo, and Mveng, and a postscript by Senghor.

The broader ambition was to make of this volume a worthy sequel to the book event, *Les prêtres noirs s'intérrogent* ("Black priests are questioning"), sometimes referred to as the founding volume of African Christian theology.[112] This is reflected in the title of Senghor's contribution: "Des prêtres noirs s'interrogent et suggèrent" ("The black priests are questioning and offering suggestions").

This volume and Mabona's contribution in particular will interest us again later (cf. Part 2, §3). Now, I want to complete the picture of his contribution to SAC's initiative in respect to Vatican II. Or rather, his views on the whole event. Not involved in the Council itself, his position is that of an outside observer. Initially, he followed reports on the event. He also recounts having met his Queenstown bishop, Rosenthal, who was in Rome for the Council. However, Mabona lost interest, especially because of what seemed to him to be the complete failure of the SAC group to find receptive ears for its proposals.[113] He highlights especially propositions that were critical of capitalism and that were pro-ecological. Regrettably, I have not been able to find any trace of these propositions.

---

[110] Meinrad Hebga, "Un malaise grave", in *Personnalité africaine et catholicisme*, Paris: Présence Africaine, 1963, p. 15.
[111] Hebga, "Un malaise grave", p. 15.
[112] Cf. the commentaries added to the fiftieth anniversary re-edition: *Des prêtres noirs s'interrogent. Cinquante ans après...*, presented by Léonard Santedi Kinkupu, Gérard Bissainthe, and Meinrad Hebga, Paris: Karthala-Présence Africaine, 2006, pp. I–XXII, 283–293, and 296–299; V.Y. Mudimbe, *The invention of Africa: Gnosis, philosophy, and the order of knowledge. African Systems of Thought*, Bloomington: Indiana University Press, 1988, pp. 56–57; and Verdin, *Alioune Diop*, pp. 219–223.
[113] Interview 3.

These were, then, the most intense experiences of Mabona's life during his time in Italy. But it was also the time of the greatest wave of independence of African colonies. Indeed it was an exceptional place for a South African to be, for instance at the time of the Sharpeville massacre on 21 March 1960 (about which he heard and which affected him greatly).[114] The brooding apartheid to which he was to return now has to be examined.

---

[114] Interview 5: "Sharpeville happened when I was in Italy. [...] it doesn't seem to me because I was so involved in it. I was involved, spiritually involved, I must say."

CHAPTER 5

BACK HOME? APARTHEID, ST. PETER'S, SPOBA

Sometime during 1963, Mongameli Mabona returned to South Africa. He was to stay only nine years before permanently leaving the country. The sociopolitical conditions under which this period of his life were spent need to be sketched briefly to understand the kinds of activity in which he engaged and the conditions which finally compelled him to leave.

1. Apartheid

In 1948, the National Party came into power in the Union of South Africa, with a programme of minority rule and advanced segregation called apartheid. The history of apartheid can be divided into three parts. The middle part, which covers the 1960s to the mid 1970s, "was a far more ambitious and unyielding phase of apartheid than the first rendition during the 1950s, when a somewhat more pragmatic and cautious approach to racial social and economic engineering was taken".[1] This is the context to which Mabona came back from Italy. I will not

---

[1] Deborah Posel, "The apartheid project, 1948-1970", in Robert Ross, Anne Kelk Mager, and Bill Nasson (eds.), *The Cambridge history of South Africa. Volume 2: 1885-1994*, Cambridge: Cambridge University Press, pp. 319–368, here p. 320. Of these contradictions and changes in apartheid even in this phase, I can only give the broadest outline (see Posel, "The apartheid project..." pp. 319–320 for details).

see the story of apartheid through to its end in this biography, since he left the country again early in the 1970s.²

At the time that the rest of Africa was gaining independence from colonial rule,³ South Africa was shifting apartheid into higher gear. True, the neighbouring countries opposed the policy, but they did not have the power to do much to counteract it.⁴ Moreover, events in southern Africa at this time unfolded in response to the global political and military context misleadingly named the "Cold War".⁵ South Africa shared with many states, including newly independent African ones, the vision of strong state intervention in modelling the internal social and economic order⁶ and widespread recourse to a rhetoric of nationalism to mobilise and consolidate power.⁷

The apartheid state inherited a segregated state and society, and endeavoured to build it systematically, starting with a set of laws implementing the policy of separate development or apartheid.⁸ Initially driven by Afrikaner ideals and symbols, it was strongly bent on spreading Afrikaners' presence in and control of major institutions.⁹ Remnants of political representation of groups other than the white population were systematically dismantled. Reserves were transformed one by one into self-governing territories from the 1960s onwards. (Some of them were destined to become independent states from the mid 1970s, but none of

---

2   I will therefore not expound any further the subsequent developments in Transkei either; a panorama of this development is in Anne Kelk Mager and Maanda Mulaudzi, "Popular responses to apartheid: 1948 – c.1975", in Robert Ross, Anne Kelk Mager, and Bill Nasson (eds.), *The Cambridge history of South Africa. Volume 2: 1885-1994*, Cambridge: Cambridge University Press, pp. 369–408, here pp. 394–398.

3   For an overview of social, political, economic, and cultural changes in Africa over the period after 1935, cf. Ali Mazrui and Christophe Wondji (eds.), *General history of Africa. Volume VIII: Africa since 1935*, Paris: UNESCO; Oxford: J. Currey, 1999.

4   Thompson, *A history of South Africa*, pp. 214–215; cf. e.g. Kenneth Kaunda, *Kaunda on violence*, William Collins: London et al., 1980.

5   Cf. Thomas Karis and Gail Gerhart, *From protest to challenge. Volume 5: Nadir and resurgence, 1964-1979*, Pretoria: UNISA Press, 1997, p. 9.

6   Posel, "The apartheid project...", pp. 319, 330.

7   Cf. David Chanaiwa, "Southern Africa since 1945", in Ali Mazrui and Christophe Wondji (eds.), *General history of Africa. Volume VIII: Africa since 1935*, Paris: UNESCO; Oxford: J. Currey, 1999, pp. 249–281, here p. 257.

8   E.g. the Group Areas Act (1950), the Native Labour (Settlement of Disputes) Act (1953), the Criminal Law Amendment Act (1953), the Mines and Works Act (1956), plus the development of the Bantu Self-Government Act (1959) – finally in the Bantu Homelands Constitution Act, 1971 (cf. Thompson, *A history of South Africa*, p. 191). Chanaiwa, "Southern Africa since 1945", pp. 257–258.

9   Posel, "The apartheid project...", p. 354.

these "Bantustans" were ever recognised by the international community.)[10] The peculiar meaning of self-governing states (and independence) in relation to the South African state is to be understood against the backdrop of so-called "separate development". Separate development, Deborah Posel concludes, was

> a strategy of reinvigorating, refashioning and rewarding 'traditional' African notions of authority and political culture – indeed, reinventing, burcaucratising and disciplining tradition as part of the wider project of creating political 'order' – at the same time as fragmenting African peoples into discrete ethnic components.[11]

This logic was partially duplicated in the townships. In the entire country, urban life was subject to a series of fanatical attempts to separate all facilities, or at least the use thereof, according to racial classification. However, this display of power only intensified the existing irony: while blacks were stripped of their South African citizenship and many were forced to live in homelands, the conditions of life there compelled people to migrate for employment, which was the only justification to enter white South Africa, but then the apartheid state needed labour from the beginning.[12]

The apartheid state was willing to accommodate the labourers without which its economy could not function – but only in increasingly populated separate townships[13] or on farms. The rest follows from there: massive forced removals,[14] increasing joblessness, high infant mortality and low life expectancy, limited public services, and poverty, not to mention endless personal trauma, for the black population (and the conditions for Indians and Coloured people were often similar).[15] For the white segment of the population, there was not only economic growth of the country and systematic elimination of most white poverty, but also the increasing need to police the state, to conscript young men to the army, and to deploy strategies of misinformation to manipulate the white citizenry. Even if one admits that a small minority of black people found their way through the system

---

[10] Thompson, *A history of South Africa*, p. 191; Posel, "The apartheid project...", p. 329.
[11] Posel, "The apartheid project...", p. 350.
[12] As confirmed, e.g. by Charles Feinstein, *An economic history of South Africa. Conquest, discrimination, and development*, Cambridge: Cambridge University Press, 2005, p. 150.
[13] Posel, "The apartheid project...", pp. 337–338, 340.
[14] Cf. Mager and Mulaudzi, "Popular responses...", pp. 385–387; cf. Laurine Platzky and Cherryl Walker, *The surplus people. Forced removals in South Africa*, Johannesburg: Ravan Press, 1985.
[15] Thompson, *A history of South Africa*, pp. 190–204; Chanaiwa, "Southern Africa since 1945", p. 259.

to enter university, achieved a better standard of living, received formal housing in townships,[16] or engaged in commerce, the general picture of discrimination and exploitation remains intact.

By the time South Africa became a Republic and withdrew from the Commonwealth in 1961, international criticism was already mounting.[17] Still, the National Party's power increased, later also supported by English-speaking voters.[18] In fact, from the 1970s, the government's policy transformed itself from an ethnic nationalism with a racist programme to a race-based nationalism.[19]

2. Apartheid education

Education was a major stake for the apartheid state. An important early objective was to gain control of the entire education system: where formerly missionaries and members of the black elite played a role in directing education for the black majority, white professionals took over.[20] The mission schools were undermined since they were seen to convey dangerous ideas to black children (which is not to say that mission education was itself without problems).[21] The state considerably increased schooling for Africans, but the entire school system was underfunded and underdeveloped. In fact, state subsidy for black schooling fell sharply from the 1950s to 1960s, maintaining severe infrastructural shortages and worsening teaching staff shortages.[22]

The 1953 Bantu Education Act established the framework for teaching to black children. Most of them would leave school with little more than basic

---

[16] Posel, "The apartheid project...", p. 339; cf. Chanaiwa, "Southern Africa since 1945", p. 257.
[17] Thompson, *A history of South Africa*, pp. 188–191.
[18] Thompson, *A history of South Africa*, p. 188.
[19] Johan Degenaar, "Afrikaner-nasionalisme", in W.P. Esterhuyse, P.V.D.P. du Toit, and A.A. van Niekerk (eds.), *Moderne politieke ideologieë*, Johannesburg: Southern, 1987, pp. 231–260, but also Posel, "The apartheid project...", p. 328.
[20] This shift in the politics of knowledge is described as the shift from the "amateurs" of the former group to the "experts" of the latter. Brahm Fleisch, "State formation and the origins of Bantu education", in Peter Kallaway (ed.), *The history of education under apartheid 1948-1994*, New York et al.: Peter Lang, 2002, pp. 39–52, here pp. 39, 48–49.
[21] Thompson, *A history of South Africa*, p. 196. On the forms of integration of black students in universities, see Thompson, *A history of South Africa*, p. 197.
[22] All of this from Mager and Mulaudzi, "Popular responses...", pp. 384–385.

literacy.[23] Academic learning content for school children and teachers was simplified. Male teachers were removed from primary education, and severely underqualified women were employed as teachers. English and Afrikaans were to be the only languages of instruction in high school. Part of the educational content for the older pupils in subjects such as languages and history, as well as in the natural sciences, lent itself to the transmission (at least at a rudimentary level) of a Western or indeed a white South African view of the world and its concomitant interests. Overall, the system was designed to prepare black people for life in the labour force with minimal potential progress.[24]

A few statistics may help to explain this situation and to understand the advent of student politics and protest in schools and universities in the 1970s:

> Data on the distribution of African pupils in 1964 showed that 72 per cent were in lower primary classes (the first four years), 25 per cent in higher primary classes (the next four years), and only 3 per cent in secondary classes.[25]

Moreover, "[i]n 1970, 34.8 per cent of economically active Africans resident in urban areas and 63.4 per cent in rural areas had no formal education. Less than 1 per cent had a degree or diploma".[26] These were important dimensions of the society in which Mongameli Mabona was to become a lecturer. At the same time, these statistics should account for the curious fact that Bantu Education also prepared its foremost opponents,[27] as we will see below.

3. The South African economy in the 1960s

In the post-World War II period, and particularly in the 1960s, the South African economy grew very rapidly. The pre-war economy was constructed around commercial farming and the gold mines; the post-war economy saw a

---

[23] Cf. Mager and Mulaudzi, "Popular responses...", p. 383; Feinstein, *An economic history*, p. 160.
[24] Posel, "The apartheid project...", pp. 339–340. This is meant as a statement of consequence and not necessarily of the initial design. On the Eiselen Commission Report (1951) and its relation to aims of Bantu Education, see Fleisch, "State formation...", pp. 39–42.
[25] Feinstein, *An economic history*, p. 160.
[26] Mager and Mulaudzi, "Popular responses...", p. 385.
[27] Hlatshwayo, *Education and independence*, p. 2.

progressive rise in industry and a relative decline in agriculture and, to a lesser extent, in mining.[28] In this period, the country was an attractive proposition for foreign investors. While the symbolic gestures opposing apartheid (e.g. sports sanctions) increased, the big Western countries took no initiatives in the period under question to advance economic sanctions.[29] This ambivalent position was maintained by most countries, with the exception of a few that lent clear support to the anti-apartheid movement, notably the Netherlands and the Scandinavian countries.[30] Since South Africa was the regional economic power (including in technical expertise) and, at the time, a collaborator with independent Rhodesia, possible economic pressure or aid that could be offered to the anti-apartheid movement by bordering countries remained very restricted.

The growing economy was hungry for skilled and semi-skilled labour beyond what the white population could offer, which opened a narrow space for some people other than whites to rise socially and economically.[31] In this way, in accordance with an irony that would remain with the apartheid state until its eventual demise, economic dictates interfered with neat political schemes. One may indeed ask what the relation was between the policy of apartheid and the pursuit of economic growth. Whereas liberal economic analysts claimed that the apartheid social order and labour policies would be detrimental to economic growth, the more radical sides of the political spectrum (for and against) were both convinced that apartheid furthered economic growth. On the one hand, the advocates of apartheid argued that "separate development" was compatible with the objective of economic growth; on the other hand, Marxist critics of apartheid also affirmed this compatibility, but they argued that the exploitative ends of the capitalist state required the cheap labour provided by apartheid policies.[32] Perhaps the economic statistics available at that time of the period that concerns us (up to 1972, when Mabona left the country) could be read as corroborating these views of the compatibility of apartheid policies and economic growth, but the statistics over a longer period of time rather support the liberal view.[33]

---

[28] Feinstein, *An economic history*, pp. 143–144.
[29] Karis and Gerhart, *Nadir and resurgence*, p. 8.
[30] Karis and Gerhart, *Nadir and resurgence*, p. 9.
[31] Karis and Gerhart, *Nadir and resurgence*, p. 10.
[32] Feinstein, *An economic history*, pp. 146, 161–164, 247.
[33] It is worth mentioning that a larger historical perspective paints a different picture. Pointing at the sharply declining growth rate of the real GDP from the beginning of the 1970s, Feinstein seems to confirm the earlier liberal interpretation. He concludes the following: Low levels of skill, inadequate nutrition, poor health, bad housing, social instability and insecurity, weak motivation, denial of industrial and political rights, the disruptive effects of migrant labour,

As in the past, the growing need for labour, and, seen from the other side, the persistent need for income, brought many people to the cities. On the law books, black labourers were in the white cities of a white country – they were migrant labourers, regulated by the pass laws.[34] In the urban environment, contexts of varying cultural mixing emerged, relativising traditional backgrounds of language and culture; at the same time, new commonalities of interest took shape, among which the conditions of life in informal housing settlements and labour stand out.[35] Mutual support – material and psychological – was found in family ties, stokvels, funeral groups, and religious meetings.[36] More will be said about some aspects of religious life below.

4. Resistance

Black resistance to encroaching white power has been discussed above[37] and continued in the period that is of interest to us here. All forms of resistance had to

---

bureaucratic interference in the allocation of workers – all ensured that 'cheap' black labour was not really cheap. On the contrary, some 80 percent of South Africa's labour force was compelled by apartheid to live and work under conditions that were profoundly prejudicial to vitally necessary improvements in productivity. Legal, social and customary barriers to occupational mobility restricted the supply of black skilled and semi-skilled workers, while the low quality of education and training depressed the standards attained by the minority of blacks who were able to move up the occupational ladder. The cost of 'cheap' black labour was also inflated by a system which imposed white supervisors on black workers. The subservience which the '*baas*' expected from his 'boys', and the racial friction and antipathy which were almost always present in such relationships, meant that the supervisory system raised rather than lowered the impediments to higher efficiency. (Feinstein, *An economic history*, p. 249)

[34] Cf. Karis and Gerhart, *Nadir and resurgence*, p. 11; Chanaiwa, "Southern Africa since 1945", p. 259; Mager and Mulaudzi, "Popular responses...", pp. 373–375.

[35] Karis and Gerhart, *Nadir and resurgence*, p. 10. The ambiguities of urban culture are captured by these two authors: [T]his process of change saw rural customs and perspectives gradually displaced by the habits and outlooks of city life. In the eyes of social conservatives, the image of the city was one of decadent materialism, outlandish fads, violent crime, and the breakdown of religious piety and parental discipline. To those already swept into the maelstrom of urban transformation, these images were not the whole picture. City life was brutal and frustrating, but it was also exciting, and for those with ambition, quick wits and a bit of luck, it held out the possibility of wealth and self-advancement. (Karis and Gerhart, *Nadir and resurgence*, p. 12)

[36] Cf. Mager and Mulaudzi, "Popular responses...", pp. 379–380. On working conditions, cf. Mager and Mulaudzi, "Popular responses..." pp. 375–378.

[37] Cf. Chapter 1, §3.3 (pp. 33) and Chapter 2, §5.

respond to the brute facts of military defeat and loss of land during the bygone era. Subsequently, reformist strategies of opposition were considered and practised. Hence, despite the events through which land ownership took the shape it did – and for diverging combinations of principled and strategic reasons – groups of resistance pursued strategies of opposition to the laws underpinning apartheid and continued to struggle for a country belonging equally to all, and governed by representatives of the people as a whole.[38] However, the more reformist strategies also provoked counter-reactions, resulting in a variety of responses, which I will outline briefly. Apartheid had to reckon with opposition from some white groups: in Parliament, from liberals; outside of Parliament, from the English-speaking churches (with some qualifications which I will discuss later[39]).[40] There were also smaller groups and individuals who could be named in a more comprehensive overview. However, here I will focus only on the African National Congress (ANC), the Pan Africanist Congress (PAC), and, a bit later, the Black Consciousness Movement (BCM). The aim is to outline the general development and orientation of each group and, in doing so, to give an impression of the range of views and strategies of resistance that people adopted.

4.1 The ANC and the PAC

As might be expected, the continuation of the political situation described above and its intensification after 1948 provoked increasing internal resistance in South Africa. This was also the era when the ANC (and then the PAC) made some headway with campaigns, before they turned to armed resistance.

Determined to affirm South Africa as a country for blacks/Africans, the ANC still advocated a nationalism inclusive of all population groups.[41] In the 1940s it was energised by the formation of its Youth League (ANCYL), whose decidedly more radical ideas were to inspire the PAC and, later, the BCM. When the Communist Party was banned in 1950, some of its members founded the White Congress of Democrats (COD), which was not destined to participate in Parliament; together with the ANC, the South African Indian Congress (SAIC), and the Coloured People's Organization (SACPO), the COD formed

---

[38] Cf. Mokgethi Motlhabi, *The theory and practice of black resistance to apartheid. A social-ethical analysis*, Johannesburg: Skotaville Publishers, 1984, p. 2.
[39] See pp. 126-127.
[40] Cf. Motlhabi, *The theory and practice*, pp. 15, 18–24.
[41] Motlhabi, *The theory and practice*, pp. 41–42.

the Congress Alliance, pursuing the aim of truly universal enfranchisement.[42] The classical formulation of this vision of a multiracial, democratic future was captured in the 1955 Freedom Charter.[43] Very practically, the ANC tackled issues of voting rights, pass laws, land ownership, labour relations, and education.[44] This was translated into mass boycotts and civil disobedience initiatives in the 1950s.

In the late 1950s, the PAC broke away from the ANC on the basis of an Africanism understood as requiring more insistence on the difference between black, Coloured, and Indian people in the political context, and thus in respect of the liberation struggle, than was usually conceded by the ANC (or was formulated in the Freedom Charter). It also placed more emphasis on a pan-Africanist vision of South Africa's present and future.[45] The role played by the Communist Party in the ANC was another bone of contention, as would be any alliance with groups with white members as long as the specific interests of such allies were not properly accounted for – at least, under the prevailing conditions of institutionalised racial inequality.[46] Yet, since the PAC insisted on eradicating the root cause of oppression – minority rule in general – in practice, it was opposed to the same specific issues instituted by the apartheid legislation as the ANC was.[47]

The authorities did not look kindly on initiatives that opposed the state. In addition to the laws mentioned above by which the apartheid policy was given legal force, the state increased restrictive laws[48] to extinguish opposition.[49] Informants were activated.[50] Resistance was repressed by banning individuals and organisations, detention (with or without trial), and later also torture and killing. The single most brutal response to peaceful resistance was the events of Sharpeville in 1960; the police killed or injured unarmed protestors in

---

[42] Cf. Motlhabi, *The theory and practice*, pp. 16, 46.
[43] But following up from the ANC's "African Claims in South Africa" (1943), cf. Motlhabi, *The theory and practice*, p. 26.
[44] Motlhabi, *The theory and practice*, pp. 50–55.
[45] Cf. Motlhabi, *The theory and practice*, p. 81.
[46] Motlhabi, *The theory and practice*, pp. 75, 77, 89–91.
[47] Cf. Motlhabi, *The theory and practice*, pp. 84–88, 102.
[48] These are the Suppression of Communism Act (1950), Riotous Assemblies Act (1956), the Unlawful Organizations Act (1960), the Sabotage Act (1962), the Criminal Procedure Amendment Act (1965), the General Law Amendment Act (1966), the Terrorism Act (1967), the Prohibition of Political Interference Act (1968), and, after the period that concerns us, the Internal Security Act (1976). Thompson, *A history of South Africa*, pp. 198–199; Chanaiwa, "Southern Africa since 1945", p. 275.
[49] Cf. Motlhabi, *The theory and practice*, Chapter 1.
[50] Karis and Gerhart, *Nadir and resurgence*, p. 17.

a PAC-initiated march against passbooks. Subsequently, both the PAC and the ANC were banned.[51] This incident dramatically confirmed the warnings of those who were convinced that peaceful opposition was going nowhere and argued that it was time to transition to violent responses (although taking recourse to violent means never was an obvious decision because of both principled and strategic considerations).[52]

Both the ANC and PAC developed underground armed movements. The ANC founded Umkhonto we Sizwe (MK), and the PAC instituted Poqo (later the Azanian People's Liberation Army, APLA). According to Mandela, MK had a strategy of progressively increasing violence, starting with acts of sabotage.[53] While Poqo planned acts of sabotage, it had fewer qualms about killing civilians.[54] The Rivonia trial of 1963–1964 is the most important historical marker for the suppression of the ANC's new initiative (and, by implication, that of the PAC). The apartheid state demonstrated its determination to render resistance futile. The military movements moved their bases outside of South Africa, first to Tanzania, then to Zambia and Botswana,[55] where they also enjoyed some support from the communist bloc countries. However, during the whole period under consideration, MK launched no attack worth mentioning on South Africa,[56] and Poqo hardly fared better.[57] The Communist Party, ANC, and PAC were neutralised – most of their leadership was imprisoned or in exile.[58] Among whites of all social groups, forms of criticism started to mount,[59] but before 1975 these dissenting voices remained a small group, with little influence.

The early part of the resistance history evoked here corresponds with Mabona's years as a seminarian and young priest. He was absent from the country during much of the intensification of the struggle, but these changes are important to the lifeworld of the country to which he returned and where he resumed his work. These political formations also represent a variety of stances on cultural politics, an issue prevalent in Mabona's work.

---

[51] Karis and Gerhart, *Nadir and resurgence*, p. 6.
[52] Mabona refers to these dilemmas in Interview 5.
[53] Mandela, "The Rivonia trail", pp. 171–172.
[54] South African History Online, "Poqo", https://www.sahistory.org.za/organisations/poqo (last accessed 18 January 2019).
[55] Karis and Gerhart, *Nadir and resurgence*, pp. 6–7.
[56] Cf. Karis and Gerhart, *Nadir and resurgence*, p. 26.
[57] Karis and Gerhart, *Nadir and resurgence*, p. 47; Motlhabi, *The theory and practice*, pp. 99–100.
[58] Cf. Karis and Gerhart, *Nadir and resurgence*, p. 19.
[59] See also the formation of the African Resistance Movement (Karis & Gerhart, *Nadir and resurgence*, 21–24), the Christian Institute, etc.

5. Life back in South Africa

> I rebelled against the spirit of [apartheid]... when I came back. I rebelled entirely. And it led to the fact that I simply disregarded many of the things – disregarded them absolutely. I simply disregarded and went when I wanted to go where I wanted to go and did what I wanted to do. It took a long time before I came back to the... by the way, [...] if you are fighting all the time and you see that your fight doesn't, you know, produce any ... [...] you sort of give up, you know? But giving up simply meant that I couldn't do anything directly, but I never accepted it again, the situation in South Africa, after coming back from Italy, never, I never accepted it.[60]

In these words, Mongameli Mabona captures his reaction to the country to which he returned. This fluctuation between defiance and despondency/dejection probably characterised his life in general. But more specifically, what were his activities during these years? Since all of these gaps can no longer be filled, I will look at some of his work for the diocese, his amateur ethnography, his poetry, and his later appointment as a lecturer.

5.1 Lumko

As before, Mabona worked in frequent consultation with his bishop.[61] From Dischl we know that Mabona also worked with Fr. Weber at Idutywa in 1964.[62] In the meantime, since the 1950s,[63] the Catechetical school (also called the Catechists' Training Centre and Missiological Institute[64]) at Lumko was established, 30 km north-east of Queenstown, and 20 km south-east of Lady Frere. It was to serve as institute for anthropology and South African languages.[65]

---

[60] Interview 5.
[61] Inteview 7, 27".
[62] Dischl, *Transkei for Christ*, p. 301. Also mentioned in Interview 3. Mabona was not sure that he was ever a full-time parish priest (Interview 7, 18").
[63] The chronology is to be verified. Elsewhere, Dischl (*Transkei for Christ*, p. 294) sets the date for the opening in 1958.
[64] Dischl, *Transkei for Christ*, pp. 219, 283.
[65] One may consult two dissimilar versions of the history of this institution: Dischl, *Transkei for Christ*, pp. 294–295; http://lumko.org/history (last consulted on 12 December 2016). Neither mentions Mabona.

By 1965, it presented two-year courses.⁶⁶ At the time, there were around thirty catechists in training. Mabona worked there for about one year, although I have not been able to determine his exact responsibilities. An anecdote from *Diviners and prophets*, however, again gives us a window on this part of his life:

> [...] in 1965 to be exact – I was teaching at a catechist school [this could only have been Lumko]. As I found that many of the men attending had had very little formal education, I tried to supplement wherever I could. One day I gave an elementary lesson in the geography of the world. I spoke about America, Australia etc. In the evening we were standing outside with a group and happened to be surveying the sky. The southern sky in the evening is a thing of beauty. One of the catechists then remarked 'Who knows if one of those stars in the west is not America and one of those stars in the east is not Australia?' I felt strangely vexed by this remark and rather testily asserted that those were merely stars and not parts of the earth. The catechist tried to defend his point of view by pointing out that the stars were surrounded by blue, and those could be the oceans I had been talking about in the lesson. My reply must have been less patient as I pointed out that the stars were in the sky and America and Australia were parts of the earth. He was not convinced, but merely said, 'Oh, they are so far away they could be up there.' I understood the meaning of this remark much later on, but my vexed embarrassment at that moment must have been some subconscious stirring or echo of that other irritating debate years ago with the two young Xhosa traditionalists [cited above, see pp. 64-65]. The concept of water as a factor separating two worlds in Xhosa cosmology seems to derive from a synchronic interpretation of reality as observed. On the other hand the perception of above and below is basically presumed to depend on distance and the position of the observer. There is a perceptual shift (*ingqondo iyaguquleleka; ingqondo iyaphenduleleka*), so that what is up may at one time be down and what is down may at one time be up. There is fundamentally a diachronic relativistic determination. Here polarity is not only a mental element but is also considered to be a physical ontological category.⁶⁷

---

66 Dischl, *Transkei for Christ*, p. 219.
67 DP, pp. 213–214.

But working at the Institute was not just about stimulating exchanges with students. He devoted himself energetically to this work and tried to develop the institution, among other things by introducing music and art to the syllabus.[68] He also developed the garden by planting fruit trees.[69] Apparently, there were some tensions with the missionaries, but this seems not to have been the rule. Mabona recalls an occasion when the priests at Lumko wanted him to go with him to the cinema; in the end, this excursion did not work out because there was a risk that the police could see him and he had to wait in the car. Several times they "disguised" him as a chauffeur or servant, or they would hide him between them in the car, to overcome the restrictive legislation imposed on the freedom of movement of black people.

Also, for whatever reason, an informant (or even two)[70] was placed (or recruited) to "spy" on Mabona and report his initiatives and teaching to the police. This is how Mabona looks back on it:

> The bishop wanted me to teach there at the catechist school. Eh, I didn't stay very long. One of the difficulties there was… the government came in and said, that man there… in fact, they said that I should not be in contact with people because I always talk politics and I poison the mind of the people. So they didn't want me in Lumko. I don't know whether the bishop minded that, their talks […].[71]

There was even question of a high-ranking official who came to Lumko with orders, including that Mabona was to be prohibited from teaching in Xhosa.[72]

Asked whether he shared his views on the state in his preaching, Mabona responded: "Yes, I had to because, you know, in the sermons, you're talking to the people you want them to go in certain ways, in certain directions. And the most interesting interactions were against government and it had to be like that."[73] While he confirmed that the police knew what he was saying, he also declares that the police did not interfere in his preaching the Transkei.

It has not been possible to confirm the exact chronology, but it was probably at this time – after he had worked at the Catechetical school for about one year[74]

---

[68] "we wanted to make Lumko a centre of African art" (Interview 5).
[69] Interview 7, 27".
[70] Interview 5.
[71] Interview 3, 1:01".
[72] Interview 5.
[73] Interview 5.
[74] Interview 7, 27".

– that a restriction was imposed on Mabona and that he was confined to the St. Theresa mission.[75] He was prohibited from going to the Queenstown "location", and people were not allowed to come to him. He was considered "a bad influence" and was accused of being a "communist". Once this restriction was imposed, the bishop apparently left it open to him how to spend his time. Mabona later recalled that Queenstown was home to many people who resisted the system and were imprisoned for it. He also testifies that the threat of imprisonment curbed his own initiative.[76] At least in that region he distinguishes between a more political resistance in the town, with its aspiration to achieve a "modern" lifestyle, and the cultural striving for a return to traditional Xhosa life in the countryside.

Of Mabona's priestly activities during this period I could discover little, except that it was from St. Theresa's that his precious box with poems, articles, and anthropological notes was stolen.[77] However, the anecdote about his conversation with students (above) puts us on another trail. In fact, it seems he was walking two paths at the same time.

5.2 Independent ethnographic studies

It would have been odd if the enthusiastic author on African culture and philosophy returned to South Africa and did not pursue these enquiries. From this perspective, returning to South Africa would have been rather an excellent opportunity to advance his research. Although he never states it in these terms, there is sufficient confirmation of this view from numerous references in *Diviners and prophets*. Thus, in the Introduction, he writes: "Chronologically, the idea of doing research on the diviner phenomenon in connection with the study of Xhosa culture took shape in my mind in 1965".[78] He may even have begun to gather information informally earlier:

> When, in the early sixties, I asked a group of diviners what was the first step in treating a person who had *ukuthwasa*, a senior man replied that he first applied *iyeza elimnyama* (black medicine) in order to free

---

[75] Interview 7, 21"; Interview 5. The curious fact that a black person was confined to a white residential area is explained by Marta Mabona (correspondence of 10 January 2019) as a measure to prevent him from having contact with other black people.
[76] Interview 5.
[77] "Jugend Mongameli", Interview 0.
[78] DP, Introduction.

the patient from ordinary disease and in order to lay a foundation of strength before applying *amayeza amhlophe* (white medicines).⁷⁹

To get an impression of how he translated this idea into practice, we can refer to a number of anecdotes he documented.

In some places, he gives an idea of how he proceeded. Speaking about testing the correctness of local perspectives on certain cosmic phenomena, he writes: "In 1966 I started a series of systematic observations carried out during the day whenever I had the time".⁸⁰ Yet, most often, he recounts rather informal interaction with people, who, three decades later, were retroactively designated as anthropological "instructors", to be connected with the information reported from other instructors. Hence, the priest-anthropologist could observe:

> The bottom decorations of the women's blankets have a theme or story which I never succeeded to obtain. Once, when she had come to town in Idutywa I appealed about the decorations to my instructor [...]. She said there was a great deal to say about these decorations but that she did not have the time there and then. I should visit her at her home and she would explain fully their meaning and give me the stories connected with them. Not very long after this I was assigned to another job in far-off Thembuland and I never had the opportunity to get the explanation. I considered it important, though, that I now knew that the decoration in the middle area is a tree called *umthiwemfene* (tree of the baboon). Since I failed to get the information about the tree from my lady instructor, I consider myself justified in bringing here information about it from another lady instructor, namely Rrasebe, Adrien Boshier's instructor.⁸¹

We get to know Mabona's keen interest in fine detail:

> Thirty years ago, when I worked there, every traditionalist woman in Gcalekaland and in Thembuland had special decorations on the outer blanket which she carried around her shoulders if her hands and arms were free and which she wrapped around her waist when busy. The decorations were divided into roughly three areas: the right, the left and a middle area. The symbols on the right and the left sides were identical

---

[79] DP, p. 341.
[80] DP, p. 186.
[81] DP, p. 216.

and consisted of black upright columns e.g. III, and then this sign: H, also in black. When I asked what these were I was told that the upright strokes were staves or sticks [...].⁸²

Apparently he did not isolate his anthropological "fieldwork" from his work as a priest – but not all colleagues shared his enthusiasm:

When I visited a hut in which girls were undergoing initiation, the recurring signs I saw on the wall were small circles and upright strokes of about 3 cm. But one would have thought the missionary I was in company of wanted to burn the whole place down. Though the hut was very well kept, he called the place filthy, especially the drawings whose meaning he did not know. This neurotic behaviour, due probably to some deep insecurity moral or ideological, made the situation finally intolerable and an uneasy silence fell or people just went away.⁸³

It was only years later that Mabona was in a position to consolidate his years of observation in writing, in the form of an anthropological study.

5.3 Poetry

It was Fr. Schimlek at Ixopo who "opened his eyes" for English literature.⁸⁴ During Mabona's time as a student in the Major Seminary at Pevensey, he "wrote a lot of articles and poems" and sent them to be published, among other places, to the Mariannhill-based newspaper *UmAfrika*.⁸⁵ Today, ten of his poems composed in this period are available – one published in 1965, seven in 1970, and two from 1974 and 1977, respectively – but the interviews lead one to understand that he wrote much more. It is not known when exactly the published poems were written or how it came about that they were published by *Présence Africaine* and in *New Coin*.

Apparently there was a time when he was extremely taken up by poetry. He explains that when he was writing poems, he could not pay proper attention to anything else, so much did the poems occupy his mind.⁸⁶ He seems to have sought

---

⁸² DP, p. 215.
⁸³ DP, p. 253. It is likely, but not certain, that this anecdote belongs to this period.
⁸⁴ "Jugend Mongameli".
⁸⁵ "Jugend Mongameli". I have not been able to establish whether any of these submissions were published.
⁸⁶ Interview 7, 1:41:30".

the company of like-minded people. In a way that I was not able to determine, Mabona was connected with the South African Poetry Society, since his name is listed[87] alongside those of Guy Butler, André de Villiers, and others in the first edition of the first issue of the society's journal, *New Coin*, in 1965. The Society's headquarters was Butler's office at Rhodes University, and he and Ruth Harnett were the editors of the journal from 1965 to 1977.[88] During this period, a number of Mabona's poems were published in *New Coin* (one each in 1965 and 1974 and three in 1977; two of these poems were also published in *Présence Africaine*). While the last publication takes us well into the 1970s, it is hard to imagine how any form of personal contact between Mabona and Rhodes University would have been practicable at any stage other than between 1963 and 1967. During the interviews, Marta Mabona read to me from a folder with correspondence a letter from Guy Butler to "Dear Fr. Mabona", dated 20 May 1973, regarding some of Mabona's poems that he was considering for publication.[89]

Finally, he felt that writing poetry monopolised his mind too much and he decided to abandon it to devote his attention to other things. Nonetheless, I note that, between the time he must have written the first poem published in *Présence Africaine* and the last poems published in *New Coin*, more than a decade has passed. The decision must have been difficult to make.

5.4 Lecturer at St. Peter's in Hammanskraal

In 1957, St. Peter's Seminary at Pevensey (where Mabona received his theological education, cf. Chapter 3, §5) was handed over to be run by the English Dominicans under the rectorship of Oswin Magrath.[90] Philippe Denis describes him as a person of progressive missionary orientation, who insisted on quality theological education for black students, advocated a stronger black clergy with more responsibilities and more representation in the church hierarchy, and who later promoted the view that black theologians and administrators had to be educated to take over their own teaching – views not commonly shared by his brethren at the time.[91] For a number of strategic reasons, the seminary was

---

[87] I stumbled across this fact in a one-page advertisement for a nameless publication (thanks to Sabinet).
[88] My information on the journal is derived from Alan Finlay, "'Pull Down to Earth ...' The story of New Coin, 1965–2014", in Monica Hendricks (ed.), *ISEA 1964-2014. A South African research institute serving people*, NISC/Rhodes University: Grahamstown, 2016, pp. 67–77.
[89] Interviews 7; 1, 45".
[90] As mentioned before, see p. 73. Denis, *The Dominican Friars*, pp. 218–219.
[91] Denis, *The Dominican Friars*, pp. 220–221, 226; confirmed by George Sombe Mukuka, *The*

relocated to Hammanskraal to the north of Pretoria, where lectures resumed from 1963.[92]

In line with these developments, Magrath wrote to the Bishop of Queenstown to request the appointment of Mongameli Mabona to St. Peter's.[93] Although he started there in 1967,[94] the link goes back earlier, since Mabona participated in the founding conference of the St. Peter's Old Boy Association (SPOBA – more about this in the next section) in July 1966, when he was still working in the Queenstown diocese.[95] Mabona considered it a big opportunity to be transferred so far away.[96]

At St. Peter's, he enjoyed good relations with his colleagues; he "had no difficulty whatsoever".[97] In 1969, there were nine lecturers – Mabona and eight white Dominicans – for fifty-nine students.[98] To his regret, he did not have any contact with professional philosophers from other institutions. His task was to teach canon law and philosophy.[99] For philosophy, he had to rely on an old, outdated handbook (unfortunately, he could not recall the title), but he did not restrict himself to this textbook.[100] He also wanted to introduce students to modern philosophy – he specifically mentioned Kant. I cannot confirm it with absolute certainty, but it may well be that Mabona was the first black lecturer of philosophy at an institution of tertiary education in South Africa (provided that one uses "black" here according to the apartheid categorisation, because Adam Small, officially "Coloured", was appointed as a lecturer of philosophy at Fort Hare in 1959, and then at the University of the Western Cape from 1960 to 1973).

---

impact of Black Consciousness on the black Catholic clergy and their training from 1965-1981. Dissertation, Master's in Theology, University of Natal, Pietermaritzburg, November 1996, pp. 45, 50, 54–55.

[92] Cf. Denis, *The Dominican Friars*, p. 222. On life and morale in the seminary, cf. Mukuka, *The impact*, p. 64; Denis, *The Dominican Friars*, pp. 224–226.

[93] This is to be confirmed – I am not sure how it could have been possible to appoint someone under restriction orders to another part of the country.

[94] Mukuka, *The impact*, p. 60.

[95] Cf. Denis, *The Dominican Friars*, p. 225, who states that, at that point in time, Mabona "was in the process of joining the staff".

[96] Interview 7, 20".

[97] Interview 7, 44". Mukuka, *The impact*, p. 55 describes them as follows: "most of whom came from the house of Studies at Oxford and other universities. They were very progressive, broadminded and far ahead of their time".

[98] Mukuka, *The impact*, p. 60.

[99] Mukuka, *The impact*, p. 60 adds Psychology.

[100] Interview 7, 34".

Mabona gives different views on his teaching. On the one hand he ascribes the problems he met with later to the fact that he was "talking freely"; he shared his views with students that the government was illegitimate and that no obedience was due to it. He adds that Rector Magrath was also strongly opposed to the apartheid system.[101] On the other hand, he affirms that he had to be careful because of the threat of informers.[102] One possibility is that he became more prudent as the years passed. He reports that the police came to the seminary several times. Once, he discovered a "listening device" at a window (one may assume of a lecture hall or office), presumably placed by a student "agent". Another time, he was confronted with a bullet, left for him to see in the window of his room, and later yet another placed conspicuously on his desk.[103]

These were eventful times at the seminary. Of the circumstances of his rectorate that were ultimately to lead to Magrath's forced resignation, two interrelated ones are of importance to us: the formation of SPOBA and the Black Priests' Manifesto.

SPOBA

One of Magrath's initiatives was to facilitate the formation of an association of former students, which held its inaugural conference on 4–7 July 1966 at Hammanskraal,[104] the year before Mabona joined the St. Peter's staff. Mabona also delivered one of the papers at this conference, under the title "White worship and black people". The body that was formed at the convention was named St. Peter's Old Boy Association (SPOBA). Combining the views of Mukuka and Mabona, I conclude that the decision to found this body came from the black participants.[105] SPOBA was to become the "black caucus group" of the Roman Catholic Church.[106] According to Gobi Clement Mokoka, SPOBA was "an organised platform to challenge and oppose the [Church] hierarchy's predilection to support the settler regime actively at the expense of the indigenous clergy, laity and the oppressed and exploited community at large".[107] In practice, SPOBA started off pursuing this goal by means of written petitions to the Catholic

---

[101] Interview 5.
[102] Interview 7, 34".
[103] Interview 7, 47".
[104] For the prehistory of SPOBA, cf. Mukuka, *The impact*, pp. 52–53.
[105] Mukuka, *The other side*, pp. 177–178; Interview 5.
[106] Cf. Mukuka, *The impact*, p. 56.
[107] Cited in Mukuka, *The impact*, p. 56.

Church hierarchy, but without eliciting much of a response.[108] At the same time, it had an influence on St. Peter's Seminary by means of the frequent contact SPOBA members had with seminary students[109] and, one should add, one of its members was a member of staff, Dr. Mabona.

In this regard, Mabona remembers[110] that students approached him (and perhaps other members of SPOBA) at St. Peter's to discuss their frustrations with the National Union of South African Students (NUSAS). They complained that the latter organisation was not addressing their problems, that they did not share the same concerns as the white students, and that they were still finding themselves discussing these separately. In practice, SPOBA extended its activities to include the student body. Mabona recounts discussions with Hammanskraal students (often while strolling together between the gates and the buildings); there were also students who came to consult with him from other institutions (he mentions the University of the North).[111] Pityana was there twice; Biko also came at least twice or thrice,[112] but at times when Mabona was not there. Mabona advised students to form an independent union as a forum for discussing their most pressing concerns; he did not see NUSAS as conducive to this. He held up SPOBA as an example of a black forum to the students.[113]

And so it came that "it was from SPOBA that SASO was formed",[114] or the new organisation "copied"[115] SPOBA, and that the "BCM started flowing into

---

[108] Cf. Gobi Clement Mokoka, *Black experience in Black Theology. A study on the Roman Catholic Church missionary endeavour in South Africa and the search for justice*. Doctoral dissertation in divinity. University of Nijmegen, 1984, pp. 152–154.

[109] Cf. Philippe Denis, "Seminary networks and Black Consciousness in South Africa in the 1970s", *South African Historical Journal* 62/1, 2010, pp. 162–182, p. 176.

[110] Interview 5. The exact chronology of events cannot be reconstructed from the different interviews with absolute certainty.

[111] Since 2005, incorporated into the new University of Limpopo.

[112] Interview 7, 51". However, the exact dates when this took place could not be determined. Mabona seems to have in mind consultations that took place between him and unnamed students before the foundation of SASO, but the interviews do not give an indication of when precisely Pityana and Biko would have been at St. Peter's. Note, in this respect, Denis, "Seminary networks...", p. 168: "An information leaflet mentioned visits of the SASO president and vice-president to St. Peter's, Hammanskraal, Umphomulo and Fedsem in March 1971. A year later the same three seminaries were still receiving visits from the SASO leadership, according to the minutes of the meeting of the Executive Council."

[113] Interview 5.

[114] Interview 5.

[115] Interview 7, 54"

SPOBA from about 1969 onwards"[116] (I understand these claims to apply only to developments at St. Peter's). But to appreciate these conclusions, let us zoom out from Hammanskraal, to present BCM and SASO as national movements.

BCM

In a national context of political near-defeat, outlined in the first sections of this chapter, a movement of action and thought emerged among black students. Such a release of political energy among students was not new in the broader African landscape,[117] but it seemed to have come quite unexpectedly in the case of South Africa. At the end of 1968,[118] the South African Student Organization (SASO) was formed to consolidate and stimulate black solidarity. It was to articulate and promote the views of black students across the country – independently of white "liberals".[119] Hence, SASO was formed as different from, and opposed to, the National Union of South African Students (NUSAS), a non-racial and liberal movement, which at the time was not able to live up to its own principles and ideals.[120] Whereas SASO's work and legacy is indeed to be found on the level of ideas (Black Consciousness, Black Theology), its aims and activities also included development projects for students and communities.[121] SASO was instrumental in the foundation of the Black People's Convention, tasked with widening the reach of its mission beyond the university milieu. However, by the time of its foundation in 1972, Mabona had already left the country.

Understanding "black" as inclusive of the groups discriminated against as "non-whites",[122] the central tenet of the BCM is the affirmation of black people's

---

[116] Cf. Mukuka, *The impact*, p. 56.
[117] Cf. UNESCO, *Le rôle des mouvements d'étudiants africains dans l'évolution politique et sociale de l'Afrique de 1900 à 1975*, Paris: UNESCO/Harmattan, 1993.
[118] But see Mukuka, *The impact*, p. 58n111: "Actually SASO was formed in December 1968 at Mariannhill, its inauguration was at Turfloop in July of 1969. That is when it entered the seminary when the students were moving from Natal to the Transvaal."
[119] Cf. Sipho Buthelezi, "The emergence of Black Consciousness: an historical appraisal", in N. B. Pityana, M. Ramphele, M. Mpumiwana, and L. Wilson (eds.) *Bounds of possibility. The legacy of Steve Biko and Black Consciousness*, Cape Town: David Philip, 1991, pp. 111–129, here pp. 111–112.
[120] Motlhabi, *The theory and practice*, pp. 108–109. On the complex history of the movement, cf. Buthelezi.
[121] Cf. Buthelezi, "The emergence of Black Consciousness...", pp. 120–121; Motlhabi, *The theory and practice*, pp. 110, 135–136.
[122] "We define Black people as those who are by law or tradition, politically, economically and socially discriminated against as a group in the South African society and identifying themselves as a unit in the struggle towards the realization of their aspirations". SASO (South

dignity as human beings and the worth of black people's culture and activities (language, history, ideas, music, etc.). Black Consciousness expounds the insight that oppression is not merely political and economic, but penetrates all aspects of black people's lives. Its claim of dignity is also a claim for autonomy, first in respect to the project of liberation, but then also to cultural life in general, including the vision of a future African-styled country. Its rejection of Bantu Education, its advocacy of citizen rights based on original African ownership of the country (and rejection of the Bantustan system), a non-racial democratic state, and a socialist or communalist approach to economics, coupled with a critique of politically insensitive foreign investment, follow directly from this.[123] Its non-racial basis has exposed it to conflicting claims about the status of people of other than African descent.[124]

But let us come back again to the origins of the BCM. Above, I described BCM as a movement, as the name indeed indicates. Its major vehicle was SASO, but other organisations and personal interactions fed into this movement too, of which the Christian sources are of interest here.[125] Focusing on the Christian roots (both in ideology and institutionally) of the movement, Denis claims that the University Christian Movement, SPROCAS,[126] and St. Peter's Old Boys Association (SPOBA) "played a direct role in the foundation and growth of BC", particularly through the intermediary role of black seminaries, "the Federal Theological Seminary (of the Anglican, Methodist, Presbyterian and Congregational Churches), the Lutheran Theological College (of the Lutheran Churches) and St. Peter's Seminary at Hammanskraal (of the Roman Catholic Church)".[127] Thus, the period when Mabona was lecturing at St. Peter's was also the time which saw the emergence of the BCM among students, as described above.

African Students Organisation), "SASO Policy Manifesto", *SASO Newsletter* 1/3, August 1971, pp. 10–11, here p. 10 http://disa.ukzn.ac.za/sites/default/files/pdf_files/saaug71.pdf). The now canonical expression of BC is Biko's essays published as *I write what I like*.

[123] Motlhabi, *The theory and practice*, pp. 115–121, 123–128, 130–132.
[124] Motlhabi, *The theory and practice*, pp. 116–117.
[125] Exploring this background from diverse perspectives are Mukuka, *The impact*; Denis, "Seminary networks…"; and Ian Macqueen, "The Christian Roots of Black Consciousness", in *Black Consciousness and progressive movements under apartheid*, Pietermaritzburg: UKZN Press, 2018, pp. 23–56.
[126] Supported by the Christian Institute and the South African Council of Churches, it was first the Study Project on Christianity in Apartheid South Africa, then the Special Project for Christian Action in Society. The latter is relevant here (cf. Denis, "Seminary networks…", p. 172).
[127] Denis, "Seminary networks…", pp. 167, 163.

Black Theology

The broader movement of Black Consciousness in turn also had an impact on the social sphere of religion. In the University Christian Movement (UCM), a Black Theology Project was launched – the beginning of Black Theology in South Africa.[128] The aim of Black Theology was understood to be a reconsideration of the Christian heritage and practice in light of this history and experience of oppression.[129] The seminal first publication was *Essays on Black Theology* of 1972,[130] edited by Mokgethi Motlhabi, who was probably once one of Mabona's students.[131] Contributors included the theologians Motlhabi, Manas Butbelezi, and Mongameli Mabona; the poet Adam Small; and the SASO activists Steve Biko and Nyameko Pityana.

To be sure, it is not clear how Mabona was connected to the Black Theology Project.[132] His chapter, which is well known and relatively often cited, has the same title as the paper he read at the founding convention of SPOBA in July 1966 (mentioned above, p. 121).[133] According to Denis, "Mongameli Mabona, while still a lecturer at St. Peter's, gave a paper on 'white worship and black people' at the national seminar on black theology organised by UCM at the Wilgespruit Fellowship Centre in March 1971".[134] Since I have not been able to find the original paper, I surmise that it is the same paper, presented a second time, and that the editor obtained permission to include it in the volume. In this sense, one should say that his contribution to the Black Theology Project pre-dated both the project and the larger BCM.

---

[128] Cf. Motlhabi, *The theory and practice*, p. 121.

[129] Motlhabi, *The theory and practice*, pp. 121–122.

[130] A second edition of this book was published as Basil Moore, *Black theology: The South African voice* in 1973. On this discrepancy, see E. Wolff, "Adam Small's shade of Black Consciousness", in Leonhard Praeg (ed.), *Philosophy on the border. Decoloniality and the shudder of the origin*, UKZN Press, 2019, pp. 112–147, here 115–116.

[131] Mokgethi Mothlabi, "Black theology in South Africa: an autobiographical reflection", *Studia Historiae Ecclesiasticae* XXXI/2, 2005, pp. 37–62, §2. In the same article, he describes Mabona as a member of SPOBA: "Perhaps the most prominent among them and one who was to be a strong advocate of black theology was Dr Mongameli Mabona. He had a Doctor of Canon Law degree from Rome, one of a few blacks in this country to have reached that level of theological education at the time."

[132] Mabona himself had no recollection of his relation to this project and was probably already out of the country by the time the volume appeared.

[133] Cf. Mukuka, *The other side*, p. 177. To be precise, the same text is published in *Essays in Black Theology* as "Black people and white worship", but in *Pro Veritate* as "White worship and black people".

[134] Denis, "Seminary networks...", p. 178.

Black Priests' Manifesto

The last event of importance in the current context is the publication of the so-called "Black Priests' Manifesto". On 23 January 1970, the *Rand Daily Mail* published a text under the title "Our Church has let us down". The authors were all SPOBA members, one of whom was lecturing at St. Peter's Seminary. That was Anthony Mabona. The other authors were David Moetapele, John Louwfant, Clement Mokoka, and Smangaliso Mkhatshwa.[135] I note that Lebamang John Sebidi (later head of St. Peter's Seminary), in speaking about Mabona's role in the Manifesto, stated: "I think he was the moving spirit behind that".[136] Yet, according to Mabona, the authors discussed the content in several meetings before it was written by all of the signatories together.[137] The aims of this Manifesto are straightforward: it denounces racial asymmetries in the Catholic Church in South Africa and calls this Church to abide by its own commitment to Africanisation in the wake of the Second Vatican Council (see full discussion in Part 2, §6). Furthermore, although it is factual and argumentative, the Manifesto articulates an unambiguous rejection of this state of affairs and calls for equal respect. The aim was not to write against the Church but to "set things right".[138]

As might be expected, this initiative provoked a response. Recounting his personal impressions, Mabona recalls that they were accused of being overly critical, that they were breaking away from the Church, and instigating dissent among students – they were labelled "rebel priests".[139] In fact, he sketches a general picture of a lack of understanding, which he also experienced from black laypeople. He had the impression that nobody was listening to them and that some people started to avoid them.

---

[135] The online *Dictionary of African Christian Biography* has articles on three of the signatories. By George Mukuka: "Moetapele, David" (http://www.dacb.org/stories/southafrica/moetapele_david.html [last accessed 5 February 2016]) and "Mokoka, Gobi Clement" (http://www.dacb.org/stories/southafrica/mokoka.html [last accessed 5 February 2016]); by Norbert Brockman, "Mkhatshwa, Smangaliso Patrick" (http://www.dacb.org/stories/southafrica/mkhatshwa1_smang.html [last accessed 5 February 2016]).

[136] Interview with Lebamang John Sebidi by Gail Gerhart on 3 July 1987 http://www.aluka.org/stable/10.5555/al.sff.document.gerhart0002 (last accessed 2 October 2016).

[137] Interview 7:46"; Interview 3.

[138] Interview 7:46".

[139] Interview 3.

A different view on the consequences of the Manifesto is outlined by Mukuka.[140] First, a discussion between the signatories of the Manifesto and the Administrative Board of the Bishop's Conference took place. Apparently, this was presented as a concession: initially, it was claimed that the Manifesto was not representative of black views in the Church, but when thousands of parishioners heeded the call by SPOBA's executive to show their support in person at the SACBC's offices, the bishops granted that discussion was needed.[141] Then an array of responses appeared in the Catholic newspaper, the *Southern Cross*, ranging between embracing and rejecting the Manifesto. Eventually, some promotions and institutional reforms were undertaken by the Catholic Church.

In the aftermath of these events, but also due to other tensions at St. Peter's Seminary and between the seminary and other Church structures, Magrath was asked to resign. He was replaced by Dominic Scholten, and responsibility for the seminary was transferred from the Dominicans to the South African Bishop's Conference.[142] Scholten, although he was not simply adverse to the issues of black students and priests, set a much higher premium on re-establishing the "normal" functioning of the seminary. In May 1972, a year and a half after Scholten's appointment, Mabona's request to be relieved of his functions was granted.

---

[140] Cf. Mukuka, *The other side*, pp. 182–186. Mukuka, The impact, pp. 74–77 and, similarly, *The other side*, pp. 181–182 present a short comparison between the Black Priests' Manifesto and BC.
[141] Mukuka, *The impact*, pp. 66–67.
[142] Cf. Denis, *The Dominican Friars*, p. 228.

CHAPTER 6

LONDON AND SWITZERLAND: POLITICS OR ANTHROPOLOGY?

Officially, the end of this period of Mabona's in South Africa came with the "withdrawal of Reverend Father Mabona from the Seminary staff in order to enable him to proceed overseas to continue his studies".[1] But from his own account, the continued threats from the police weighed heavily in his decision and he considered his departure as fleeing into exile.

This return to Europe was to have quite a different significance for him than his first sojourn there. As much as his first journey to Italy was imposed on him, he invested a lot of energy during his years in Italy to master what that milieu had to offer: Catholic theology, and Latin; African culture, and the expatriate intellectual milieu were an additional boon. By contrast, his departure from South Africa the second time did not really assume the form of embracing a new world. Rather, he left because his 1965 return to South Africa became unsustainable, and henceforth he had to find an alternative way to return to Xhosaland, for which he never ceased to long. My impression is that by that time the most significant formative events were already behind him and that, apart from events in his personal life, the most significant context of reference for him remained South Africa.[2] For this reason I will not say much about the sociopolitical contexts in which Mongameli Mabona subsequently lived and I will refocus this historical presentation on the personal aspects of his life.

His initial plan to depart into exile was to take an opportunity to pursue studies in Biblical Sciences in Israel, but he had to abandon this idea because the

---
[1] Mukuka, *The impact*, pp. 89–90.
[2] Explicitly suggested by Marta Mabona.

available bursary was too small to live on.³ In the end, his path led to London, where he started a Master's degree in Religious Studies at the School of Oriental and African Studies (SOAS) at London University (1972–1973).

Whether he received any funding for this is not known, but it is true that he continued his activities as a priest. For some time, he worked at the Guardian Angels Parish in the east of London,⁴ where he was housed by a South African family.⁵ He said mass, supported sick and dying people, and stood in for his alcoholic colleague – in short, performing the full duties as parish priest – while pursuing his studies at SOAS.⁶ Subsequently he also worked with Jesuits in Birmingham.⁷ Then, after twenty years' service, he left the priesthood.⁸ His ultimate reasons for this decision remain unknown to me. He started to make his living as an employee in hotels.

Having sketched the stage, let us take a look at two important activities from this time.

1. SOAS

From 1972 to 1973, Mongameli Mabona was enrolled in a Master's in religious studies. Next to his course work, he also had to submit a research essay – the "long essay" to which he repeatedly refers in *Diviners and prophets*. The supervisor for this project was Richard Gray, who was to become a family friend for the rest of his life. Gray⁹ was appointed to the SOAS in 1963 as a specialist in African history, a field in which he was considered a pioneer. Already an established academic, he was promoted to professor the year Mabona studied with him.¹⁰ During these years, Gray did extensive research on precolonial African history.

---

[3] Interview 0, 9"; Interview 5.
[4] Interview 0, 4".
[5] Interview 7, 1:06"
[6] Interview 5.
[7] Interview 5.
[8] Interview 7, 1:14". Ordained at the end of 1954, this takes us to 1974. The interviews also give the impression that he had left the priesthood even earlier. However, in the Introduction to DP, he indicates the "church-work" dimension of his life as spanning from 1954 to 1975.
[9] The information below is obtained from Roland Oliver, "Professor Richard Gray. Incisive historian of Africa", *The Independent*, 14 September 2005 and Andrew Roberts, "Richard Gray, 1929–2005", *Azania: Archaeological research in Africa* 40/1, 2005, pp. 166–167.
[10] Incidentally, he was the supervisor for Walter Rodney's PhD too.

A late convert himself, he later worked on the history of Christianity in Africa and he also helped to establish a department for the study of religions at SOAS.

While realising lucidly that he "couldn't go back to South Africa"[11] – at least in those years it would have been inconceivable – Mabona embarked on a study which was going to occupy him for close to three decades after the formal completion of the project. The title of the dissertation was "The interaction and development of different religions in the Eastern Cape in the late eighteenth and early nineteenth centuries, with special reference to the first two Xhosa prophets". This is the project on which he would much later comment:

> A long and close personal study of the mythology of the Khoisan and Southern African Bantu peoples, started at SOAS in 1972, eventually served to convince me that, the remarkable apparent ethnic differences between these two groups notwithstanding, there must have existed at the beginning a basic unity in a common stock. This conclusion even in this tentative form raised a host of pressing questions which were well-nigh unmanageable in the field of historical inquiry. All these questions will be posed and answers to them will be suggested as we go along.[12]

And hence it serves as a point of entry to his anthropological work, which he concluded with *Diviners and prophets*.

2. The Azanian People's Liberation Front and other politics

At least during the first years of exile, Mabona maintained ties with South African acquaintances (in addition to maintaining contact with his family). He devoted time rallying support for the group of BC activists who had gathered in Botswana, the short-lived Azanian People's Liberation Front (APLF).[13] This group was formed in 1972 by SASO members who were convinced that the BCM had to move on to an armed strategy to oppose the apartheid state. A combination of

---

[11] Interview 5.
[12] DP, p. 45.
[13] The information that follows is derived from Toivo Asheeke, "'Arming Black Consciousness': The Formation of the Bokwe Group/Azanian Peoples' Liberation Front, April 1972–September 1976", *Journal of Southern African Studies* 45/1, 2019, pp. 69–88.

strategic decisions and banning orders motivated them to settle in Botswana. There, they recruited members and negotiated with other groups (the ANC and its Umkhonto we Sizwe, but more so the PAC/APLA, to which it was ideologically closer). They planned and trained for action; some were also trained as far afield as Libya or the Golan Heights. At its peak, the APLF counted more than 100 members. In the aftermath of Soweto 1976, the members decided to join the ANC. The APLF is also known as the Bokwe group. Bokwe Mafuna, formerly a freelance journalist for the *Rand Daily Mail*, joined SASO in the early 1970s and became a major driving force behind the APLF.

Mabona's contact person in Botswana was Mafuna.[14] The speeches Mabona gave were occasions to find funding for this group. It involved a lot of travelling. He received support for this from different people, including Bettina Stein from Wiesbaden.[15] She would have organised his trips to Berlin and accompanied him to both the western and the eastern sides of the city.[16] He recounts that he got some support at least from German students.[17]

Mabona still received information from the group in Botswana and visisted them at least once.[18] He highlights their objective of serving as a connector

---

[14] Interview 0, 9". In an interview with Daniel Magaziner, Mafuna responded to the question: "[...] given that you were a Christian, how was the armed struggle legitimized in your eyes?" by referencing three of the signatories of the Black Priests' Manifesto: "It was a just struggle. I had no problems at all with that. I understood, I can't quote now from the bible exactly, but I think it is in Saint Luke, Chapter 3-around there, when Christ says he has come to liberate the poor, and that was in a sense the legitimising verse for me and for many other people. When priests like Mabona, Anthony Mabona, he had been a Catholic priest and Clement Mokoka, even Mkhatshwa, who is the mayor of Pretoria, people believed that a just struggle had to be conducted and it would have God's blessing. And in order to achieve our objectives, we were able to see that we could and we had to do everything that was necessary to destroy the evil of apartheid. I don't think we ever had a problem about that. I don't think that Christians have ever had a problem in defending what they truly believed in whether through war or any other means. So maybe we were just ordinary Christians, we were just doing the normal thing, that should have been done a long time ago in this country" (page 21). "Interview with Bokwe Mafuna", 3 November 2005, http://www.aluka.org/action/showMetadata?doi=10.5555/AL.SFF.DOCUMENT.MAGAZP1B1001 (last accessed 3 June 2019). It may be that Mafuna was one of Mabona's students during his short stint at St. Peter's, but I have not been able to establish the exact chronology.

[15] Interview 7, 1:13".

[16] In Interview 0, his daughter Nomsa remarks that he had many stamps from the German Democratic Republic (East Germany) in his old passport.

[17] It thus seems likely that Mabona engaged in these activities at least for some time while he was still an ordained priest.

[18] Interview 7, 56".

between the student movement and the "outside" world and trying to get them aid through this way. However, as far as he could see, relations between the Botswana group and their allies on the "inside" were not always simple, and the Botswana group grew apart from the others.[19] He also remembers this group's opposition to the ANC in those years – principally directed at the latter's inefficiency. Yet, in the end, he had doubts about the Botswana group's own efficiency.[20]

Mongameli Mabona himself met with ANC members (probably in London), but the discussion brought to the fore unbridgeable differences. In fact, it ended with his receiving the warning that he would not be able to do anything in South Africa without the ANC.[21] One may thus safely conclude that Denis was right in claiming vaguely that "[h]e went to London where he joined the liberation movement", but was mistaken when he states elsewhere that "he eventually joined the ANC in London".[22]

For his first year in London, Mabona succeeded in obtaining a travel permit. But thereafter he was a political refugee and often did not have regular papers. This made him an interesting target: he was once offered British citizenship, but under the condition that he act as an informant – a proposition which he rejected.

3. Family life

The day before Pope John XXIII's death, on 2 June 1963, Mongameli Mabona met a young Swiss woman on St. Peter's Square in the Vatican.[23] Marta Giger came to Rome to learn Italian, which was in vogue with her peers at the time. A native of the countryside outside of Lucerne, she was the daughter of a prison warden and a housewife, and the eldest of three sisters. She started her professional education in a commercial school before moving on to study social work. But, since childhood, she had dreamt of working in Africa or India at a mission, as a layperson.

---

[19] Interview 5.
[20] This is confirmed by Asheeke, "'Arming Black Consciousness'...", pp. 86–87.
[21] Interview 7, 1:03".
[22] Denis, *The Dominican Friars*, p. 225 and Denis, "Seminary networks...", p. 178.
[23] Interview 7, 1:59"; Interview 5.

Late in the 1960s, the opportunity came to realise something of that dream, when she joined her cousin, Dr. Hermann Kunz,[24] in Angola. At that stage, he was working as a surgeon at Tchindjendje, midway between Lubito and Nova Lisboa (now Huambo), and she helped him with the office administration. "It was beautiful. We were in the bush. It was fantastic", she reminisces. She also explains that the hospital there was modern and on the same standard as what she had known in her home country. People came there from all over Angola and even from neighbouring countries.[25] Her cousin wanted to open a nursing school and asked Giger to go home to study nursing in preparation for this project. So, after two years in Angola, at the end of 1970, she returned to Switzerland and started at the nursing school. However, when she was close to completing her training, tensions in Angola flared up and her cousin had to leave the country in a hurry. Since the civil war then broke out, nothing came of the project; her cousin later started a project in Tanzania. Marta Giger was never to settle in Africa again. However, as she quips, Africa came to her…

While she was in Angola, she wanted to visit her friend, Mongameli Mabona, in South Africa, but he forbade her to do so, fearing that either or both of them would run into problems with the law.[26] But somehow Mabona managed to get together the means to visit her in Angola sometime during 1970.

During his stay in London, he again took up contact with her and, in his own words: "From 1977 onwards she has been an unfailing source of encouragement".[27] This is the year when he resettled in Switzerland. They were married the next year in London, where they found a way of overcoming the administrative difficulties.[28] At that stage, the question was raised (by correspondence?) whether they were going to follow only the European marriage customs or if there would also be a Xhosa celebration – the latter did not take place, I assume, principally because of the practical implications.[29]

In Lucerne,[30] where they have lived ever since, three children were born to the couple: Themba (1978), Sipho (1980), and Nomsa (1982). In the meantime,

---

[24] Correspondence with Marta Mabona (10 January 2019).
[25] Interview 5.
[26] Interview 7, 2:01".
[27] DP, "Gratitude".
[28] Interview 5.
[29] Interview 6, 1:01".
[30] According to Mabona, the feature that is fairly striking is that Lucerne is near a lake, Interview 5.

Marta Mabona continued to work as a nurse, while Mongameli Mabona looked after the children. Their mother's view on this was: "You know, my husband, he's a wonderful father and he has always been. He was the one who was looking after our children and you can't imagine the dedication he had". He affirms this: "Yes, because I had learnt to look after children of my stepmother. She always gave the children to me to look after, so I had learnt that at the time. So when they came, I was I was used to it". And Themba adds: "I remember talking about when you were a little boy, I remember that you told us a lot about stick-fighting [...]".[31]

After a couple of unhappy experiences as an English tutor, he succeeded in getting an appointment as a porter at the hospital. From 1984 to his retirement in 1994, this is where he worked.

4. Continued research

As stated earlier, Mabona did not have much interest in European politics. Over many years, he remained preoccupied with his anthropology project, specifically with "an investigation into the roots of Xhosa culture and history".[32] He explains:

> I had just started my course at SOAS [i.e. 1972[33]] when I met the late Mr. Alioune Diop, founder of Présence Africaine, who was attending a conference in London. He highly praised my work to his learned friends and said it would be of great value. At that time I had a still very inadequate idea of my project and was in a state of vacillation, but Alioune Diop, the icon in matters of African culture and his words, bolstered my courage and made me determined to rise up to his high expectations.[34]

---

[31] Interview 1.
[32] DP, "Blurb".
[33] The chronology is not entirely sure. In the introduction to DP, he writes: "But I did not get the time to dedicate myself formally to such research till 1972 when, [...] I was admitted to the School of Oriental and African Studies (SOAS) at the University of London. My work in SOAS started in 1973, and I had Professor Gray as supervisor when writing the "long essay" required at the end of the MA course which I completed in the same year". This raises the question what Mabona did in London after his arrival in 1972. It may be that the course work component was done from 1972 and the "long essay" completed in 1973.
[34] DP, "Gratitude".

From the earlier interest in philosophy, and theology, the core of anthropology remained as his lasting interest. Finally, he sent some of his writings to Prof. Wolfgang Marschall at the Ethnologisches Seminar of the University of Bern, on the basis of which he was accepted to the doctoral programme in anthropology in 1984.[35]

Originally from Silesia, Marschall studied in Cologne and Munich. As a specialist on South East Asia, he did a lot of fieldwork in Indonesia, but also some in Mexico. After a few years as professor of anthropology in Tübingen, he moved to Bern, where he worked until his retirement in 2003.[36] Mabona described him as experienced in supervision.[37]

During these years, it seems that Mabona filled every available moment with work on this project. In fact, he presents the broader frame as follows: "This work reflects the results of a long drawn-out research programme executed in moments snatched from real life engagements: Church-work (1954-1975); the struggle against apartheid (1948-1991); work in the market place (1975-1994); domestic occupations (1977)".[38] Hence, he expresses his gratitude for the freedom to do so during his hours in service of the hospital:

> Frau Ida Dommen, who was head of the physiotherapy ward at Kantonsspital Luzern, was the first to provide me with a room that I could use for reading at every free moment I had at my disposal. She set a precedent for all the other departments in which I subsequently worked (1984-1994).[39]

But holiday times were devoted to this project too. Thus we know that, between 1984 and 1987, he did research at the Commonwealth Institute Library in London and at the Library of the Frobenius Institute in Frankfurt. He enjoyed the practical support of Richard Gray and his wife, Gabriella Cattaneo, in London, Dr. Beatrix Heintze assisted him at the Frobenius Institute. He particularly mentions the library team of D. H. Simpson and colleagues at the Commonwealth Institute Library. The list is longer:

---

[35] Interview 7, 1:19"; DP, "Introduction".
[36] This information is based on the short presentation on "Interviews with German anthropologists" webpage: http://www.germananthropology.com/short-portrait/wolfgang-marschall/144.
[37] Interview 5.
[38] DP, "Introduction", first sentence.
[39] DP, "Gratitude".

Later, when I visited the bookshop of Présence Africaine in Paris, Madame (Mama) Yande C. Diop also proved very ready to help with a number of sorely needed texts. I wish here to express my deep gratitude to Présence Africaine for all their generous assistance. In the matter of texts, I wish to say that, particularly at the start of my research, I was in great need of Xhosa texts, as I have spent a considerable time of my adult life in Europe. My niece, Babalwa Lujabe, BA (Business Admin.) was the first to give me all the Xhosa readers at her disposal. [...] In this matter of texts I also got tremendous and generous help from Prof. Dr. Katesa Schlosser of Kiel University, as well as from Professor O. F. Raum, formerly of Fort Hare. Professor Marschall had kindly furnished me with the necessary introductions.[40]

For his research travels, he received financial support from the University of Bern and from Miss Margaret Feeny.[41] This catalogue of names and institutions paints a picture of a network of support and exchange, invaluable for such a project.

However, there were also setbacks. Apart from the practical difficulties of juggling his research with his family and professional life, Mabona intended to spend more time in South Africa to further his project. He wanted to consult the National Archives and conduct interviews with people who were intimately acquainted with Xhosa culture. This plan did not work out, although he had a number of opportunities, beginning in 1991, to return to South Africa. It was during such a visit that Mabona conducted the interviews published in *Présence Africaine*.[42] In fact, in that year, 1996, he again submitted a number of contributions to the journal: two interviews, an article on women's resistance to apartheid, two book reviews on South African authors, and an article on the impact of *Présence Africaine* on South African struggle history, in particular on black consciousness (see Part 2, §8).

As a consequence of not being able to pursue his studies more actively in South Africa,[43] he remained unsatisfied with the fact that most of his work was based on the published material he could find in Europe. His study ended up being much more historical than he would have liked.

---

[40] DP, "Gratitude".
[41] DP, "Gratitude".
[42] Mabona, "Interviews", *Présence Africaine* 153/1, 1996, pp. 82–85.
[43] But he seems to have kept his eye on the research during these visits; cf. "In 1998 I was again back in South Africa and I happened to be standing in a queue in front of a bank in Queenstown." DP, p. 415.

Finally, Mabona's second doctorate, under the title "Diviners and Prophets among the Xhosa (1593 -1856). A study in Xhosa cultural history", was "[a]ccepted by the Philosophico-historical Faculty on the recommendation of Prof. Wolfgang Marschall and Prof. Reinhard Schulze, Bern, 7 July, 2000".[44] The published version from LIT Verlag appeared in 2004. Interestingly, the blurb identifies the author as a "South African anthropologist" (bear in mind that he obtained Swiss citizenship in 1990).[45]

These were two extremely different theses: one in Catholic canon law, the other in the cultural history of the Xhosa. Yet, I wonder if there is not a subterranean connection between the two. This similarity would reside in the question of understanding the task of mediating between two cultural worlds. This is the task of the new convert or catechist (as Mabona's father was); this is the role assumed in different ways by Xhosa diviners and prophets.[46] This is, in my view, a major question of Mabona's whole intellectual journey.

In the early 1990s, the last dominos of apartheid history fell. In 1991, amnesty made it possible for political exiles to return to South Africa.[47] A message from Uncle Babana, who had looked after Mabona as a small child, weighed on the Mabona family's spirit; Uncle Babana said that he would not die before his nephew Mongameli had returned. Thus it came about that the family all went to the Transkei in 1991. They made a second return to Queenstown soon after Mabona's retirement and, since then, he has returned a number of times.

On 5 June 2019, Mongameli Mabona celebrated his ninetieth birthday.

---

[44] According to the Copyright page of DP.
[45] Interview 7.
[46] It is perhaps relevant to mention in this context that "Chronologically, the idea of doing research on the diviner phenomenon in connection with the study of Xhosa culture took shape in my mind in 1965" (DP, Intro), i.e. two years after completing the first doctorate.
[47] Zosa Olenka De Sas Kropiwnicki, "The meeting of myths and realities: The 'homecoming' of second-generation exiles in post-apartheid South Africa", *Refuge* 30/2, 2014, pp. 79–92, especially pp. 81–82.

PART 2 – WORK

From his life narrative, we have come to know Mongameli Mabona's explorative temperament and his unceasing reflection. It is therefore appropriate that we turn from his life and work in general to take a closer look at his intellectual work, insofar as the extant texts allow.

Regrettably, the sources are not readily available. One needs access to the facilities of a university library even to find some of his texts. For others, even that will not suffice if the library concerned does not have a very strong international network to borrow material. I have gone to great lengths to establish Mabona's full bibliography – which is added as an addendum – but even so, there may be some more texts yet to be discovered. Because of the difficulty of accessing his texts, my primary objective in this part of the book is to provide a survey of the content of Mabona's written work – principally theology, philosophy, anthropology, and poetry – for the wider scholarly and interested public. Here and there, I will allow myself some critical comments, but the emphasis in this section is to highlight the lines of development and the conjunctions and discontinuities in his thought. To give an impression of the reception of his publications, I also note secondary literature devoted to or citing Mabona's texts, as far as I could locate any. Finally, I punctuate the discussion with a few sections of general appraisal regarding the character of parts of his work.

Together, the biographical and sociopolitical contextualisation of Mabona's biography (Part 1) and the survey of texts (Part 2), offer a starting point and a tool for those scholars who would like to continue this exploration, for instance by comparisons of Mabona's writings to that of his contemporaries or by advanced critical examinations.

1. *Lux*: The first impetus

Mongameli Mabona's first three published articles appeared in the annual journal of the African Association of St. Augustine, *Lux* (see Part 1, Chapter 4, §4).[1] These publications provide a clear view on the young writer's first intellectual experimentations and the blooming of his concerns and interests.

His very first published venture into the world of independent thinking is an attempt to situate Africa historically and culturally, in his article "Africa's true position and destiny" (1958–1959). He typifies the contemporary period as a time of "spiritual reawakening" of the whole of humanity (p. 14). He argues that the present was also a significant moment in history for the African continent, since it was the "judgement hour of Europe" (pp. 13, 14). Both the spiritual and material aspects of the broader Western civilisation stand to be judged. In Mabona's appraisal, Europe can claim on the side of its spiritual achievements the foundation of vibrant Christian communities in Asia and Africa. He reserves his critical indictment for the West's material developments, notably Western military technology – the development of nuclear weapons in particular weighs on his mind. He posits that what underlies the negative aspects of the West's material development is its "lack of charity" (p. 15). Africa in particular has been on the receiving end of what he refers to as "harassment" from Europe.[2]

This ambiguous state of affairs under the dominance of the West results in a crisis for the whole of humanity, and it is not possible to see where this is heading. However, Mabona cites Pope Pius XII's view that humanity is at the brink of a springtime[3] in which the good is bound to gain in strength. This springtime holds the promise of progressive integration of Africa into the greater human family (p. 17) – an integration not in the sense of improved connectivity by means of new transport and communication technologies, but in the sense of an "awakening of man's awareness of his kinship with and need of his fellow-men" (p. 18).

---

[1] The existence of these articles came to my attention in a bibliographical report published in *Rivista trimestrale di studi e documentazione dell'Istituto italiano per l'Africa e l'Oriente*, 15/1, January–February, pp. 43–49.

[2] However, Mabona asserts that Asia is protecting Africa (partially) from this harassment. Since he does not give any geopolitical specification for these intercontinental relations, his claim remains highly speculative.

[3] In fact, Mabona cites the Pope's own word, "primavera" (Italian for springtime), but renders it repeatedly with "springtide", which is a different, but not unrelated, image. I therefore replace "springtide" with "springtime".

Following the Pope on this point, Mabona senses in this integration the growth of the Mystic Body of Christ, and indeed of the Kingdom of God.

Such is the situation in which he sees Africa emerging on the world scene (at the time when he wrote his article). Although the continent boasts considerable material resources, he argues that its "spiritual progress" is of more significance, and he advances the permanence and growth of Christianity as the central point of this progress.

The article is both argumentative and speculative. Mabona supports his main points with reference, indeed, with deference, to the teachings and writings of Pope Pius XII and to Bishop Fulton Sheen, a member of the Catholic hierarchy. One may describe the article as a *theological cultural critique* on a global scale. Its basic assumption is that, in order to address the issues he raises, theology is an appropriate, indeed the most appropriate, form of questioning and reflection. It is noteworthy that the central concern of all these articles is the African continent. Furthermore, from his first article onwards, for many years to come, Mabona holds that such a critique of global tendencies needs to proceed by means of a comparison of cultures or blocks of humanity on a scale for which continents are the appropriate unit of comparison.

This article is an invaluable vantage point from which to obtain a perspective on the nature and extent of the subsequent development of Mabona's thought.

"African mentality in a world frame" (1958–1959), Mabona's second *Lux* article, continues his argument and perspective on the formation of humanity as a "World Community" and the laborious and painful, but inevitable, dawn of a spiritual springtime. The "universal struggles" of humanity in this period are divergent:

> Ideological, Political, Ethnic. Expressed in simpler terms, this means that there is tension between the Theistic and Atheistic outlooks in the world, there is tension in the Master-and-Servant relations among peoples, and lastly there is tension in the different mental outlooks of the various Ethnic Complexes of the globe. (p. 32)

How is one to deal with these tensions? By tackling, first of all, the last of the three: divergent ethnic-mental outlooks. Mutual fear, distrust, and ignorance can be overcome by gaining insight into one another's "deepest mental structures" (p. 32). If that can be achieved, pressure regarding the other two points will also be released. One can hope to make headway in this respect by turning to *anthropology*. To be sure, Mabona rejects all theories which categorise "cultural outlooks or mentality" (p. 33) from a universal historical perspective, on the basis of the supposition that there is one humanity where some are more, and others less, advanced. But this rejection obliges Mabona to face two difficult problems at the same time. First, how does one reject the idea of progress without rejecting the historical formation of cultures? Second, how does one describe cultural differences without sacrificing the idea of one humanity?

His attempt to resolve these dilemmas consists of affirming the simultaneous differences between cultures in respect to their myths, legends, and folklore, and taking them as expressions of the deepest aspirations of each cultural group. Working his way through the complex debates on the nature of myths, Mabona concludes that a sympathetic reading of these tales is invaluable as a way to access the thought of people of different cultural origins.

Having thus determined the general approach, he suggests that one can proceed to study different families of myths – Indian, Latin, Nordic, Japanese, Chinese, etc. – by comparing them, or, as the article's title says, placing them, in a world frame. He does not argue for a comparison of the minute details, but rather of the most general traits,[4] perhaps one could say the essence, of each collection of myths. Hence, the European collection would be typified primarily by reason and intellect, the Indian by mysticism and desire, the Chinese and Japanese by beauty, etc. These broad classifications then allow for further specification of the typical temperaments, for instance, of English, German, Italian, or Slavonic Europeans, each with their own typical forms of manifestation.

This points the way to consider the specificity of Africa. Mabona describes African mythology as monotheistically inclined, and he claims that discourse on divinity is restricted to myths (it does not infuse everyday history). Furthermore, this form of discourse is linked to a cult of ancestor worship. The sources which Mabona reviews critically include the works of Willoughby, Smith and Frobenius. Likewise, he reviews the "French school" (p. 41) (mainly Tempels, Lefrou, Aujoulat, although he also includes Westerman, Driberg, and Young) and the central place this trend of enquiry accords to the life force in the African view of reality. Note that, at this stage, the approach Mabona adopts – the form of thinking he considers appropriate for dealing with the stated problem – is still anthropological. This is evident when he concedes the viability of a philosophical

---

4   Although the essentialising thrust of the argument is undeniable, Mabona qualifies it by specifying that the characteristics he identifies "are found predominantly in the one system and are *comparatively* lacking in the other" (p. 42, my emphasis).

reading of culture,[5] while insisting that this metaphysics of the vital force would *not* be a philosophy in the strictest sense. Subsequently, rather than entertaining the philosophical import of myths, he presents, in detail, one "African" myth: the Xhosa tale of the brides coming to the kraal of the dragon, Namba.[6] Humanity, figured in the myth by a bride, faces obstacles and has to assume an appropriately virtuous attitude to overcome life's difficulties. However, following Eliade, Mabona insists on the plurality of the layers of meaning on which such a symbolic narration may be understood, in turn or at the same time.

But Mabona also applies the same symbolic reading to customs, taking initiation as his primary example. He argues that initiation should be viewed, and participated in, as a part of biological life, a beat of the rhythm of life, as an event of regeneration and a concentration of wisdom, a catching up, etc. At the same time, the entire rite is enveloped in symbols. In all, such *symbolic* thinking is more dialectical than expressive of strict, mutually exclusive, and non-contradictory categories. At the same time, Mabona contends that the work of Griaule and Dieterlen on the Dogon people testifies to the "metaphysics, sociology and psychology" (p. 48) advanced by symbolic thought.

With this detour through a detailed exploration of a myth and a cultural practice, Mabona returns to the broader characterisations of cultural families: the European intellectualist bent, the Eastern axiological bent, and the African symbolic bent (p. 50). In more elaborate terms, Mabona ventures to capture the essence of the African mode of thought as follows:

> The African sees life as a mystery, and his characteristic expression of that primal intuition is Rhythm. MYSTERY and RHYTHM.... I think that is the formula for the African mind: the vision of being as the Unum – the One. Rhythm has always been the classic expression of mystery as can be seen in the rituals, dances, music, and poetry. The symbol is the intellectual mode for the expression of the mystery of the reconciliation of opposites because logic refuses to oblige. (p. 50)

---

[5] "The French thinkers have done a world of good in bringing systematic philosophical thought to bear on the apparently unpromising field of African Metaphysical speculation" (p. 42).

[6] Mabona refers to A.C. Jordan's reworking of this myth in *The wrath of the ancestors* (1940). Originally published in Xhosa as *Ingqumbo Yeminyanya*, it "deals with history and the changing traditions of the Mpondomise people, and with the familiar themes of conflict between the new and the old, between Westernized 'school' and traditional 'red ochre' people, and between mission religion and traditional belief", according to the synthesis by Patricia Handley in Eugene Benson and L.W. Conolly (eds.), *Encyclopedia of post-colonial literatures in English* (second edition), London and New York: Routledge, 2005, p. 742.

But this essence is not without ambiguity – quite the contrary. Mabona claims that such a general orientation has its strengths *and* weaknesses, which he identifies in the case for the African bent, as characterised by spontaneity and humour, but also "slowness, indecision, and duplicity" (p. 50).

When people from one cultural group use their own frame of reference to assess the acts and thoughts of people from other cultural groups, this may easily lead to the identification of insufficiencies in the others. A more prudent approach, Mabona suggests, would be to consider all viewpoints as complementary: "[A]ll ethnic complexes are equidistant from the centre of the Fullness of Being, though at definitely diverse starting points or angles from it" (p. 52). He even ventures the lyrical speculation that there is "a secret love affair between Europe and Africa" – which accounts in his mind for the "lovers' quarrels between these two Continents" (p. 52).

From his first to his second article, Mabona clearly gained confidence. The second article reflects a much broader intellectual orientation. The bibliography reveals his readings in theory regarding myth and anthropology, which are amply reviewed in the article; he reviews works by Lévy-Bruhl, Cassirer, Malinowski, Singer, Bergson, Rosenberg, Boas, MacIver, and Otto. Apart from the first paragraph, which evokes the earlier essay, and an oddly inserted paragraph with practical advice on religious representations in catechism in Africa at the end, there is hardly anything left of the Christian theological perspective of his first article. The argument is now conducted in a much more social-scientific way. He does not mention Senghor, but Mabona's idea of universal human civilisations, the complementary cultural essences, corresponds with the Senghorian view.[7]

Undoubtedly the most salient change brought about by the third and last of Mabona's *Lux* articles – "Towards an African philosophy"[8] (1959) – is its

---

[7] In a later chapter, "The depths of African philosophy" (reviewed below), he includes Senghor explicitly in his list of authors who gave him direction and claims that this influence stretches as far back as the date of his first publications: "In a former article which I wrote for the Lux Magazine in 1958 and which I later passed on to Présence Africaine I made it clear that my point of departure in the subject of African Philosophy was constituted by the masterly analyses of such men as Leopold Sedar Senghor, Father Tempels, Father Alexis Kagame, Aimé Césaire and the researches of Marcel Griaule and Miss Dieterlen. To this I must also add the most valuable reading of the Book of the Dead of the Ancient Egyptians and other works on Egyptology" (pp. 31–32). However, it is not clear to which article Mabona refers in this citation.

[8] There are references to this article (in any of its three publications) in the following secondary literature: L.V. Thomas, "Un système philosophique sénégalais: la cosmologie des Diola",

philosophical intention. As the citation from "The depths of African philosophy" (in the previous footnote) demonstrates, Mabona himself traces his work *in* African philosophy back as early as 1958, in particular in connection with his study of the "ethnophilosophers", *négritude* authors, and the anthropologists Griaule and Dieterlen (and probably also Cheikh Anta Diop in the same years). If "an African philosophy" is the essay's aim, what does it take as its starting point?

Seemingly, this starting point is an observation about the enduring hegemony of the Western view on the world and a declaration of Mabona's counter-hegemonic ideal: "[W]hat the world really needs is the complete image of humanity patterned on the various ways of thought and forms of culture of the diverse ethnic complexes composing the human family" (p. 56).[9] The utopian imagery of a global family is carried over from the first article ("Africa's true position and destiny"), and the vision of complementary ethnic and cultural groups from the second ("African mentality in a world frame"). Instead of looking for a solution to global conflict and violence in the direction of universal similarities among people, Mabona advocates a view that puts human diversity at the centre. For only through insight into one's own weaknesses and understanding of another can one hope to recognise "human interdependence and solidarity" (p. 57). From such a perspective, each group has a contribution to make.

And his point is about groups – relatively uniform cultural groups, like those of Africa.[10] Following the work of Gabriel Hanotaux, Cheikh Anta Diop, E.A. Wallis Budge, and Eugene Guernier, Mabona not only includes ancient Egyptian

---

Présence Africaine 32/33, June–September 1960, pp. 64–76, here p. 64. Walter Markov and Fausto Codino, "Appunti sulla storiografia Africana", *Studi Storici* 4/4, October–December 1963, pp. 759–782, here p. 776. Paulin Hountondji, *Sur la "philosophie africaine"*, Paris: François Maspéro, p. 57; English translation: *African philosophy. Myth and reality* (second edition), Bloomington and Indianapolis: Indianapolis University Press, 1996, pp. 58 and 194. Austin J. Shelton, "The ideology of blackness and beauty in America and Africa", *Présence Africaine* 79, third term 1976, pp. 126–136, p. 131. Austin J. Shelton, "African attitudes and values: Generalizations for Africanist teaching", *Présence Africaine* 97, "Science politique" / "Political Science", first term 1976, pp. 117–131, here p. 124. Théophile Obenga, "Cheikh Anta Diop et les autres", *Présence Africaine* 105/106, first and second terms 1978, pp. 29–44, here p. 34. Oladimeji I. Alo, "Contemporary convergence in sociological theories: the relevance of the African thought system in theory formation", *International Journal of Sociology and Social Policy*, 4/2, 1984, pp. 60–76, here pp. 70–71. Wilfred Okambawa, "Who is the father of African theology?" *Hekima Review* 9, June 1993, pp. 23–39, p. 27.

9   The page numbers follow the *Présence Africaine* edition.
10 "This Civilisation was made of a complex of cultures which in their structure showed a marvelous formal and thematic uniformity as attested by their artefacts, literature, and mythologies" (p. 57).

culture in African culture, but affirms the Africanness of the ancient Egyptians and the role ancient Egypt played as a source of Greco-Roman culture (pp. 57, 59). In the same breath, the ancient kingdoms of West Africa, Congo-Angola and Zimbabwe,[11] are evoked, presumably to pre-empt any objection by an ignorant reader about the very existence of African civilisations.

Next, the "values" and "philosophical basis" (p. 61) of such big cultural units must be studied. Again, Mabona first applies this procedure to European culture. This is a significant point because Mabona is at pains to convince his readers that the reconstructive procedure by which he will identify the values and philosophical basis of African culture is not determined by that specific object of study, but could, and should, be applied equally to all vast cultural spheres. Thus, with reference to literature and religions, European culture is again presented as deeply imprinted by the "search for final illumination" (p. 61), to which are added the "belief in a multiplicity of gods" and the "belief in the divine origin of (their) race" (p. 62). Mabona speculates in a theological register that the Occident's striving for clarity, logic, and truth is an indication that it was not for nothing that the gospel of incarnation was entrusted to Europe. Similarly, Mabona subsequently surveys Indian, Chinese, and Japanese culture (pp. 63–71).

As for Africa, its cultural life has had to deal with enormous setbacks, particularly military defeat and subjugation, but also purposeful misrepresentation of its history (pp. 60, 71). Yet, the extant sources, written or oral, art or dance, suffice for the attentive observer to extract the continent's cultural essence – just as Mabona has done in "African mentality in a world frame", when he stated: "Symbolism is the natural expression of the African mind" (p. 72). Whereas the ethnophilosophers would focus on linguistic sources, Mabona focuses in the first place on figurative symbols, "the circle and semicircle and the triangle and cone" (p. 72). Subsequently, he attempts to demonstrate that the "use of [these] symbol[s] is too consistently and widely diffused among Africans to be compared to the casual manifestations of a similar usage by members of other racial groups" (p. 72). He refers to Frobenius, Griaule/Ogotemmeli, Egyptian writings, and Hampâté Bâ[12] to support his claim of the general use and regular recurrence

---

[11] At this point, Mabona diverges into a historical reconstruction of the name Zimbabwe (relying on the oldest Portuguese travel sources and linguistic argumentation) and a demonstration that the inhabitants and rulers of the kingdom of Zimbabwe were African (with reference to the sources of African historiography at his disposal), as was still his practice in DP.

[12] Mabona may have been present when Hampâté Bâ presented his study on animism at the Second Congress of Black Writers and Artists, a study which Mabona cites in this article.

of these symbols. Once these recurrent symbols have been described, Mabona traces the corresponding references from the symbolic level to the biological, social, religious, and metaphysical levels (following the precepts of Eliade, already alluded to in Mabona's second article). Likewise, he examines animal symbols (the bird, snake, ram, and lion) and colour symbols (red, yellow, white, and black). His basic conclusion relates the major symbols to an intricate system of references:

> the circle and the triangle, and the confrontation of bird and snake or woman and dragon – do not only refer to linear or biological realities, but signify at the same time the contrast between death and life, the confrontation of humanity and reality of the irrational element and the rational, and the mutual transformations of these realities one into the other. (p. 77)

Ultimately, this study of symbols leads to the following conclusion:

> [T]he African [is] symbolistic, universalist or transcendentalist in his mentality. His basic tendency or orientation is towards Being as One. We say he is transcendentalist, because he does not take the principle of contradiction or identity, with their sequel of almost infinite distinctions, as the starting point of his thought, but adopts rather the dialectical and polyvalent principle of the Oneness of Being. This principle is not arrived at logically, otherwise it could have been just another form of monism. This principle is arrived at by extrapolation from the attentively observed vital rhythm of the world. (p. 78)

And, thus, Mabona arrives at the connection between Africa and rhythm – a cherished topic for Senghor, whom Mabona takes as his guide here.[13] Mabona, in fact, accords rhythm equal status in African culture to that of symbolism. But how did he make the leap from symbolism to rhythm? First, one has to understand Mabona's very specific understanding of rhythm: he sees it as generative and not merely as repetitive. Once this premise has been established, it becomes possible to relate the core symbols of the circle and triangle with this view of rhythm, as the circle is rhythmically generated by a succession of triangle-like segments. Rhythm itself is the articulation of the relatedness between things in general.

---

[13] He cites Senghor's contributions to both of the Congresses for Black Writers and Artists.

If I follow the argument correctly, it is this layered symbolism and the rhythmic relatedness which Mabona considers the metaphysical foundation of African culture (p. 79). Abstraction of an aspect of one's existence from the whole (which he also calls "objectivization") is foreign to this mode of existence. It is more spontaneous to live the tension between the person and the world, between different layers of meaning, as one is confronted by them. How one understands life, law, society, religion, nature, etc. is mediated by this basic attitude. One may conclude that the ideal of humanity as a family and the complementarity of cultures, evoked at the beginning of the article, reflect this cultural stance towards the "oneness of being", despite its inherent tensions.

But that is not all. Mabona concludes his article by offering a short "scheme of being" on the basis of "two principles of African thought" (p. 82). Here, I take "principle" to mean a basic structuring element of thought as transmitted in African culture, since the first principle is "generative repetition" (i.e. repetition). The second is the "vibrational principle of Sudanese philosophy" – referring to "contained or internal movement as opposed to local external movement", p. 83 – and the construct is introduced without any indication of how it had been derived or how the Sudanese particularity is to be related to African culture in general.[14] It is also not clear how Mabona presents the metaphysical claims that follow from these principles as logical implications of them, or as his own philosophical development permitted by following these principles.

His metaphysical schema of being maintains that being is continuous self-assertion of beings. Such self-assertion is an act of vibration, which allows for a series of four modifications: interiorisation (or self-preservation), externalisation (or growth), return to self as an object (or consciousness), and self-exteriorisation as an object (or expression). Mabona envisages that the whole range of classical philosophical questions can be rethought from this culturally specific vantage point. He describes this as work in progress and expresses the hope "that African young men will examine more and more deeply the thought-structure which underlies African culture in the whole extent of its millennial history and of its area of diffusion" (p. 85). Such a metaphysics, developed from cultural anthropology, I take to be what Mabona aimed "toward", as he formulated it in the title of his article. In fact, this suspicion will be confirmed by "The depths of African philosophy", in which the metaphysics of four modifications of being are expanded (see p. 162 below).

---

[14] The term "Sudanese" is to be understood here in the old, geographic sense of the wide region south of the Sahara from West to Central Africa.

This grand programmatic article is the first published consolidation of Mabona's independent reflection. One way to gain a perspective on this project is to recall that, at the time of writing, the author was on a mission in Rome to further his competence in Catholic theology and to specialise in canon law. While the first article clearly shows how the young Mabona absorbed what the theological milieu in Rome could offer, his energetic study of anthropology and history is striking. Clearly, a second agenda was already forming in his mind, one that was more focused on the African continent than on the kingdom of God. Mabona allows himself some grand theorising, but one also senses that, at this point, he was still searching for the exact form that his intellectual engagement had to take. His contact with other African students and the Second Congress of Black Writers and Artists stimulated his process.

The vibrancy of his new intellectual project caught the eye of others. "Towards an African philosophy" was republished by *Présence Africaine* the next year (1960) and subsequently elsewhere. As late as 1975, A.J. Smet included this article in the first volume of his anthology *Philosophie africaine. Textes choisis*. A survey of the reception of this article in other publications (see p. 147n8) testifies to the fact that Mabona was subsequently identified as a philosopher and a social scientist who was to be taken seriously in this respect.

However, although it may have been clear to his readers that he had something philosophical to offer, he does not seem to have made a final decision in favour of philosophy. On the one hand, he did indeed continue to call part of his work "philosophy". On the other hand, a lot of it rather fell into the ambit of anthropology, and, in his later work, he simply left the philosophical aspirations by the wayside. Furthermore, his theological ink had not yet dried up.

2. *Présence Africaine*: Writing for a wide public

Including the republication of "Towards an African philosophy", Mabona's next six works were all published by *Présence Africaine* (except for the short intervention on film and education in Africa, discussed below). With the exception of the chapter "The depths of African philosophy", the journal also made these texts available in French. All of these studies continue the work described thus far, but build on it in different directions. For the sake of continuity, I discuss the five articles first and then discuss the chapter which, as we will see, holds quite a singular place in Mabona's work.

In his short paper "Elements of African culture"[15] (1962), Mabona returns to the question of ancient African civilisations. He references the state of research and affirms again the Africanness of different African kingdoms, as well as of Ancient Egypt. Whereas previously he strongly affirmed the unity of African culture, he now concedes that the idea of the development of a variety of African cultures is not entirely implausible (even while he insists that, in distant pre-history, culture must have been fairly homogenous). At the same time, he considers almost the opposite argument in respect to world cultures: despite the superficial similarity of myths and rites in the cultures of different continents, there are underlying differences between them – differences allowing us to group together large cultural regions. This is illustrated in the case of African culture with the same reference to symbols, arts, and rites as in "African mentality in a world frame" and "Towards an African philosophy", but this time he also evokes social organisation as illustration. He describes African morality as anthropocentric; adult individuals are considered free, but they "yield" freely to the interests of the group. "At this level", he explains, "no disorder is tolerated" (p. 111). He argues that this traditional schema is co-opted in contemporary politics, where the governing party is responsible for legislation and the opposition represents the freedom of individuals. Thus, society holds individual freedom and duty towards the collective in a dialectical balance. However, this tension is often internalised by individuals and brought to expression as "coresponsibility" or solidarity. This was typical of traditional African societies, according to Mabona.

African religion typically affirms a supreme creator God to whom people pray, but who is not the object of adoration (strangely, Mabona concedes that this was different in ancient Egyptian religion, without commenting on the significance of this difference). The ancestors and natural spirits populate the invisible realm. The desire for mystic or post-life unification with God is foreign to African religion (again, in contradistinction to Egyptian religion). However, in this life, people may be possessed by spirits, allowing for a vision of continuity between everyday human existence and the realm of spirits.

In conclusion, Mabona reiterates the importance of symbolism and rhythm in African culture. He also has a word of advice for those who communicate the Christian gospel to Africans on how to take African culture into account (pp. 112, 114).

---

[15] This article is cited by Henri Maurier, *Philosophie de l'Afrique noire*, Sankt Augustin: Verlag des Anthropos-Instituts, 1976, p. 38.

At first sight, "The vocation and presence of Africa in modern scientific life" (1963) adopts a completely different line of exploration. Yet, in fact, Mabona just sets the bar higher for the relevance of his ongoing research programme. Playing devil's advocate, he concedes that it may seem presumptuous to speak of an African vocation in relation to modern science when nuclear arms, global communication technologies, and space vessels have been developed without a need for African collaboration. His rebuttal consists, first, of a simple observation, namely about the presence of Africa in the world of technology: current technology is the outcome of a history of human technological inventions all over the globe. Second, he notes that the contemporary advanced technologies have been produced by a small segment of the world's societies. But he advances the thesis that there is no evidence to support the view that the current state of technological progress is at its highest point; in fact, one may assume that technological invention would progress much further if a much bigger segment of the world's population, with their various backgrounds and experiences, were included in the process. In a spurt of optimism, Mabona also evokes the rich material resources of the African continent, resources without which technological and industrial developments are impossible.

The second component of his argumentation is based on Mabona's distinction between a reductive view of intelligence as mere knowledge (which he sees as prevalent in contemporary technology and science) and intelligence as a broader wisdom or understanding of human life. Once it is divorced from such wisdom, science remains a superficial and dangerous kind of knowledge. Wastage of resources serves as an illustration of this. Curiously, Mabona sees the beginning of such an abstract knowledge in Socrates. Socrates' misanthropism and critique of myths set the tone for an irresponsible detachment of human beings from the cosmos. Only ironically could one call this attitude the "love for wisdom" ("philosophy") (p. 72). In opposition to this view of "wisdom", Mabona advocates a broader or deeper understanding of human reason – true wisdom – which would accord scientific abstraction as we know it its rightful place as an abstraction, in order to adopt a more holistic, integrated, and responsible view of wisdom.

If Mabona's call is heeded, it may well turn out that the scientific progress of modern times is only an interlude. Subsequently, he argues,

> [t]he next step will consist in a diffusion of wisdom and a close study of the fundamental natural laws. I will define wisdom in terms of the concept of human values like the sense of responsibility, human dignity and brotherhood; and I will define fundamental natural laws as those laws implied in the operation of the natural forces of vibration. (p. 73)

One cannot fail to observe how the metaphysical principle of vibration (presented at the end of "Towards an African philosophy") is remobilized here in an ambitious redesign of science as a component of a much vaster wisdom regarding the responsible interrelation between people and nature. How precisely this plea for a reinterpretation of the laws of nature in terms of a principle of vibration is to be undertaken remains undeveloped. Moreover, the prediction that other scientific laws will be discovered along this path is surely somewhat hasty. But the broader intention is clear: to call for rigorously approaching science as a *human* undertaking. And since humans are of different cultures, Mabona can venture a bold prediction or wish:

> The vanguard of the scientific progress of to-morrow will be formed by those countries or peoples who will have bent their necks to the laws of wisdom by accepting sincerely the human values of responsibility, human dignity, human brotherhood, etc…; countries or peoples, moreover, that will make a close study of the fundamental laws of energy. (p. 73).

In this utopian vision, there is ample room for Africa.

In all, Mabona's position is much like that of his contemporaries, Senghor, Alioune, Diop, or, in a different way, that of Fanon: Africa's contribution to the contemporary world is that of a rehumanization. In a way, this is still an affirmation of the complementarity of different cultures, where the current excellence of the West in matters of science and technology is recognised, but not without postulating Africa's normative excellence.

This is perhaps the best place to evoke again Mabona's contribution to the "First international congress on the use of audiovisual media for vocational education and training in Africa" (1962) (cf. Part 1, Chapter 4, §4). In a different way, this speech also deals with what is required for Africa to play its role in global science. Mabona frames his speech as an invitation to Italy to engage in mass education in Africa.

In his opinion, Africa enjoys a significant geographical position in relation to the other continents. Despite the frail economic state of the continent, it has wealth in the form of water, minerals, and agricultural production. It is only a "lack of training and expertise" (*mancanza di preparazione*, p. 197) that obstructs the continent from reaping the benefits of its real wealth. The continent cannot provide in this need without help from others. However, the painful reality is that the recent history of interaction between Africa and a number of European countries is an impediment to such exchange.

Yet, in Mabona's view, Italy is in a singular situation: for a long time, it was not involved in colonisation and then it made a speedy end to its short colonial ambitions. This instills confidence in Italy on the African continent. Furthermore, Italy is geographically relatively close to Africa and has a long history of ties with Africa. Mabona encourages Italians to overcome their shame regarding the recent past in order to get involved in Africa. He considers it perfectly realistic that a new cooperation based on friendship could be established. Besides, the world has entered a new era of "global awareness" (*coscienza mondiale*, p. 198) that humanity's problems cannot be dealt with in a piecemeal, local way alone. He cites Pope John XXIII's encyclical "Mater et magister" as a valuable guide in this respect.

As valuable as traditional schools are, the time has come, according to Mabona, to step up the education of the masses. A number of practical difficulties could be overcome by deploying audiovisual technologies. He lends his unambiguous support for the initiatives of the International Committee for the Development of Educational and Cultural Activities in Africa (CIDAECA) in this domain.

The framework for Mabona's brief meditation on "African spirituality"[16] (1964) is his identification of a global, ideological conflict, but this time in terms different from those with which he opened "African mentality in a world frame". The two opposing camps of this conflict are the personalist view (misnamed spiritualist by its adherents and idealist by its adversaries) and the impersonalist or mechanistic view (misnamed realist by its adherents and materialist by its adversaries). This tense opposition is due to the fact that each camp identifies the root of nihilism in the other. Yet the contingent historical developments that, in a specific era, accord one culture centre stage while relegating another to the wings, makes it hard to see and appreciate this ideological conflict for what it is.

If Mabona, then, claims that all people have "a spiritual outlook", this is not to be understood (or at least not primarily) in religious terms, but in terms of these basic ideological orientations. It may therefore strike as odd, initially, when Mabona gives us not two but three major types of spirituality: personalist-individualistic, realist-collectivistic, and anthropocentric-animistic (p. 159). This apparent anomaly is dispersed when Mabona comments on the apparent void that separates the two major ideological positions – everything happens

---

[16] Cited in Paulin Hountondji, *Sur la "philosophie africaine"*, Paris: François Maspéro, p. 57; English translation: *African philosophy. Myth and reality* (second edition), Bloomington and Indianapolis: Indianapolis University Press, 1996, pp. 58, 194. Wilfred Okambawa, "Who is the father of African theology?", *Hekima Review* 9, June 1993, pp. 23–39, p. 27.

as if no communication, no relation, is possible. And it is in this space that he situates "man and his interests" (p. 159). This "man" is the human of the anthropocentric-animistic spirituality of African culture which was "never much engrossed in conceptual views of the universe", but should essentially be typified as "anthropocentric, rhythmic and symbolic" (p. 159) – not as exclusively African but as predominantly characteristic of this cultural family. By this time, we are well acquainted with this portrayal of African culture by Mabona. But how does he fit this description into his view of the ideological conflict? By virtue of emphasising the "generative power" of language over its "noetic" capability, he sees the predominant position of African culture as *between* these two camps. The human being, speech, symbols, and rhythm all share a dialectical constitution of aspects of the two major orientations, yet, without their anxious self-elevation to a single absolute (even rendering the ultimate ideological determinations "immaterial", p. 161).

The obverse of not aspiring to the absolute (as in religion, aspiring to mystical unity with God), is a view on human reality as fundamentally in communion – communion with other humans and with the environment. Correspondingly, truth, as a function of language, consists much less in the utterance of claims that correspond with reality and much more with the real generation of a positive relation between people. Emanating from this communion with others is an ethics of community and of human dignity. "African spirituality" explores in detail how these major orientations fan out into more detailed virtues, and the cultural institutions by which they were instilled in people.

In the final conclusions of the article, Mabona claims that African spirituality is the most appropriate for the African context, and certainly preferable to either of the two dominant ideologies offered to the world at that time. Without evoking the complementarity of cultures (as he did in earlier writings), he suggests that the world has much to learn from this African spirituality.

A footnote to "The religious concepts of the Nguni" (1965) describes the article as "A follow-up to the author's 'African Spirituality' in P.A. [*Présence Africaine*] No. 52. This was originally written as a letter to an Englishman" (p. 12). The last part of the article explicitly takes over this correspondence, but without naming the interlocutor.

There are different motivations for looking at Africa's past and present, in view of anticipating its future. One of them is the desire to prove that there is no real African future, but that Europe, having achieved universality, already holds the image of what Africa will become. In response to such an attitude, Mabona retorts that one has to at least entertain the possibility that Africans may want to respond to modernity in a different way than Europeans, that such differences could be accounted for by the differences in cultural starting points and that modern civilisation has itself become the object of critique due to its destructive potential, a realisation which prompts people to reconsider their deepest values.

What the question ultimately comes down to, for Mabona, is how people assess their relation to others – not so much relatives and friends, but strangers. Here Mabona points out that modern society devalues the significance of strangers through the density of communication, the density of habitation, the formalisation of the economy, the spread of "mechanistic values" (p. 178), and secularisation.

However, Mabona also seeks to approach the question from another angle. All people have an awareness of being an "I", but this is not to be separated from an awareness of being part of a "we" (at least in the sense of having the same attributes as others, for example, being African, or being a man). Hence, feeling part of a "we" means to self-identify while identifying with others. This identification can stretch as far as the whole of humanity. Still, African modes of self-awareness or self-consciousness go even further to embrace identification with animals, plants, and stones: the self-awareness "has a kind of instinctive attention to, and spontaneous sympathy with, all elements of the universe and this not in a superficial, condescending manner but in a deep and earnest search for communion" (pp. 179–180). Hence, by another route, we again come across this fundamental communal "matrix" or "situation" (p. 180) from which people are considered to live. Again, Mabona is willing to translate this cultural fact into metaphysical parlance, but now, instead of reverting to "personalist" and "impersonalist" as the main categories, he simply rejects dualism and monism in favour of "relative dualism and dynamic pluralism" (p. 180). As we might expect by now, Mabona considers the layeredness of symbolism to be the most appropriate way to articulate this human situation.[17]

One would anticipate that Mabona would comment on the ways in which the traumatic history of Africa has adversely affected the transmission of this cultural view. However, he claims that the "universal conspiracy on its very existence" (the existence of the "African race", p. 180) has strengthened the lived reality of community. And, according to Mabona, since African resistance leads to revolt and revolution, Africans will forever side with the oppressed of this world.

---

[17] In fact, he is willing to accept "analogical imagery" and "convertibility of categories" as equivalents for "symbolism" (p. 180).

On the theme of revolution, Mabona clarifies that the revolution of Africans he has in mind is more than the resistance of one class – "Africa is revolting in terms of the oppression of a whole race !" (p. 181). The "Revolution of the Poor" would only be a smaller component of this. Ultimately, his target is the "scandalous perversion constituted by the fundamental denial in theoretical or practical terms of the humanity of a whole section of mankind" (p. 181) – having in mind, perhaps, first of all his native South Africa, to which he must have returned by the time this article appeared in print.

At this point, Mabona addresses his original English correspondent explicitly, to explain his research project on Nguni culture. He wants to explore the "attitudes, positions, things" which are "suggested" by this culture, without these ever being expressed "in absolute, clear-cut lines" (p. 182). In this context, he responds to his interlocutor's questions about the future of Nguni religion and its concepts. Rather than a direct response, Mabona's long-term research aims to explore the inevitable change of Nguni convictions and attitudes (p. 183). Apart from a few general observations about cultural change in general, Mabona's only pointer is a vague anticipation of a more Africanised Christianity in which Nguni norms and customs will probably play a significant role.

Readers who expect an exposition on Nguni religious concepts will thus be frustrated by this article. It has much more to say about general cultural and philosophical concerns. Whatever his attitude to the question of his interlocutor may have been at the time, it is worth noting that the question of Nguni religion is the central theme of both his Master's dissertation at SOAS and his doctoral dissertation at Bern (see §7 below). Two other themes in this article need to be highlighted: first, the minor but persistent reference to African Christianity; second, political resistance against global racism. These two themes apparently belong (together) to Mabona's anticipation of the continent's future.

3. "The depths of African philosophy" and *The outlines of African philosophy*

In the biographical part of this book, we saw how Alioune Diop launched a broad consultation with African Catholics in preparation for the second Vatican council (cf. Chapter 4, §6). A major outcome of the open letter "On the contribution of African personhood to the vitality of Catholicism" was the publication of the volume *Personnalité africaine et catholicisme* ("African personhood and Catholicism"), which appeared in 1963. As one of the contributors, Mabona gained splendid international visibility and some formal recognition by his peers as an important new African intellectual voice.

Meinrad Hebga's introductory contribution, "A severe malaise", set the tone for the volume by forcefully evoking the accumulated historical burden of the African continent, citing "[c]enturies of slavery and deportations, the Afrikanders [*sic*], racism and segregation, the subjection of Black Peoples, the history of Africa humiliated by self-assured peoples and their 'Christianity'" (p. 8). It is this history of injustice and the question of the ambiguous relation of Christianity to it – an ideology of oppression or the gospel aiming at the liberation of the oppressed? – which the volume intended to bring to the heart of debates at the Second Vatican Council: "As we approach the Ecumenical Council, the essential problem for us African Christians is this: what is, what will henceforth be the status of African Christians in universal Christianity? What is, what will be Christianity's attitude towards non-European cultures?" (p. 11) The titles of various contributions speak to this theme: "A council for Africa's moment" (Sastre), "The church, the black world and the council" (Ela), "God and Africa" (Tchouanga), "Malagasy wisdom and Christian theology (Rahajarizafy), "The bantu view of reality vis-à-vis Christianity" (Lufuluabo), "Liturgical language and catholicity" (Ngango), "Fundamental structures of black-African prayer" (Mveng), "For a church of the poor" (Souffrant), "Catechism and preaching" (Nioka), "The church of Africa: economic and social development" (Obama), and finally "The black priests are questioning and offering suggestions" (Senghor).

Furthermore, the volume was conceived as a follow-up from *Le prêtres noirs s'interrogent* – the groundbreaking volume on African theology published in 1956.[18]

The nature of Mabona's chapter in it, "The depths of African philosophy", is easier to appreciate within the big picture of the whole volume. From this perspective, it is startlingly evident that his chapter does not in any direct way contribute to the objectives of Diop's overarching project or to the theme of the book (an impression which is reinforced by the fact that it is the only chapter written in English). It is left to the readers to conjecture how this chapter could

---

[18] However, the historical and critical texts on this volume, added to its 2006 re-edition, make no reference to *Personnalité africaine et catholicisme*. See *Des prêtres noirs s'interrogent. Cinquante ans après...*, presented by Léonard Santedi Kinkupu, Gérard Bissainthe, and Meinrad Hebga, Paris: Karthala-Présence Africaine, 2006, pp. I–XXII, 283–293, and 296–299.

be reconstrued as a contribution. One may glimpse part of the reason for this odd fact, as well as some of the backstage events that accompanied the submission of the chapter, in its last paragraph:

> I beg readers to pardon the diffuse form of this short treatise. For certain reasons and especially on account of insistent demands from my distinguished friend, Alioune Diop, conclusions drawn over a number of years of thought and study were put together in a hurry. I hope that final publication of the work in book form could be done in two or three years. (p. 58)

The citation also invites the reader to follow up reading the chapter by studying the book, which, as we have seen, was written, but never published. However, I had the opportunity to make a duplicate of Mabona's own copy during a visit to Lucerne in September 2018. Although the epilogue of the book is signed 28 August 1962 and the chapter was published only in 1963, the chapter is to be read as a preparation for the book (as the last citation confirms). Indeed, the content of the two texts overlaps substantially.[19]

But let us turn from the formal considerations to the content. The reader quickly discovers that this is Mabona's first attempt to fulfil his promise to write an African metaphysics compatible with science, a promise initially formulated in "Towards an African philosophy". These two texts are the concrete manifestation of his first labours to build on his working hypothesis, with the hope of stimulating others to join the exploration. Here I focus on the content of the chapter, but I still give some impression of the further developments in the unpublished *The outlines of African philosophy*.

The first section of "The depths of African philosophy"[20] is devoted to an apologetic preamble. Somewhat grudgingly, Mabona grants that, at the time of writing, it was still unavoidable for an author to defend the very idea of African

---

[19] The chapter is published on pp. 29–58 of *Personnalité africaine et catholicisme*. Of these, pp. 29–44 correspond with the Introduction and first chapter of Part I (i.e. pp. 1–30) of the book manuscript. Pages 44–53 of the chapter do not seem to have a counterpart in the book. Then, Part II, Chapter 4, pp. 146–153 of the book manuscript is inserted as pp. 53–56 of the chapter. Finally, the conclusions of pp. 56–58 of the chapter are unique again.

[20] Cited in Paulin Hountondji, *Sur la "philosophie africaine"*, Paris: François Maspéro, p. 57; English translation: *African philosophy. Myth and reality* (second edition), Bloomington and Indianapolis: Indianapolis University Press, 1996, pp. 58, 194. Wilfred Okambawa, "Who is the father of African theology?", *Hekima Review* 9, June 1993, pp. 23–39, p. 27. Fidelis U. Okafor, "In defense of Afro-Japanese ethnophilosophy", *Philosophy East and West*, 47/3, July 1997, pp. 363–381, here p. 369.

philosophy. His basic point is to remind the reader of the cultural embeddedness and roots of philosophy in Greek culture, and he asks just the same for African philosophy: if philosophy can be Greek, so can it be African. Following Cheikh Anta Diop, he insists on the functional dimension of culture – a means by which to master a specific environment. Without claiming to be able to cover the whole range of African cultural phenomena, the material available to him suffices to launch his exploration and in this way invigorate African thought in all disciplines. Not that he is reinventing the wheel – his declared orientation draws from the early "ethnophilosophers", *négritude* authors, African ethnography, and studies on ancient Egypt.[21] According to his self-presentation, these authors provided the principles that he applies in this study. Most of what follows represents only the outcome of this study and not a running commentary on the ways by which he appropriated the work of these predecessors or his own for the material it is applied to.

According to Mabona, the study of African thought should be pursued on two levels: first, that of *symbolism* which functions as a sort of language and logic; second, the *analogical* extension of the first level, which allows for mythology and metaphysics.[22]

African ontology understands being as dynamic, rather than static, namely as a vital force or vibration (the internal movement of self-repetition of being). We recognise the terrain opened three years earlier by Mabona. He elaborates on the four basic modalities of vibration: (1) interiorisation or self-preservation, (2) growth or outward movement (presupposing the former), (3) consciousness (returning to self as an object), and (4) self-exteriorisation or expression (of an "I"). But now Mabona adds two more dimensions to this discussion. For each form of vibration, he adds and elaborates on a *diagrammatic* representation.[23] Thereafter, the diagrammatic representation is used as support for a *quantification* of all the movement possibilities, on the basis of which calculations of the units of different forms of movement may be undertaken. Later (p. 50), we learn that

---

[21] As mentioned in the citation in the footnote above.

[22] This argumentative procedure is attributed to the Dogon people in the preface to Marcel Griaule and Germaine Dieterlen, *Signes grafiques soudanais*, Paris: Hermann, 1951, Mabona's reference work for all his claims on Sudanese thought and symbols. The ethnographic account of this book gathers information from Dogon, Bambara, and Bozo people from Mali.

[23] Among all the elaborate diagrams presented by Mabona in "The depths of African philosophy" and *The outlines of African philosophy*, I could find only one that corresponds with the Sudanese diagrams documented by Griaule and Dieterlen (see *Signes grafiques soudanais*, p. 21, figure 40).

the four modalities of vibrational movement are responsible for four degrees of autonomy: autodynamism, passive autonomy, active autonomy, and an unnamed, more radical form of autonomy on the fourth level. Although Mabona does not seem to be concerned with illustrative examples, we could relate the first form of movement with that of dead matter, the second with vegetative life, the third with animal life, and the fourth with human existence (cf. p. 49).

Finally, this ontological speculation is extended briefly up to a tenth order of being (p. 56), which would be the place of a unique, supreme being (p. 58).

The basic objective of "The depths of African philosophy" was to discuss and develop the "general principles of African Philosophy" (p. 32), so it remains in *The outlines of African philosophy* (p. 95). Although this is a more substantive study, its author is nonetheless aware of the limits of his enterprise. The epilogue starts with a disclaimer:

> In this work I have tried to give in a summary and shortened form what I consider to be the main lines of development of philosophical concepts starting from principles of African thought. The work is naturally incomplete and far from mature. (p. 154)

Taking the metaphysics of the four modalities of being as his foundation, Mabona's exposition elaborates on the relations between units of existence, between their core and periphery. This involves developments on energy and the relative force or velocity of different energies too (e.g. p. 124). Natural phenomena such as gravity, magnetism, electricity, heat and light, sound and odour are accounted for in this theoretical frame. He ponders geography and meteorology (pp. 84–85). Life and death (p. 68), the foundation of the universe, and the origin and genesis of matter (pp. 67, 69, 121–122) are expounded on and there is even a calculation of the time it took for the universe to bring forth life (p. 98). All of these discussions together represent the "first stage" or "order" of being, and this spans Part 1 of his book.

The second part, a kind of "appendix" to the first, gives a condensed overview over the "other orders of being" (p. 99). The most significant aspects of these are certainly the emergence of consciousness (p. 140ff) and imagination (p. 142ff).

In some places (for example, pp. 46–47), Mabona discusses the parallels between aspects of his metaphysical account and documented forms of African thought: the Egyptian Book of the Dead, or Sudanese thought.[24] However,

---

[24] But note that, in the Epilogue (p. 154), he states that he purposefully limited references to *The Book of the Dead* and to Dogon/Sudanese symbolism to the minimum.

overall, the specific Africanness claimed for these thoughts remain under-clarified – which is even more surprising in light of Mabona's own immersion in an anthropology or ethnomethodological paradigm.

Formally, this book (and the chapter) could be typified as a metaphysical speculation of the rationalist type (in the sense of not working from observation to abstraction, but starting from pure ideas and constructing a schema on them). The author hardly makes any attempt to apply these principles to reality. Rather, he sometimes evokes similarities between his schemas and cultural artefacts from different localities in Africa. Although there is some reference to African cultural and historical points of orientation, the general thrust is clearly philosophical, and more specifically metaphysical, and not anthropological. My current set of competences allows me no reason to conclude that Mabona succeeded in pulling off his ambitious project. As reported in the biographical account, he himself is rather sceptical about its success.

3.1 General appraisal: South Africa's first African philosopher?

Looking back now at all Mabona's writings discussed thus far, we can make a number of more general observations. Except for the first article and a few references to Christianity in Africa in later ones, none of the above would intimate that we are dealing with an author whose first preoccupation must have been finishing his PhD in Canon Law. To this we will turn later. We see the emergence of an active interest in anthropology (coupled with historical studies) and a specific type of early African philosophy – "ethnophilosophy" as it has become known since Hountondji.

There is another intriguing detail to be derived from this. Whatever one's assessment of Mabona's work may be, one cannot deny that he was contributing to African philosophy, at the very least to a level sufficient to convince some of his philosophical contemporaries that he was a serious interlocutor. Is Mabona, then, South Africa's first African philosopher? For the sake of caution, let it be stated that the answer to this question depends on one's understanding of what philosophy is, and, in particular, of what African philosophy is. African philosophy can be traced back as far as the thought of ancient Egypt or, indeed, to the oral traditions spanning centuries. But one may also be interested in the history of the written thought, presented to the world as philosophy, published for an academic or intellectual readership, after a process of review by scholarly peers. If this is the definition in mind, Anton Muziwakhe Lembede is certainly relevant.²⁵ However, his writings are more political debate,²⁶ and his 1945 Master's thesis is a historical exploration in Western philosophy.²⁷ As far as I could establish, Mabona is indeed South Africa's first African philosopher. It may be that future research will disprove my claim, but at the time of writing, I have not been able to find any specialist of South African philosophy who could cite a text of African philosophy from a South African author dating before the mid 1970s. To this, I should add what I have argued in the biographical part of this work, namely that Mabona was possibly the second non-white lecturer of philosophy at a South African institution of tertiary education.

The fact that the South African scholarly community has never known about this work, and indeed about Mabona himself (except for a few rare exceptions),²⁸ does not invalidate the facts. The numerous citations of his articles from this period demonstrate that he was recognised as a philosopher of African philosophy by his scholarly contemporaries.

4. Dissertatio ad lauream in Facultate Juris Canonici apud Pontificiam Universitatem Urbanianam

If one considers the energy and enthusiasm with which Mabona threw himself into studying African history, culture, and philosophy during his years in Rome, it is surprising that he still had the time or the desire to complete his doctoral thesis in theology. Yet, he did not merely complete his thesis – the study reflects a long

---

25 Anton Muziwakhe Lembede, *Freedom in our lifetime. The collected writings of Anton Muziwakhe Lembede*, Robert Edgar and Luyanda ka Msumza (eds.), Athens: Ohio University.
26 A limited case may perhaps be the article "Know thyself" (1945), *Freedom in our lifetime*, pp. 86–88, but even this article is not presented to the reader as a philosophical meditation.
27 It was entitled "The conception of God as expounded by or as it emerges from the writings of great philosophers – from Descartes to the present day", cf. *Freedom in our lifetime*, pp. 104–105.
28 In Part 1, I have cited studies such as those of Mukuka, Denis, and Motlhabi, who discuss Mabona in the context of SPOBA and the Black Priests' Manifesto. The only reference to Mabona as philosopher I could find thus far is in Mogobe Ramose's article, "I doubt, therefore African philosophy exists" (*South African Journal of Philosophy* 22/2, 2003, pp. 113–127), but this is limited to the generic claim "that many African philosophers such as Abanda Ndengue, Abiola Irele, Alexis Kagame, Mulago gwa Cikala Musharhamina, Lufuluabo, Chiri, Ntumba, Towet, Mongamelli [*sic*] Mabona, N'daw, Nkrumah, Nyerere and many others have contributed to the already existing edifice of African philosophy" (p. 120).

and serious engagement with the scholarly community relevant to his study (as described in the biographical section, Part 1, Chapter 4, §3), as well as with the complex methodology and material of the dissertation itself. It is admittedly a fairly short document (VII + 131 pages). The bibliography of eighty-one items consists of ecclesiastical and scholarly works, most in the domain of canon law and the lay apostolate, the bulk of which spans the last four centuries. Apart from a handful of publications in English, German, and French, the majority are in Latin. The complete absence of any apparent trace of his other lively research interests of that period is conspicuous. Does this reflect implicit or explicit institutional censorship? Or did he want to demonstrate that he could master the discipline on its own terms to the required level of perfection? Or were the two domains of research simply separate in his mind? The answer to these questions will remain pure speculation.

The thesis is designed as an exploration of the gradual transformations of the juridical status of catechists, an ecclesiastical function which has always existed in the Western and Eastern Church (p. II). The approach is thus theoretical rather than practical (p. IV). This general design fans out into five chapters (see outline, p. IV). First, the earliest tradition of the institution of lecturer-catechist is traced from its inception in the life work of Christ, through the time of the apostolic fathers and through the middle ages to demonstrate that the institution has an uninterrupted existence up to the Council of Trent (p. 1) in the middle of the sixteenth century. Then, in two separate chapters, the specific functions of the catechist and the "universality" of this institution are examined. The spread of this institution, as witnessed in authoritative ecclesiastical documents, stretched from Africa (in the historical sense, before the modern invention of "Africa") and Europe (France/Gallia, Spain, England, Germany) to the East (Constantinople, Edessa, Antioch, Armenia, Hungary, Russia). However, especially in the period after the Council of Trent, there was a temporary suspension of the office of the catechist, as is documented in Chapter 4 of Mabona's thesis. In conclusion, the fifth chapter argues in favour of a rehabilitation of this neglected institution. To do so, Mabona has to work his way through a number of relevant obstacles: tradition, canonical law, the Church's understanding of ordination, and prescriptions in respect of celibacy.

Considering this thesis in conjunction with Mabona's other scholarly work during his period in Rome, one may safely claim that, by the time Mabona went back to South Africa, he had laid a solid foundation for a life of study and writing. Was philosophy going to be his primary orientation? Or rather anthropology or theology? Or would he prefer to follow all three lines of enquiry at the same time?

For some years, this question remained unsettled, while an entirely different mode of expression came to the fore: poetry.

5. "The nuclear blast of spring": Poetry

Since there is something quite inappropriate in trying to summarise the expressiveness of poetry, I will limit this discussion to a short rendering of the themes that occupied Mabona in his poems and provide a number of illustrative citations.[29]

In "The sea", a stand-alone poem from 1965, the poet reproaches the sea for its treacherous duplicity. What appeared at first to be a depiction of a scene of nature turns out to be a recollection of past trauma:

> I saw your burning gold –
> Yesterday,
> As the sun rose
> But was not deceived.
> For I have tasted
> Your bitter brine,
> Cold grave of my fathers,
> As they were brought
> In galleyfuls
> To far-off hells.

The poet is left with a confusing ambiguity between the attraction and repulsion towards the oceans.

Let us now turn to the six poems published in 1970. Addressed to an unidentified reader, "Chrysalis" is a call to a change of mind. The reader is urged not to remain locked into a moribund repetition of past ideas (like an eternal chrysalis); the reader is instead invited to give passions and thought free rein to participate in the creative rhythm of the universe (like an escaping butterfly).

---

[29] I have benefited greatly from the opportunity to work through these poems together with Pol Peeters, emeritus professor of French literature.

As a note indicates, the title "Gazer-at-the-dawn" was a praise name of the Xhosa king Maqoma, who led the last significant military campaign against British troops before he was caught and sent to Robben Island, where he died.[30] The Amathola Mountains, where King Maqoma fought the colonial attack still brave the elements today. With the rains, blowing in from the sea, come the whispered messages from another place surrounded by the sea: Robben Island. But now the wind blows inland from these mountains, carrying the battle cries of the Amatholas to "cities, homestead, guts and men's hearts". The end of the poem evokes the dawn of liberation which King Maqoma may not have seen, but which is bound to arrive one day.

The unsettling question which the next poem, "The answer", ponders is the "legitimacy of genocide". This answer – or its counterargument, rather – is only subtly suggested: in a fundamentally obscure world, only life itself can provide the light of living intensity. Genocide, depriving humanity of that light, is self-defeating.

"Dead freedom-fighter"[31] is addressed to an unnamed fallen "comrade brother", and reflects remorse for not being present to do anything to prevent his death ("Oh, where was I?"). Such a wound to the survivor's conscience is, however, not entirely futile:

> You fought
> For mother Africa
> And your atrocious death
> Is the keen lash wherewith
> She'll whip her enemies
> To cowering shame
> And her sons to redeem her name.

In "Contestation", the narrator stands up in a posture of defiance to the "slanderous universe". This stance for truth, or truthfulness, against overpowering defamation (one may assume the situation of the poet in South Africa) counts on the same universe's responsiveness to truth.[32]

---

[30] Cf. "Gaser-at-the-dawn", *Présence Africaine* 76/4, 1970, pp. 167–168, here p. 168.
[31] This poem is cited in Stephen Finn, "Poets oppressed, poets of protest: a comparison of pre-Israel Hebrew poets and pre-Azania black poets", *Journal of Postcolonial Writing* 30/1, 1990, pp. 103–131, here p. 112.
[32] It is possible that the confrontation between the women and the snake, discussed in "Towards an African philosophy", forms the symbolic key to this poem.

The previous poem was addressed to the universe; the next is entitled "Prayer". The first part of this prayer expresses grief, while the second part calls on "fury and laughter". The grief is evoked by the foundation of the world which is depicted as "monstrous" and "aged with quarrels". But through fury and laughter, this world can be reshaped

> To the seething rhythm
> Of our flicking
> Hands
> And the restless beat
> Of our bouncing
> Feet.

Whether this dance is religious, whether the dance is a preparation to restorative action, is left to the reader to decide.

Is "Futility" a come-down from the celebration of the ability to change the world in "Prayer"? The scene is set for a breakdown, when the poet starts with an evocation of autumn which dies too young. Under such autumn-like circumstances of life

> Man holds the coiling rope of life
> As if it were a serpent whose fangs he dreads,
> Should he lose his tightened grip.

But are humans the mere objects of forces greater than themselves? So it seems, and thus life seems futile. However, the same universe which plays with and mocks people's "passion for life's precarious flame" has more in store than inevitable winter, death, and decay: "the nuclear blast of spring".[33] If this predominantly natural imagery has a political meaning, then, it turns out, it is resistance to the coming resurgence that is futile.

Four of Mabona's poems were published by *New Coin*: "The sea" (twice, in 1965 and 1977), "Chrysalis" (1977), "Rich harvest" (1974), and "Black theology" (1977). The last two still require our attention.

Someone, looking up in search of signs by which to get a grip on pressing questions, is disappointed and withdraws into the night. Like an otter chasing after prey, he darts in pursuit of dreams. Here he obtains a "Rich harvest" of seeds left by "his sleeping ancestors".

---

[33] One may recall here that the image of an unstoppable spring was already used in Mabona's first *Lux* articles.

"Black theology" calls on a Jesus who, according to the proclamation, rose from the dead and in doing so broke through the natural order of things. But the poet has no intention to play along with this message:

> Well, leave our shores, Lazarus-Jesus
> We want none of your reversals. Go away

The poet objects to the unnatural thrust of the gospel message and pleads for exorcism from the corresponding "mind therapy".[34] Yet in a surprising about-turn, the poem ends in Xhosa and Tswana/Sepedi,[35] by pleading with "Buth' Yesu" (brother Jesus) rather to stay, even expressing affection for him.

Looking back at these poems, one notices the recurrent descriptions of natural phenomena (mountain, sea, seasons, etc.), animals (especially snakes, but also otters, birds, insects, etc.), and plants. The question of historical injustice or the trauma inflicted by the sociopolitical conditions in South Africa at the time seem to be nearly always present –sometimes very explicitly and at other times under the surface. Often, the poems sketch a troubled present which had been in the making through a history of confrontations, a present which may (or may not) open into a future. What the role of people is in bringing about a new future remains undecided – at stake – in these poems.

6. Writings of a South African priest

Of Mabona's intellectual work as a priest and seminary lecturer only a fragmentary picture remains. If one considers his theological specialisation in canon law and the theme of catechism – after all, the consummation of his formal education – in a narrow sense, the texts that he wrote later seem to present a clean break. And indeed, the abrupt change of his form of argumentation and presentation is striking. However, following my suggestion that the interest in the role of the catechist was, for him, the location of mediation between two cultural worlds, it becomes possible to notice a concealed continuity. The tension between worlds is thematised in the essay "Black people and white worship" ([1966] 1972).

---

[34] Echoes of his own contribution, "Black people and white worship", to *Essays in Black Theology* (see discussion above) are evident.
[35] I thank Ms. Rose Kgwete and Dr. Mpho Tshivhase for helping me translate these phrases.

Mabona's approach is, in the first place, anthropological: worship is a phenomenon of human culture which engages the whole person. Second, it has a specific character, in that worship belongs to religious practice with a transcendent or eschatological dimension. He rejects the idea that Christian faith is centred on divine intervention to compensate for the remaining limits of human mastery over the world. Rather, the core of this faith is a divine calling to establish a family of all humankind – a unity which still transcends contemporary reality. This perspective allows Mabona to consider liturgy "an expression of family relationships with a cosmic dimension" (p. 82). But instead of portraying worship then as a kind of investment in the afterlife, he explicitly downplays the significance of death and the afterlife as a point of orientation in worship: worship is a "function of life" (p. 82), not an attempt to step out of it.

And since this is the case, the form of worship is important: mystification through obsolete symbols contradicts the very idea of worship. His plea is for a radical and persistent reform. He rejects worship as a spiritual exercise in "cringing" in favour of one that aims at the generation of "freedom" (p. 83). In particular, he considers the existing spiritual training of the clergy to be "foreign to our traditions" (p. 84). But why strike at the exercises striving at moral excellence? Because it promotes the idea of self-perfection by "entering into oneself" (p. 84). At this point, the orientation of African tradition is deployed as a counter-model:

> A sensible person in our society was supposed to be one who knew and performed his or her duties towards ancestors and members of the community. [...] It was supposed to make a person a sensible and well-adjusted member of society and the universe. (p. 84)

Hence his concluding advocacy is a call to resist sterile exercises in spirituality and rather to promote relations of communion between individuals, humanity, and nature.

In direct continuity with this line of thought is the "Black Priests' Manifesto", which Mabona wrote with Mkhatshwa, Moetapele, Louwfant, and Mokoka (see pp. 126-127). This piece, which appeared on 23 January 1970 in the *Rand Daily Mail* was entitled "Our church has let us down". For its republication in the same year in *African Ecclesiastical Review*, it was entitled "Africanisation in South Africa". Partly a list of grievances, partly an outcry ("ENOUGH! ENOUGH!", p. 424[36]), this article was an unprecedented gesture by the black clergy, taking recourse to

---

[36] Cited from the Karis and Gerhardt republication.

public media in the hope of finally being heard by the Church. Yet, reading the text today, the collegial, albeit firm, expression of the points of dispute and the authors' explicit loyalty and devotion to the Church and the Gospel is striking.

Their plea is presented from the perspective of a desire for the well-being of the Church. Their plea for the Africanisation of the Church in South Africa echoes the contemporary views of the Catholic hierarchy, notably that of Pope Paul VI (who declared during his visit to Uganda in 1969 that there was a need for the Church to embrace the contribution of "negritude") (cf. p. 424). Such views were affirmed by Cardinal Paul Zoungrana, at that time Archbishop of Ouagadougou, who insisted on the need to accord the "African soul" its rightful place in the Church – as the authors also point out (cf. p. 424).

Although the Catholic Church in South Africa claimed to reject apartheid, the five signatories complain that its clergy was divided on the subject. Its institutions ("seminaries, convents, hospitals, schools, monasteries, associations and churches", p. 425) often followed the lines of racial segregation. This is the core of the problem, in their assessment:

> The Whites would never accept a Black or multi-racial government. Whites in South Africa are not prepared to serve under Africans in any capacity. Socially, culturally and intellectually, the Whites consider themselves quite different from the Blacks. The obvious conclusion is that most Whites have opted out of the concept of integration. (p. 425)

These five authors not only oppose this attitude but also express their view on the true Christian alternative: "As Christians we believe in a multiracial society. We feel this is the only way in which real Christianity can be practised" (p. 425).

They are painfully aware of the limitations this policy imposes on black people's aspirations in all dimensions of life. Yet, for the time being, they do not realistically see an end to apartheid. Given this context, the signatories list eight points of detailed grievances, aimed to improve the conditions for black members and clergy. Negatively, these points deal with the racially profiled inequalities and knock-on effects of apartheid in the Church; positively, they call for the Africanisation of the Church's practice and governance.

In response to this *Rand Daily Mail* publication, *Pro Veritate* invited Mabona to further his reflection and to stimulate debate on the "Africanisation of the Church" (1970), as his article was entitled.

In general, Mabona recommends that Africanisation be understood as "a 'taking over' of authority, responsibility and initiative by people of native African origin in the political and cultural life of their nations or communities" (p. 3). Under the name "indigenisation" or "adaptation", this idea has been used in churches too, but Mabona feared that these attempts had steered discussions to that date in a more theoretical direction and lacked the urgency transmitted by the term "Africanisation". Although he granted some understanding of the real issues among some missionaries, the churches in general seemed unwilling to deal with this question. Instead through "moral or physical violence" (p. 3) they maintained the authority of whites over blacks when the blacks had long known that they did not need such guardianship any longer, if they ever did.

Mabona justifies his position on the basis of principled theological argumentation:

> As for adaptation or indigenisation, it has been realized that it is not the Word of God which has to be adapted to a culture or religion but it is the cultural-religious idiom of a people that ha[s] to be penetrated by the Word of God and hence imbued with His Spirit. It is bad theology to use Scripture to prove theses posed by the human mind; rather Scriptural themes are hermeneutically interpreted to enlighten a certain question or critical situation suggested or constructed by concrete historical circumstances. (p. 3)

The Western robe in which the Gospel arrived in Africa is not essential to its message.

Africanisation would obviously have an impact on narrowly cultural forms of religious life, such as the music of celebrations. But it would penetrate deeper, for instance, in cultivating the spiritual dimension of people's interaction with objects of everyday usage (as it used to be in earlier African societies). Likewise, Africanisation would entail a recognition of the ancestor cult, the essence of which is the feeling of "gratitude, solidarity, and human dependence" (p. 4).

Westernisation was an inevitable fact of history, but had to be undone in the African context. This, Mabona advocated, had to be done through a broad process of intra-Church dialogue.

Whereas dialogue is certainly preferred to violence, Mabona is compelled to think about violence and counter-violence when the World Council of Churches[37]

---

[37] For background, cf. Ian Macqueen, "Ecumenism and the global anti-apartheid struggle: The World Council of Churches' Special Fund in South Africa and Botswana, 1970-75", *Historia* 62/2, 2017, pp. 87–111.

announced its support for movements of antiracist "guerrilla movements". His contribution to the debate, "God and violence" (prepared in response to an invitation from the *South African Outlook*) sets two big principles. First, racialism is "arrant nonsense" (p. 186); second, separation imposed on "adult, free, and responsible persons, violates the freedom of those persons and is an insult to their dignity as responsible individuals" (p. 186). Where such violence reigns, counter-violence cannot simply be rejected. At the same time, Mabona acknowledges the complexity of historically conditioned relations which makes it hard to guarantee that counter-violence effectively targets a real aggressor (rather than a potential or real ally). For this reason, even legitimate recourse to violence should never brush aside all dialogue, without which no lasting relations can be established.

7. Anthropology and religion

Mabona's most important remaining studies are strictly academic dissertations. The first of these, the "long essay", prepared at the School of Oriental and African Studies (SOAS) in London, was indeed submitted as a "Religious studies essay" in 1973. On the basis of its contents, it may also be considered a study in historical anthropology, focused principally on the world described above, in Part 2, Chapter 1. The dissertation's full title gives an impression of the wide, interdisciplinary dimensions of the study: "The interaction and development of different religions in the Eastern Cape in the late eighteenth and early nineteenth centuries, with special reference to the first two Xhosa prophets".[38]

---

[38] Cited by Terence Ranger, "From Humanism to the Science of Man: Colonialism in Africa and the Understanding of Alien Societies", *Transactions of the Royal Historical Society* 26, 1976, pp. 115–141, p. 132. Terence Ranger, Review of Janet Hodgson's *The god of the Xhosa: a study of the origins and development of the traditional concepts of the supreme being* [1983], *Bulletin of the School of Oriental and African Studies* 47/2, 1984, p. 410. Terence Ranger, "African initiatives and resistance in the face of partition and conquest", in A. Adu Boahen (ed.), *General History Of Africa*, Volume 7: Africa under Colonial Domination 1880-1935, Berkeley: UNESCO/University of California Press, 1985, pp. 45–62, p. 52. J. B. Peires, "The Central Beliefs of the Xhosa Cattle-Killing", *Journal of African History* 28/1, 1987, pp. 43–63, p. 62. Olatunji Oyeneye and Margaret Peil, *Consensus, Conflict and Change: A Sociological Introduction to African Societies*, Nairobi: East African Educational Publishers, 1998, pp. 28–29.

If one merely pages through the essay, one's first impression is that it starts without any announcement of the theme, a problem statement, a demarcation of its scope or subtitles – relying only on the lengthy title to orient the reader. However, the text (consisting of 16 pages of exposition, followed by 15 more pages with endnotes) is very well-structured (paragraphs are tagged with major and sub-numbers) and the argument unfolds very neatly.

The essay starts with a reference to the first documented case of interethnic marriage between Xhosa and San (in the 13th century) and the formation of Xhosa-Khoi communities in the 16th and 18th centuries. To this, he adds evidence to the linguistic sedimentation in the Xhosa language of their appreciation for the Khoi. These facts serve as a lively illustration of his point that "Khoisan-Xhosa interaction took place at a deep cultural level" (p. 2). Once this has been put on the agenda, Mabona can launch the orientation of the whole essay:

> The upshot of this long-lasting interaction between the two cultures was the emergence of a Xhosa religious system of such vitality that it threw up, at the beginning of the nineteenth century, a counter-challenge of remarkable strength to missionary Christianity and colonial invasion. This challenge was embodied especially in the two prophetic figures who arose about this time amongst the Xhosa: Makhanda, better known as Makana, and Ntsikana. (p. 2)

The reader cannot overlook that Mabona has exchanged the exploration of quite static continent-wide essences of African culture (in his earlier articles) for a much more historically sensitive description of the formation of cultural variations in interactions between groups, irrespective of whether that interaction was more collaborative or more confrontational.

The dissertation aims at providing a profile of the convergences and divergences of Xhosa and Khoisan elements in Xhosa religious views and practices as a point from which missions and colonisation were engaged with and resisted. Whereas attention to Khoi and San culture and history was a new theme for Mabona, we recognise his earlier interest in the study of myths (albeit now with a significantly different approach) and of Xhosa religious concepts as part of a broader Nguni cultural landscape. But true to his new dynamic view on human interaction, the relation between Xhosa and Christian *beliefs* among Xhosa prophets is studied. The varied mixtures resulted in what he describes as "a bedrock of ideology both for resistance and for a process of controlled accommodation in a new situation of cultural alienation" (p. 3).

Hence, he presents mythological personae and animal, plant, and stone symbolism as they are represented in the myths of the different groups. Views on cosmogony, life and death, and the formation of peoples are also described. His painstaking accumulation of historical and ethnographic detail is evident – gone is the metaphysical speculation detached from any application which we encountered in "The depths of African philosophy". Since the "emergent Khoisan-Xhosa religious system was the launching pad of the prophets" (p. 10), Mabona can proceed by focusing on prophets, while always viewing them as a part of broader social trends.

For the period under consideration in this dissertation and from the point of view of the study of religion, the major event is the Xhosa people's encounter with Christianity. The latter differed markedly in theology, rites, and ethics from the religious complex described thus far. In Mabona's view, the most significant difference was between two respective views of humanity. So important was this difference that Makana[39] made the case for taking them as reflecting two different kinds of human reality, a black and a white one, each with its own divinity (Mabona insists on the political dimension of Makana's views) (pp. 12–13). However, this also meant that Makana accorded a place to the Christian deity, albeit in a relation of separation and subordination to the Xhosa one (pp. 14–15).

However, this conflictual instrumentalisation of salient differences between the two religious complexes was contemporaneous with other, contrary, developments. In Mabona's view, "[w]hen this Khoisan-Xhosa 'religious cocktail' came into contact with Christianity, its piquancy was increased by the absorption of congenial elements from the new religion" (p. 11). This tension between the tendency to willing appropriation and the accentuation of differences together resulted in a range of cultural and religious strategies, each with its own political roots and consequences. Hence the position of Makana represented only one alternative; that of Ntsikana represented another notable one. Ntsikana preached the existence of a single deity, which he presented as a composition of Khoisan, Xhosa, and Christian ideas (pp. 13–14).[40]

Whereas the prophets, who also acted as diviners, should be understood against the backdrop of their sociocultural environment, one should also note the significant influence they in their turn exercised on that environment. Thus, the

---

[39] Also called Mak(h)anda or Nxele – as referred to in the biographical part of this book (see p. 33).

[40] However, elsewhere, Mabona places more emphasis on the Christian dimension of his message: "Ntsikana was advising the adoption of the Christian message and warning against social and cultural alienation bound up with money economy" (p. 13).

tension between Makana and Ntsikana led to the polarisation of the Xhosa people. This then led to two opposing political strategies: Mabona typifies Makana's strategy as a politics of "resistance" and that of Ntsikana as "collaborationist and accommodationist" (p. 14). Makana's view was characterised by his hard refusal to mix Khoisan-Xhosa religious views with Christian ones, but Mabona is reluctant to construe this view as merely conservative. In Mabona's opinion, this stance, as much as that of Ntsikana, demonstrated the "ability to adapt and to innovate" (p. 14). Mabona attributes the very emergence of prophets to this ability. In fact, his definition of prophets as "traditional royal diviners who had learned from their contact with Christianity the importance of having a message of salvation" (p. 14) applies to Makana too.

Mabona's appreciation for the Makana option is attested by the pages of careful description of the strategic composition of Makana's religious outlook from pre-existing elements of the three religious families. The echo of the scholar's personal situation at that time and that of the South Africa he had left is unavoidably audible when he concludes his study as follows:

> Makana's doctrine was repeated by Mlanjeni, Nongqause, and Mhlakaza and lost its force only in 1890, when Xhosa national resistance finally collapsed. It was in this year as well that Makana's personal effects were at last buried by his relatives who had given up the hope of his return. He himself had died in 1820 in the ocean after an unsuccessful attempt to escape from Robben Island where he had been brought after the disastrous defeat at Grahamstown. Ntsikana died of natural causes in 1821. (p. 16)

It is quite evident that the cultural politics of Makana and Ntsikana resonates with the question on the relation between the different population groups in South Africa (particularly the debates between the PAC/BC or ANC views, described in the bibliographical part, Chapter 5). Or, to put it differently, working through the historical material of religious responses to the colonial reality in the early nineteenth century, may well be – for Mongameli Mabona, but also for others – a means by which to contemplate the pressing issues of the apartheid years (and beyond, as we will see in §9, below).

8. Interlude: The publication spurt of 1996

As far as publications go,[41] the "long essay" would be the last the world would see from Mabona for more than twenty years (and even then, its submission would have to be considered a publication). Then, in 1996, he came out again with a bouquet of articles. The democratic turn in South African history clearly forms the background for this burst of writing. Another part of the justification for this collection of texts is given in the second one, which I will present below:

> At the request of the staff of the magazine Présence Africaine, made at its offices in Paris on 10-10-95, I visited the Transkei in the first half of November 1995 to find out who were the recipients of the copies of Présence Africaine sent to the Transkei in 1964 and to assess the influence which the magazine exercised on the political struggle of the Blacks in South Africa at that critical juncture. (p. 77)

The common thread running through these texts is the attempt to recall some of the smaller histories that led to the fall of the "granite wall" that apartheid was supposed to be, as Mabona states in the article "'Présence Africaine' and South African freedom" (1996). The historical perspective on the liberation presented in this article serves as a background for the other articles too.

Mabona sets apartheid in a longer and broader history of the European Enlightenment, technological development, and the spread of Christianity – which he reads critically. Subsequently, the history of colonisation and of racial segregation is portrayed as outgrowths of these three components. But he also passes in review a history of divergent strategies of resistance: Ntsikana is evoked, as are important historical figures of the ANC, PAC, and BCM. To this, he adds initiatives of cultural resistance, the mobilisation of women, and initiatives by some black members of the clergy and students. Then he turns to the real theme of his article:

> Into this buzzing and humming situation of political high tension a bombshell was dropped. In 1964, copies of *Présence Africaine*,[42] a

---

[41] While the text was not published in the ordinary sense, it is in the public domain as a submission for an advanced degree.

[42] Mabona does not specify which copies and how many copies were sent. His argument does not require this specification. However, one may mention that the second 1964 edition of *Présence Africaine* included a dossier on apartheid in South Africa.

Cultural Review of the Black World published in Paris, made a surprising and sudden appearance in the Transkei. [...] The late Mr. Alioune Diop, the Editor of this prestigious review, could not have chosen a more strategic moment to administer this shot in the arm for the black struggle in South Africa. The news of this literary bonanza went round like wild fire. But it was all hushed because all kinds of 'communist' literature were banned and forbidden. (p. 60)

Interviews with two recipients of copies (a clerk and a teacher) were conducted by Mabona and included in his 1996 dossier.

Mabona claims a direct link between the influence of these missives and the emergence of Black Consciousness (pp. 61, 62). The fact that Biko and Pityana drew on Fanon and Césaire – both linked with *Présence Africaine* – is cited as an example of this. Long citations from these authors and a prison letter from Mandela serve to illustrate the spirit of defiance. The article closes with a celebration of all the heroes who contributed to the struggle against apartheid.

His next, shorter, article continues the discussion under the title "'Présence Africaine' in Transkei, 1964: Report". The report reflects the conditions under which Mabona, after decades of exile, found his native Transkei and, on top of that, attempted to accomplish a relatively specific information-gathering mission. The two interviewees were old acquaintances of his: a school teacher and a relative who had worked at the Revenue Office. In the 1960s, both were in Idutywa. Bear in mind that the moment when the copies of *Présence Africaine* arrived in that area corresponds with Mabona's personal contact with these individuals (it was just after his return from Rome and just before he left that area; in other words, 1964–1965). The verbatim transcriptions, in the form of two page-long testimonies, echo Mabona's views, outlined above.

In line with his objective of highlighting liberation narratives, Mabona subsequently turns to "Women's role in the South African struggle for freedom" and the role of literature in two separate articles. In the form of a testimony, Mabona recounts the emergence of women's music groups in townships and their ability to articulate people's frustrations and ambitions.[43] He also hails the role women played to encourage disheartened exiles – as he saw in London from 1971 to 1977. Finally, he acclaims the help and support given to exiles in Germany, not by the state, but particularly by young German women.

---

[43] On this point, Mabona cites an earlier article of his, apparently dated 7 October 1979, which I have not been able to locate.

The next article is a review of *Littérature d'Afrique du Sud* (two volumes), which was prepared by the journal *Notre Librairie* on South African literature and which appeared in April and September of 1995. Covering the whole period from the mid seventeenth century to the date of publication, the emphasis in these volumes is the role of literature as a means of resistance and liberation. The works presented excel as literary achievements, but also as expositions of the violence of oppression. Mabona typifies this literature in terms of its "politics of human dignity and freedom" (p. 210). He critiques the work, first, as an oversimplified presentation of South African literature, as either in English or Afrikaans – underestimating the "Bantu" voice, even when it is expressed in English. Indeed, Mabona declares that "[t]he essence of the South African voice is Bantu-English-Afrikaans. This voice of the new rainbow nation is now free to sound its clarion call of human dignity and freedom" (p. 210). A second point of critique is that the volumes' focus resulted in the exclusion of a number of important authors. Thirdly, he reminds the reader of the wealth of oral literature that is not reflected in this work.

In continuation of this review, Mabona submitted another, entitled "Le regard de l'antilope" ("The antelope's gaze"). This is the title given to the French translation of James Gregory's autobiographical account *Good bye Bafana*. The review consists mainly of a summary of Gregory's developing relationship with Mandela while Gregory was a prison warden.

9. *Diviners and prophets*: The last, incomplete, work

As the ultimate accomplishment of his desire to study diviners among the Xhosa in 1965 and in explicit continuation of his SOAS "long essay",[44] the full name of Mabona's doctoral dissertation in anthropology is *Diviners and Prophets among the Xhosa (1593 -1856). A study in Xhosa cultural history* (2000).[45] In monograph

---

[44] Cf. DP, Introduction, no page numbers.
[45] This book is cited in the following: A short anonymous review in *Etnofoor* 18/1, 2005, 1 unnumbered page. Roger S. Levine, "Cultural innovation and translation in the Eastern Cape: Jan Tzatzoe, Xhosa intellectual and the making of an African Gospel, 1817–1833", *African Historical Review* 42/2, 2010, pp. 84–101, here p. 92. Tony Dold and Michelle Cocks, *Voices from the Forest: Celebrating Nature and Culture in Xhosaland*, Johannesburg: Jacana, 2012, p. 227. Lourenço Casimiro Pinto, "Contact rock art of the eastern cape and third spaces of enunciation", *The South African Archaeological Bulletin* 69/200, December 2014,

format, published by LIT-Verlag in 2004, the text (from the acknowledgments to the bibliography) spans 463 pages.

The *first chapter* is devoted to a description of the physical and natural landscape of Xhosaland – not only as a substrate which impacted on patterns of movement, settlement, and interaction (p. 40), but also from the perspective of the cultural appropriation of that environment.

In *Chapter Two*, Mabona takes up the question of Khoisan-Xhosa cultural interaction and devotes particular attention to a reconstruction of the earliest reconstructable origins of proto-Bantu and Khoisan migrations from East Africa (pp. 45, 83, 100–101). He defends as probable the thesis that these two groups have a common origin (p. 56). Hence, he takes up the hypothesis, merely suggested in the "long essay", that Khoisan-Xhosa interaction had millennial historical roots (pp. 96, 163). Thereafter, he traces the subsequent migrations of the ancestors of the "southeastern African Bantu" (p. 124) from these old localities, and in particular from the region of Lake Chad (pp. 107–109), via what is now Angola (p. 128ff), turning past Lake Malawi and moving southward via what is now Mozambique (p. 141) to the south-eastern part of present-day South Africa, where Xhosaland is situated (p. 105ff).[46]

Chapter Three is again devoted to background issues.[47] The first of these is a discussion of euphony[48] and polysynthesis[49] as structuring principles of the Xhosa language. In his exposition of euphony, Mabona includes a reflection on the logical possibilities opened by similarities (homology) of opposites and

---

pp. 152–163, here pp. 161–162. Emily McGiffin, "Oral poetry and development ideology in South Africa's Eastern Cape", *Third World Thematics: A TWQ Journal*, 2/2-3, 2017, pp. 279–295, numerous citations. Brent Sinclair-Thomson and Sam Challis, "The 'bullets to water' belief complex: a pan-southern African cognate epistemology for protective medicines and the control of projectiles", *Journal of Conflict Archaeology* 12/3, 2017, pp. 192–208, here p. 197.

[46] Conclusions summarised pp. 152–153, 162.

[47] With the following words, Mabona summarises the scope of Chapters 2 and 3: "Whereas in the second chapter I tried to study the cultural history of the Xhosa speaking peoples in synthesis from pre-historic times on through the iron age to historical times, in this chapter my intention has been to disclose the inner structures of that culture at all its stages. Neither the historical aperçu in the second chapter nor the efforts at socio-linguistic analysis in this chapter were pursued as ends in themselves and must, therefore, remain in their highly tentative and summary form. My hope is, however, that as summary as they are, these studies will be helpful in understanding the background and nature of the cultural forces at work in the profession and practices of diviners." (DP, p. 265)

[48] Shaping of words and phrases to sound more pleasing.

[49] Integrating divergent elements of meaning into a single word.

contrasts:[50] whereas formal logics works with the principles of identity and the exclusion of the third,[51] homological expressions allow for both contradictory things to be valid. The former logic presupposes an immutable state of affairs; the latter gives expression to a dynamic, changing world (pp. 167–169, see also p. 286).[52] Furthermore, Mabona discusses the formative influence of the social lifeworld and cultural practices on language by examining ritualisation (the layering of concrete terms with ritual significance), as well as oaths, adages, and verses. The contribution of this detour into Xhosa linguistics for the book seems to be captured by Mabona's observation that "when I examined the inner structure and the roots of Xhosa linguistic formations I found myself face to face with Xhosa cultural themes and elements of the Xhosa worldview" (p. 198).

The second major theme of Chapter Three is mythology. Mabona explains that these "*intsomi*" are essentially tales of wisdom, which also convey cosmological and ethnographic ideas (p. 214), and he proceeds with a narration of and commentary on three examples: the story of Mbulukazi, the story of the five heads, and the story of Ironside and his sister.

Thereafter, Xhosa iconography is passed in review. Numerous pages of photos of symbolic figures, animals, human and mythological depictions, and sculptures are commented on. Together, they open a panoramic view on the depiction of recurrent symbols and ideas in traditional Xhosa culture. While focusing here on the culture of one group, the iconography in particular is a testimony to "how widely cultural universals are spread over the Continent".[53] At least superficially, there is some continuation with the themes of study that occupied Mabona during his time in Rome.

Finally, considering the long Xhosa history, Mabona feels himself rather inclined to insist on the changes: the formation and receding of cultural elements. He documents changes in Xhosa culture over five phases ("the prehistoric stage, the West African stage, the Angolan Sojourn, and the East African stage", and the present[54]) focusing on phenomena such as burial practices, initiation

---

[50] E.g. *vala* ("shut") – *vula* ("open"), DP, p. 169, but according to Mabona, this phenomenon abounds in the Xhosa language to such an extent as to warrant considering it a structural principle of the language.

[51] The principle of identity determines that A is always identical to itself (A = A), and the exclusion of the third states that A is either B or non-B; there is no third possibility.

[52] This discussion is anticipated by a similar one on logic in the *Lux* article "African mentality in a world frame".

[53] DP, "Introduction".

[54] DP, "Introduction".

rites, means of transport, terminology, religious practices, the transmission of customs, customary law, and others.[55] However, despite his focus on the broad changes, Mabona still finds it appropriate to identify the salient, long-term stable tendencies or "thought structures" of Xhosa culture. In this respect, Mabona describes the values attributed to colours, conceptions of time and space, religious representations, counting, etc.[56]

Only in the *fourth chapter* does the discussion of diviners and prophets really start. Diviners are presented as the original guardians of cultural transmission. Whereas prophetism is associated with the arrival of Christianity in southern Africa and thus is a fairly recent phenomenon, divinerhood dates back to times immemorial; in fact, Mabona considers it "coeval with Bantu society" (p. 292, likewise p. 314). Mabona's basic stance on the relation between these major social roles is that "[p]rophetism can justly be regarded as a [C]hristian epiphenomenon of the office and functions of a diviner among the Bantu. There is admittedly a basic continuity between the two roles in the historical process of development and self-adaptation" (p. 265). In order to shed light on these twin phenomena, he provides an overview of significant historical instances, covering the period demarcated in the title of his book, 1593 to 1856. The first of these dates corresponds with the first instance of a diviner recorded in writing.[57] As an example of the workings of divinerhood in precolonial times, Mabona describes the dependency of King Tshiwo (born 1675, DP, Introduction) on diviners, both in his personal and family concerns and in matters of diplomatic and military strategy (p. 298).

For the institution of divinerhood, a major turning point came with the arrival of Europeans in Xhosaland (that is, during the period described in Part 1, Chapter 1). Within this broader context, Mabona considers the arrival of (British) missionaries (which he established as 1816) to have been a "massive and direct confrontation with an alien culture that caused in the Xhosa polity an acute crisis of identity" (p. 300). Mabona's objective is to describe the responses, adaptations, and inventions of diviners in response to this situation. For this

---

[55] Cf. DP, p. 264: "To sum up, therefore, it seems that central east Africa is the area in which the Bantu, with the Xhosa-speaking peoples included, increased and broadened the ritual and conceptual framework on which their agricultural and pastoral activities were based. But the centre of gravity for survival and further achievement was based on cattle culture."
[56] Not shying away from making comparative observations with ancient Greek philosophy (cf. DP, pp. 282–283, 284–285).
[57] However, Mabona also cites a reference from the year 922 to a diviner who was not Xhosa (DP, p. 295).

purpose, he reconstructs the approaches of Makhanda/Makan(n)a and Ntsikana – both of whom were directly involved in the first encounters and confrontations with missionaries and the colonial powers.[58] As in the "long essay", Mabona describes the differences between Makana and Ntsikana. Makana was a properly trained diviner, who, despite initial rapprochement to Christianity, remained within the ambit of traditional Xhosa culture, albeit in his specific, innovative way. Ntsikana was a borderline case for this study, since he was never trained as a diviner and his public action and the role he played depended much more on an individual experience of vocation. He was also not a real Christian convert, refusing baptism. However, Mabona also highlights their similarities, which make for interesting comparisons: "The two social factors that established the legitimacy of both Makana's and Ntsikana's roles were the authority of the chief and popular consensus. The personal factors, on the other hand, were their divinerhood and prophets' messages of national salvation" (p. 304). Both died in the early 1820s. The implicit, but tangible, preference for Makana in the "long essay" seems to have made room for a more equal, descriptive, presentation of these two figures.[59]

Mlanjeni, born in 1833, represented a new generation of diviners. His specialisation seems to have been his opposition to witchcraft. His objective was to cure people of witchcraft, in the sense of changing their "inner disposition" (p. 306), rather than merely stopping the external ceremonies. He won the esteem of chiefs and exerted some influence on them, but also attracted the suspicion of the colonial powers. It is not very clear from the discussion what the particularity of his short active life as a diviner was.

The last two figures singled out by Mabona are Mhlakaza, probably a trained diviner, perhaps a specialist, and his (adoptive?) daughter and apprentice, Nongqawuse (p. 309). A lot of the difficulty in grasping their work resides in the conflicting traditions of interpretation: "while the Xhosa disown and reject Nongqawuse and Mhlakaza, colonial history seeks to ennoble them and attach them onto Xhosa society – it depicts them as an endogenous and worthy product of this society" (p. 309, cf. p. 310f). It is not the disastrous consequences of their prophecy (in the case of Nongqawuse, the infamous cattle killings of 1856–1857) on which the Xhosa rejection is based, since the other figures discussed were not exempt from failure. It is rather that their work was and is disowned as fake.

---

[58] However, Mabona mentions that both Makana and Ntsikana had been followers of the Dutch missionary Van der Kemp years earlier (DP, pp. 301, 303).

[59] However, Mabona's wording still reflects a soft spot for Makana.

Mabona's reading of the history of their public work puts them neatly in the pocket of the British colonial powers. In conclusion, he declares the

> obvious futility to engage in the exercise of analysing the ideas contained in their 'prophecies' from a religious point of view. In fact their 'prophecies' were nothing but green ivy and blue death, they were a macabre and deadly charade of both the Xhosa and [C]hristian religions. (p. 312)

After this overview of major historical figures, Mabona considers divinerhood on its own with a more descriptive intention. Issuing from a vocation, diviners needed training (traditionally, among the Xhosa, five years) and the authorisation of a chief to practise. They were consecrated by a public ceremony. Their varied social functions stretched from healing people to offering strategic advice to chiefs. The whole practice was situated in a larger context of a particular view on life, the ancestors, animals, the cosmos – much of what had been described earlier in *Diviners and prophets*. The phenomenon of trances is specifically treated, in the form of a comparison with similar phenomena in Europe (pre-Christian and Christian mystic forms) and in Asia (in Hinduism and Buddhism). The comparison of metaphysical presuppositions of the respective practices is somewhat reminiscent of similar comparisons as far back as Mabona's early articles "African mentality in a world frame" and "Towards an African philosophy". An overview of the symbolism used by Xhosa diviners rounds off the chapter. According to Mabona's interpretation, the "over-arching ideal trajectories or modalities connecting this whole system of comprehension and organisation are homology, analogy, and symbology" (p. 382). All three of these salient features, which are typical of Xhosa culture in general, have been discussed already, either earlier in *Diviners and prophets* or in "The depths of African philosophy". But the metaphysical speculations of the early texts are absent, and analogy and symbolism are now discussed with a view to anthropological description (there is even a short theory of symbolism, pp. 387–390).

The main text of the book finally, and surprisingly, stops abruptly with the following declaration:

> The underlying idea for me in undertaking this study was to show how, when armed resistance against colonial invasion was flagging, the diviner prophets of the last century among the Xhosa stepped into the frontline of leadership. The prophet diviners, benefiting from the training for their office, fashioned an ideology drawn mostly from

> traditional sources, and used it as an effective weapon to mobilise the flagging forces of resistance and help save the cultural identity of the Xhosa. Their power was based upon their dependence on the ancestors. They made the people feel that when they were going back to their ancestors they were going back to their future and when they were going forward towards their ancestors, they were going forward to their real healing past. (pp. 400–401)

This declaration has the great advantage of revealing the author's overarching objective. At the same time, one cannot fail to notice that despite the laborious research that went into it and the already bulky text, the book still has not arrived at what it set out to accomplish. This would be part of the justification for Mabona's own reservations about this book.

9.1 Final appraisal

This overview suffices to demonstrate that there are numerous continuities between Mabona's earlier and later work: logic, symbolism, the focus on Xhosa culture, the emphasis of religious ideas. In this sense, Mabona's final book had been long in the making. However, he does not seem to have been consciously concerned with rounding off projects in *Diviners and prophets*; except for the "long essay" to which he returns numerous times, he does not refer to any of his own previous publications.

This axis of his work, which links the "long essay" to *Diviners and prophets*, points to arguably the single most striking feature of *Diviners and prophets*: the turn to anthropology. Traces of the competence he built up as a student of theology are found in the text; issues of African philosophy are touched on here and there. But both of these remain quite marginal. It is in anthropology that Mabona seems to have found his voice. Or rather, after having left behind both Italy and South Africa, this seems to have been the form of scholarly work that best suited his intellectual quest under the conditions of exile. Still, this point should not be exaggerated, since the bibliography[60] of his book reflects, amongst other things, ample readings in both African and European philosophy.

---

[60] Since not all of the works listed in the bibliography are cited or discussed in the book, Mabona's readers are led to understand it as a broader view on both the sources cited and publications that were useful in shaping the author's mind during the course of compiling the study.

These more formal considerations aside, one needs to ponder the overall theme of the book. In Part 1 of this book, I have already hinted at an implicit continuity that links a lot of his work: the question of how to cope with cultural and religious traditions in contexts of social and political turmoil and uncertainty. The pearls of this string link his father as a catechist, his personal experience as a Xhosa Christian and later as a Xhosa Catholic priest, the figure of the catechist in the centre of his dissertation in theology, the major figures of Makana and Ntsikana, and finally the other major diviners and prophets of the nineteenth century. I do not want to reduce the content and significance of each text to self-analyses, as if Mabona always wrote in front of a mirror. But I do maintain that the question of cultural improvisation, coupled with both fidelity and critique of tradition, seems to be a major means by which to confront difficult sociopolitical questions. In this respect, one may recall his exclamation: "[P]ersonally, I find nothing wrong with miscegenation. Shades of 'bastard tribes'!" (DP, p. 55) This reflects his view not only on crude biological racism but also on artificial cultural purity. In my view, his last text took the constituent parts of his own personal complexity to the extreme: writing about the religious-intellectual phenomena of a previous century in a distant region of Xhosaland – in English, while sitting in Lucerne, reading for a dissertation at the University of Bern. Mabona is not one or the other, but both: his most loyal embrace of Xhosa tradition is by means of European practices of excellence.

However, a caveat should be raised by mentioning an idea Mabona insisted upon in his writings on black theology – a kind of allergy to channelling the good life to the interior. One might rephrase his position as the axiom that health is with others, with a world. If this is taken as a guide to his orientation, one should resist reading his anthropological work as no more than projections of the internal conflict of a tormented soul. I would rather read it as a point of entry – albeit an oblique or uncertain entry – to his political engagement, or at least to his social and political commentary. It is a more studious and indirect approach – but undertaken in the hope of contributing to real and lasting solutions. As much as the quest for solutions is tangible in his work, one has the impression of an unfinished project, leaving the reader to take on the fulfilment of the task, despite the confusion of the high stakes in the present.

TIMELINE

5 June 1929	– birth, Qombolo
1930	– mother dies
?	– moves with father and brother to Sabalele
1937(?)–1942(?)	– moves to Zigudu and starts school; in state school up to Standard 4 (now called Grade 6).
1943(?)–1948(?)	– continues schooling at Ixopo Minor Seminary; completes matriculation
1949(?)–1954(?)	– Major Seminary St. Peters, Pevensey
1953 or 1954	– father dies
1953 or 1954	– brother dies
1954	– ordination; starts working as a priest in the Queenstown area
1957–1963	– Rome: three years of canon law; four years of study and research for thesis; Second meeting of black writers and artists; Vatican II.
1958(?)–(?)	– editor of *Lux*; first articles
1960	– first article in *Présence Africaine* published
1963	– completes PhD in canon law; back in South Africa;[1] teaches at Lumko, St. Peters
July 1966[2]	– SPOBA founded
1967	– appointed at St. Peters[3]
1970	– Black Priests' Manifesto published
May 1972	– leaves South Africa[4]; starts at SOAS; London
1973	– "long essay"

---

[1] August 1963, according to Martha Mabona (Interview 3).
[2] According to Dictionary of African Christian Bibliography.
[3] Mukuka, *The impact*, p. 60.
[4] Denis, "Seminary networks…"

1975	– leaves priesthood[5]; works in hotels in London; advocacy for Mafuna group
1977	– moves to Switzerland
1978	– marries Marta Giger
1984	– enrols for PhD in Bern
1984–1994	– works in hospital
1991	– first visit to South Africa from exile
1996	– visit to South Africa; reports for *Présence Africaine*
2000	– completion of PhD in Anthropology at the University of Bern
2004	– publication of *Diviners and prophets*
2019	– celebrates ninetieth birthday

* *This timeline is only a guide for the most important dates. The uncertainties are discussed in the biographical part of the book.*

---

[5] DP, "Introduction"

MABONA
PRIMARY BIBLIOGRAPHY

Dissertations

— 1963: Doctorate in canon law. *De statu catechistarum in Ecclesia: studium historico-canonicum*, Propaganda Fide, Rome.
— 1973:[1] Master's in Religious Studies. "The interaction and development of different religions in the Eastern Cape in the late eighteenth and early nineteenth Centuries, with special reference to the first two Xhosa prophets", School of Oriental and African Studies, London.
— 2000: Doctorate in cultural history. *Diviners and prophets among the Xhosa (1593-1856). A study in Xhosa cultural history*, University of Bern.
  • Published by Münster: Lit Verlag, 2004.
  • Abbreviated in this book as DP.

Unpublished book

— 1962: *The outlines of African philosophy*, Rome, 155 pages.

Articles

— "Africa's true position and destiny", *Lux* 1958–1959, pp. 13–20.
— "African mentality in a world frame", *Lux* 1958–1959, pp. 32–53.
— "Towards an African philosophy", *Lux* 1959, pp. 56–85.

---

[1] In DP, the date of this dissertation is repeatedly indicated as 1974. However, SOAS catalogued the dissertation with the date 1973 (author's correspondence with Mia Barrow-Sullivan and Catherine Martin on 23 August 2016).

- Republished: "Towards an African philosophy", *Présence Africaine* 30/2, 1960, pp. 59–77.
- Republished: "Towards an African philosophy", *Rivista trimestrale di studi e documentazione dell'Istituto italiano per l'Africa e l'Oriente* 22/1, March 1967, pp. 3–14.[2]
- Translation: "Philosophie africaine", *Présence africaine* XXX/2, February–March 1960, pp. 40–59.
- Translation republished as "Philosophie africaine", in Alphons Josef Smet, *Philosophie africaine*, volume I, Kinshasa: Presses Universitaires du Zaïre, 1975, pp. 207–225.

— With Alhaji Isa Kaita, Jean Christophe Mackpayen, Sy Mamadou, Mohamed Said Samantar, Doudou Gueye, E. E. Esua, Godwin Paul Doe, F. Lukusa, Gian Luigi Pezza, and Camillo Bonanni: "Impiego degli audiovisivi per l'educazione in Africa", in *Africa: Rivista trimestrale di studi e documentazione dell'Istituto italiano per l'Africa e l'Oriente* 17/4, July–August 1962, pp. 179–198 (Mabona's contribution is on pp. 197–198).

— "Elements of African culture", *Présence Africaine* 41/2, 1962, pp. 109–114.
- Translation: "Eléments de culture africaine", *Présence Africaine* XLI/2, 1962, pp. 144–150.

— "The depths of African philosophy", *Personnalité africaine et catholicisme*, Paris: Présence Africaine, 1963, pp. 29–58.

— "The vocation and presence of Africa in modern scientific life", *Présence Africaine* 48/4, 1963, pp. 71–74.
- Translations: "Vocation et présence de l'Afrique dans la vie scientifique moderne", *Présence Africaine*, XLVIII /4, 1963, pp. 206–209.

— "African spirituality", *Présence Africaine* 52/4, 1964, pp. 158–162.
- Translation: "La spiritualité africaine", *Présence Africaine* LII/4, 1964, pp. 157–161.

— "The religious concepts of the Ngunis", *Présence Africaine*, 54/2, 1965, pp. 177–184
- Translation: "Sur l'avenir des concepts religieux chez les Nguni". *Présence Africaine* LIV/2, 1965, pp. 173–180.

Theology

— With Smangaliso Mkhatshwa, David Moetapele, John Louwfant, and Clement Mokoka, "Our Church has let us down", *Rand Daily Mail*, 23 January 1970.

---

2 A.J. Smet catalogues two further republications of this article, notably in the journals *Africa* (Rome) and *Africa Report* (New York). As far as I could establish, this is an error. See A.J. Smet, "African philosophical bibliography / Bibliographie de la philosophie africaine / Bibliografie van de afrikaanse wijsbegeerte" http://www.isp.ucl.ac.be/recherche/philafr/M.html (last consulted 2 October 2019).

- Republished: Smangaliso Mkhatshwa, David Moetapele, John Louwfant, Clement Mokoka, and Anthony Mabona, "Africanisation in South Africa", *African Ecclesiastical Review* 12/2, 1970, pp. 175–177.
- Republished: "Black Priests' Manifesto, January 23, 1970", Thomas Karis and Gail Gerhart, *From protest to challenge. Volume 5: Nadir and resurgence, 1964-1979*, Pretoria: UNISA Press, 1997, pp. 424–427.

— "Africansation of the church", *Pro Veritate* VIII/11, 15 March 1970, pp. 3–4.
— "God and violence", *South African Outlook* 100-101, 1970, 185–187.
— "Black people and white worship", in Mokgethi Motlhabi (ed.), *Essays on Black Theology*, Johannesburg: Black Theology Project of the University Christian Movement, 1972, pp. 81–84.
- Republished: "Black people and white worship", in Basil Moore (ed.), *The challenge of Black Theology in South Africa*, London: Hurst, 1973; Atlanta: John Knox Press, 1974, pp. 104–108.
- Republished: "White worship and black people", in *Pro Veritate*, May 1971, pp. 10–11.
- Translation: "Schwarze Menschen und weisser Gottesdienst", in Basil Moore, *Schwarze Theologie in Afrika*, Ulrich Hühne (trans.), Göttingen: Vandenhoeck & Ruprecht, 1973, pp. 122–126.

Later publications

— "'Présence Africaine' and South African freedom", *Présence Africaine* 153/1, 1996, pp. 53–64.
- Translation: "'Présence Africaine' et la liberté en Afrique du Sud", *Présence Africaine* 153/1, 1996, pp. 65–76.
— "'Presence Africaine' in Transkei, 1964: Report", *Présence Africaine* 153/1, 1996, pp. 77–79
- Translation: "'Présence Africaine' au Transkei. Evaluation", *Présence Africaine* 153/1, 1996, pp. 80–82
— "Interviews" [with Timothy Mlityalwa and Victor Lujabe], *Présence Africaine* 153/1, 1996, pp. 82–84.
- Translation follows without a new title, *Présence Africaine* 153/1, 1996, pp. 84–85
— "Women's role in the South African struggle for freedom", *Présence Africaine* 153/1, 1996, pp. 158–159.
- [there seems to have been no translation published]
— "'Littérature d'Afrique du Sud'", *Présence Africaine*, *Présence Africaine* 153/1, 1996, pp. 209–211 [in English].
— "'Le regard de l'antilope'", *Présence Africaine* 1954/2, 1996, pp. 307–310 [in English].

Poetry

— "The Sea", *Présence Africaine* 56/4, 1965, p. 98.
  • Also *New Coin* 1, 1965, p. 8.
  • Republished in dossier "South-Africa", with poems by Denis Brutus and Mazisi Kunenein in *Présence Africaine* 57/1, 1966, pp. 312–318 (Mabona's poem is on page 318).
  • Republished *New Coin* 13/1-2, Apr 1977, pp. 1–38, 3–4.
— "Chrysalis", *Présence Africaine* 76/4, 1970, pp. 166–167.
  • *New Coin* 13/1-2, Apr 1977, pp. 1–38, 5–6
— "Gazer-at-the-dawn", *Présence Africaine* 76/4, 1970, pp. 167–168.
— "The Answer", *Présence Africaine* 76/4, 1970, p. 168.
— "Dead Freedom-Fighter", *Présence Africaine* 76/4, 1970, p. 169.
— "Contestation", *Présence Africaine* 76/4, 1970, pp. 169–170.
— "Prayer", *Présence Africaine* 76/4, 1970, pp. 170–171.
— "Futility", *Présence Africaine* 76/4, 1970, pp. 171–172.
— "Rich harvest", *New Coin*, 10/1-2, April 1974, p. 36.
— "Black Theology", *New Coin* 13/1-2, April 1977, p. 7.

NOTES ON THE SOURCES FOR INTERVIEWS AND BIOGRAPHY

Interview number	Date	Participants
0	8 January 2016	Family interview
1	15 January 2016 (morning interview)	Mongameli, Marta, and Themba Mabona
2	15 January 2016	Mongameli, Marta, and Themba Mabona
3	15 January 2016 (afternoon interview)	Mongameli Mabona
4	15 January 2016 (short interview)	Mongameli Mabona
5	16 January 2016 (lunch interview)	Mongameli and Marta Mabona
6	18 September 2018	Mongameli, Marta, and Themba Mabona
7	19 September 2018	Mongameli Mabona

Note on the interviews

Early in January 2016, before my first meeting with Mongameli Mabona, members of his family conducted an interview and sent it to me (Interview 0). Together with the family interview, I received a one-page document, "Jugend Mongameli", with a few biographical facts in the first person.

Sometimes I was alone with Mongameli Mabona during the interviews; sometimes Themba or Marta was present, and at points they also participated. This was of great help, since they could remind Mongameli Mabona of certain facts or correct information. Sometimes they also asked questions that I would not have thought of.

Whenever I render the interviews, I either stay as closely to the original formulations or cite from the interview directly. In citations from the interviews, I have had to make small editorial changes.

Note on sources for biography

I have only two sources to portray Mabona's childhood and youth: the interviews and notes from *Diviners and prophets*. The latter are of immense value, since they provide a glimpse of the lifeworld of the young Mabona. At the same time, one has to recognise that, taken together, they represent only one angle on his life, namely those recollections that could be meaningfully referred to in a doctoral thesis on Xhosa culture.

I have made ample use of these self-references. In a few places, it is not clear in which part of his life an anecdote has to be situated. Here, I have had to conjecture.

More rigorous historical research would include expanding the archive work, conducting more interviews, etc. Regretfully, I have neither the time nor the means to do so. However, I do not hesitate to present this work as an invitation to those who are better equipped to correct and complete it – in fact, I would be most grateful if people were to do so.

REFERENCES

This bibliography lists only the texts referenced in Part 1.

Adhikari, Mohamed. *Not white enough, not black enough: racial identity in the South African coloured community*. Athens: Ohio University Press, 2005.

"African student parley opens in London". Broadcast from Monrovia Liberia on the ELWA Radio Station, as cited by the Foreign Broadcast Information Service (USA), *Daily Report, Foreign Radio Broadcasts* 75, 1963, p. 11.

Asheeke, Toivo. "'Arming Black Consciousness': The Formation of the Bokwe Group/Azanian Peoples' Liberation Front, April 1972–September 1976". *Journal of Southern African Studies* 45/1, 2019, pp. 69–88.

Aymans, Winfried. "Mörsdorf, Klaus". *Neue Deutsche Biographie* 17, 1994, pp. 683f. https://www.deutsche-biographie.de/pnd118734474.html#ndbcontent (last accessed 27 September 2019).

Beinart, William. "Chieftaincy and the concept of articulation: South Africa circa 1900-1950", in William Beinart and Saul Dubow (eds.), *Segregation and apartheid in twentieth-century South Africa*. London and New York: Routledge, 1995, pp. 176–188.

Bonner, Philip. "South African Society and Culture, 1910-1948", in Robert Ross, Anne Kelk Mager, and Bill Nasson (eds.), *The Cambridge history of South Africa. Volume 2: 1885-1994*. Cambridge: Cambridge University Press, pp. 254–318.

Borruso, Paolo. "Catholic Italy and post-colonial Africa: the new subjects of an informal commitment in the 1960s". *Cahiers de la Méditerranée* 88, 2014, pp. 99–111.

Bouamama, Saïd. *Figures de la révolution africaine. De Kenyatta à Sankara*. Paris: Découverte, 2014.

Brockman, Norbert. "Mkhatshwa, Smangaliso Patrick". *Dictionary of African Christian Biography*. http://www.dacb.org/stories/southafrica/mkhatshwa1_smang.html (last accessed 5 February 2016).

Buthelezi, Sipho. "The emergence of Black Consciousness: an historical appraisal", in N. B. Pityana, M. Ramphele, M. Mpumiwana, and L. Wilson (eds.), *Bounds of possibility. The legacy of Steve Biko and Black Consciousness*. Cape Town: David Philip, 1991, pp. 111–129.

Castells, Manuel. "The rise of the fourth world: informational capitalism, poverty, and social exclusion", in *End of millennium*. Oxford: Blackwell, 1998, pp. 70–165.

Catholic diocese of Queenstown: http://dioceseofqueenstown.mariannhillmedia.org/history/ (last accessed 3 June 2019).

Chanaiwa, David. "Southern Africa since 1945", in Ali Mazrui and Christophe Wondji (eds.), *General history of Africa. Volume VIII: Africa since 1935*. Paris: UNESCO; Oxford: J. Currey, 1999, pp. 249–281.

Cherki, Alice. "Préface à l'édition de 2002", in Frantz Fanon, *Les damnés de la terre*. Paris: La Découverte, 2002, pp. 5–15.

Clark, Martin. *Modern Italy 1871-1995*. Second edition. London and New York: Longman, 1996.

Collective. *Des prêtres noirs s'interrogent. Cinquante ans après...*, presented by Léonard Santedi

Kinkupu, Gérard Bissainthe, and Meinrad Hebga. Paris: Karthala-Présence Africaine, 2006.
Collective. *Personnalité africaine et catholicisme*. Paris: Présence Africaine, 1963.
Contemporary Cultural Studies Unit [University of Natal] (CCSU), "Community and the Progressive Press: A Case Study in Finding Our Way". *Journal of Communication Inquiry* 12/1, 1988, pp. 26-44.
"Cyril Bernard Papali". *Wikipedia, The Free Encyclopedia*. https://en.wikipedia.org/wiki/Cyril_Bernard_Papali (last accessed 1 June 2019).
Degenaar, Johan. "Afrikaner-nasionalisme", in W.P. Esterhuyse, P.V.D.P. du Toit, and A.A. van Niekerk (eds.), *Moderne politieke ideologieë*. Johannesburg: Southern, 1987, pp. 231-260.
Deliège, Robert. *Gandhi*. Paris: Presses Universitaires de France, 1999.
Denis, Philippe. *The Dominican Friars in Southern Africa. A social history (1577-1990)*. Leiden, Boston, and Cologne: Brill, 1998.
Denis, Philippe. "Seminary networks and Black Consciousness in South Africa in the 1970s". *South African Historical Journal* 62/1, 2010, pp. 162-182.
Derouck, Stefan. Correspondence with E. Wolff on 5 October 2018.
Dischl, Marcel. *Transkei for Christ. A history of the Catholic Church in the Transkeian territories*. No place: no publisher, 1982.
Duggan, Christopher. *A concise history of Italy*. Cambridge: Cambridge University Press, 1994.
Danquah, Joseph Boakye. "The 'force' of Ghanaism", in *The Ghanaian establishment. Its constitution, its detentions, its traditions, its justice and statecraft and its heritage of Ghanaism*. Accra: Ghana Universities Press, 1997, pp. 183-185.
Elphick, Richard. "Mission Christianity and interwar liberalism", in Jeffrey Butler, Richard Elphick, and David Wels (eds.), *Democratic liberalism in South Africa: its history and prospect*. Johannesburg and Cape Town: David Philip, 1987, pp. 64-80.
Etherington, Norman, Patrick Harries, and Bernard Mbenga. "From colonial hegemonies to imperial conquest, 1840-1880", in Carolyn Hamilton, Robert John Ross, and Bernard K. Mbenga (eds.), *The Cambridge history of South Africa, Volume 1: From early times to 1885*. New York: Cambridge University Press, 2010, pp. 319-391.
Feinstein, Charles. *An economic history of South Africa. Conquest, discrimination, and development*. Cambridge: Cambridge University Press, 2005.
Ferro, Marc. *Histoire des colonisations. Des conquêtes aux indépendances XIIIe-XXe siècle*. Paris: Seuil, 1994.
Fanon, Frantz. *Les damnés de la terre*. Paris: La Découverte, 2002.
Fanon, Frantz. "Mutual foundations for national culture and liberation struggle", in *The wretched of the earth*. New York: Grove Press, 2004, pp. 170-180.
Finlay, Alan. "'Pull Down to Earth ...' The story of *New Coin*, 1965-2014", in Monica Hendricks (ed.), *ISEA 1964-2014. A South African research institute serving people*. NISC and Rhodes University: Grahamstown, 2016, pp. 67-77.
Fleisch, Brahm. "State formation and the origins of Bantu education", in Peter Kallaway (ed.), *The history of education under apartheid 1948-1994*. New York et al.: Peter Lang, 2002, pp. 39-52.
Frémeaux, Jacques. *Les empires coloniaux. Une histoire-monde*. Paris: CNRS éditions, 2012.
Freund, Bill. "South Africa: The Union Years, 1910-1948. Political and economic foundations", in Robert Ross, Anne Kelk Mager, and Bill Nasson (eds.), *The Cambridge history of South Africa. Volume 2: 1885-1994*. Cambridge: Cambridge University Press, pp. 211-253.
Giliomee, Hermann. *The Afrikaners. Biography of a people*. Charlottesville: University of Virginia Press, 2004.

Giuliani, Gaia and Cristina Lombardi-Diop. *Bianco e nero. Storia dell'identità razziale degli italiani*. Florence: Mondadori Education, 2013.

Gueye, Abdoulaye. "De la religion chez les intellectuels africains en France. L'odyssée d'un référent identitaire". *Cahiers d'études africaines* 162/2, 2001, pp. 267–291.

Hart, Keith and Vishnu Padayachee. "A history of South African capitalism in national and global perspective". *Transformation: Critical Perspectives on Southern Africa* 81/82, 2013, pp. 55–85.

Hassan, Salah D. "Inaugural Issues: The Cultural Politics of the Early 'Présence Africaine', 1947-55". *Research in African Literatures* 30/2, 1999, pp. 194–221.

Hebga, Meinrad. "Un malaise grave", in *Personnalité africaine et catholicisme*. Paris: Présence Africaine, 1963.

Hlatshwayo, Simphiwe. *Education and independence. Education in South Africa, 1658-1988*. Westport and London: Greenwood Press, 2000.

Howlett, Marc-Vincent and Romuald Fonkoua. "La maison Présence Africaine". *Gradhiva* 10/2, 2009, pp. 106–133.

Pope John XXIII. "His holiness replies". *Présence Africaine* XXIV-XXV/1, 1959, pp. 469–470.

Johns, Sheridan and Gail Gerhart. *Protest and hope, 1882-1934*. Volume 1 of *From protest to challenge. A documentary history of African politics in South Africa, 1882-1990*. Second edition. Pretoria: Jacana, 2014.

Kaita, Alhaji Isa, Jean Christophe Mackpayen, Sy Mamadou, Mohamed Said Samantar, Doudou Gueye, E. E. Esua, Godwin Paul Doe, F. Lukusa, Gian Luigi Pezza, Camillo Bonanni, and Antonio Mabona. "Impiego degli audiovisivi per l'educazione in Africa". *Africa: Rivista trimestrale di studi e documentazione dell'Istituto italiano per l'Africa e l'Oriente* 17/4, July–August 1962, pp. 179–198.

Karis, Thomas and Gail Gerhart. *From protest to challenge. Volume 5: Nadir and resurgence, 1964-1979*. Pretoria: UNISA Press, 1997.

Kaunda, Kenneth. *Kaunda on violence*. London et al.: William Collins, 1980.

Kesteloot, Lylian. "1956 – 1959. D'un congrès à l'autre". *Présence Africaine* 2007/1 (N° 175-176-177), pp. 125–129.

Kinyongo, Jean. "La philosophie africaine et son histoire". *Les Études philosophiques* (Philosophies africaines) 4, 1982, pp. 407–418.

Kocka, Jürgen. *Geschichte des Kapitalismus*. Munich: Verlag C.H. Beck, 2017.

Kropiwnicki, Zosa Olenka De Sas. "The meeting of myths and realities: The 'homecoming' of second-generation exiles in post-apartheid South Africa". *Refuge* 30/2, 2014, pp. 79–92.

Legassick, Martin. "British hegemony and the origins of segregation in South Africa, 1901-14", in William Beinart and Saul Dubow (eds.), *Segregation and apartheid in twentieth-century South Africa*. London and New York: Routledge, 1995, pp. 43–56.

Lambert, Michael. "The classics and black South African identities", in *The classics and South African identities*. London: Bristol Classical Press, 2011, pp. 91–124.

Lievens, Jos. Personal correspondence with E. Wolff on 1 July 2018.

Lock, Etienne. *Identité africaine et Catholicisme: problématique de la rencontre de deux notions à travers l'itinéraire d'Alioune Diop (1956-1995)*. Doctoral dissertation in history. Université Charles-de-Gaulle – Lille-III, 2014.

M'Bokolo, Elikia. "Les pratiques de l'apartheid", in Marc Ferro (ed.), *Le livre noir du colonialisme. XVIe – XXIe siècle: de l'extermination à la repentance*. Paris: Fayard and Pluriel, 2010, pp. 627–639.

Macqueen, Ian. "The Christian Roots of Black Consciousness", in *Black Consciousness and progressive movements under apartheid*. Pietermaritzburg: UKZN Press, 2018, pp. 23–56.

Mafuna, Bokwe (and Daniel Magaziner). "Interview with Bokwe Mafuna", 3 November 2005, http://www.aluka.org/action/showMetadata?doi=10.5555/AL.SFF.DOCUMENT. MAGAZP1B1001 (last accessed 3 June 2019).

Mager, Anne Kelk and Maanda Mulaudzi. "Popular responses to apartheid: 1948 – c.1975", in Robert Ross, Anne Kelk Mager, and Bill Nasson (eds.), *The Cambridge history of South Africa. Volume 2: 1885-1994*. Cambridge: Cambridge University Press, pp. 369–408.

Mamdani, Mahmood. *Citizen and subject. Contemporary Africa and the legacy of late colonialism*. Princeton: Princeton University Press, 1996.

Mandela, Nelson. "The Rivonia trail", in *No easy walk to freedom*. Essex: Heinemann, [1965] 1990, pp. 162–189.

Mokoka, Gobi Clement. *Black experience in Black Theology. A study on the Roman Catholic Church missionary endeavour in South Africa and the search for justice*. Doctoral dissertation in divinity. University of Nijmegen, 1984.

"Motions". *Présence Africaine* 1959/1 (N° XXIV-XXV), pp. 461–463.

Motlhabi, Mokgethi. *The theory and practice of black resistance to apartheid. A social-ethical analysis*. Johannesburg: Skotaville Publishers, 1984.

Mothlabi, Mokgethi. "Black theology in South Africa: an autobiographical reflection". *Studia Historiae Ecclesiasticae* XXXI/2, 2005, pp. 37–62.

Motlhabi, Mothlabi (ed.). *Essays on Black Theology*. Johannesburg: Black Theology Project of the University Christian Movement, 1972.

Mpisi, Jean. *Le Cardinal Malula et Jean-Paul II. Dialogue difficile entre l'église "africaine" et le saint-siège*. Paris: L'Harmattan, 2005.

Mudimbe, Valentin Yves. *The invention of Africa: Gnosis, philosophy, and the order of knowledge*. *African Systems of Thought*. Bloomington: Indiana University Press, 1988.

Mudimbe, Valentin Yves (ed.). *The surreptitious speech. Présence Africaine and the politics of otherness 1947 - 1987*. Chicago: Chicago University Press, 1992.

Mudimbe, Valentin. "'À la naissance de *Présence Africaine*: La nuit de foi pourtant'. Lettre à Éric Van Grasdorff". *Rue Descartes* 83/4 2014, pp. 117–136.

Mukuka, George Sombe. *The impact of Black Consciousness on the black Catholic clergy and their training from 1965-1981*. Dissertation, Master's in Theology, University of Natal, Pietermaritzburg, November 1996.

Mukuka, George. "The establishment of the Indigenous Catholic Clergy in South Africa: 1919-1957". *Studia Historiae Ecclesiasticae* XXXIV/1, 2008, pp. 305–334.

Mukuka, George Sombe. *The other side of the story. The silent experience of the black clergy in the Catholic Church in South Africa (1898-1976)*. Pietermaritzburg: Cluster Publications, 2008.

Mukuka, George. "Moetapele, David". *Dictionary of African Christian Biography*, http://www.dacb.org/stories/southafrica/moetapele_david.html (last accessed 5 February 2016).

Mukuka, George. "Mokoka, Gobi Clement". *Dictionary of African Christian Biography*, http://www.dacb.org/stories/southafrica/mokoka.html (last accessed 5 February 2016).

Nußbaum, Karin. "Klaus Mörsdorf und Michael Schmaus als Konzilsberater des Münchener Erzbischofs Kardinal Julius Döpfner auf dem Zweiten Vatikanischen Konzil. Eine Untersuchung aufgrund des Konzilsnachlasses Kardinal Döpfners". *Münchener Theologische Zeitschrift* 55, 2004, pp. 132–150.

Oliver, Roland. "Professor Richard Gray. Incisive historian of Africa". *The Independent*, 14 September 2005.

Peires, Jeffrey. "Ethnicity and Pseudo-ethnicity in the Ciskei", in William Beinart and Saul Dubow (eds.), *Segregation and apartheid in twentieth-century South Africa*. London and New York:

Routledge, 1995, pp. 256–284.

Peires, Jeffrey. "How the Eastern Cape lost its edge to the Western Cape: The political economy in the Eastern Cape on the eve of Union", in Greg Ruiters (ed.), *The fate of the Eastern Cape. History, politics and social policy*. Scottsville: UKZN Press, 2011, pp. 42–59.

Peires, Jeffrey. *The house of Phalo: A history of the Xhosa people in the days of their independence*. Berkeley and Los Angeles: University of California Press, 1981.

Platzky, Laurine and Cherryl Walker. *The surplus people. Forced removals in South Africa*. Johannesburg: Ravan Press, 1985.

Posel, Deborah. "The apartheid project, 1948-1970", in Robert Ross, Anne Kelk Mager, and Bill Nasson (eds.), *The Cambridge history of South Africa. Volume 2: 1885-1994*. Cambridge: Cambridge University Press, pp. 319–368.

Reader's Digest. *Illustrated History of South Africa: The Real Story*. Third edition. Cape Town: Reader's Digest Association South Africa, 1994.

Ranger, Terence. "The invention of tradition in colonial Africa", in Eric Hobsbawm and Terence Ranger (eds.), *The invention of tradition*. Cambridge: Cambridge University Press, 1983, pp. 211–262.

Roberts, Andrew. "Richard Gray, 1929–2005". *Azania: Archaeological research in Africa*, 40:1, 2005, pp. 166–167.

Romano, Sergio. *Histoire de l'Italie du Risorgiomento à nos jours*. Paris: Seuil, 1977.

South African Students Organisation (SASO). "SASO Policy Manifesto". *SASO Newsletter* 1/3, August 1971, pp. 10–11. http://disa.ukzn.ac.za/sites/default/files/pdf_files/saaug71.pdf.

Scheffczyk, Leo Kardinal. "Schmaus, Michael". *Neue Deutsche Biographie* 23, 2007, pp. 123–124. https://www.deutsche-biographie.de/pnd118608495.html#ndbcontent (last accessed, 27 September 2019).

Schimlek, Francis. *Against the stream. Life of Father Bernard Huss, C.M.M. The social apostle of the Bantu*. Mariannhill Natal: Mariannhill Mission Press, 1949.

Sebidi, Lebamang John (and Gail Gerhart). "Interview with Lebamang John Sebidi" on 3 July 1987, http://www.aluka.org/stable/10.5555/al.sff.document.gerhart0002 (last accessed 2 October 2016).

Southall, Roger. *South Africa's Transkei. The political economy of an 'independent' Bantustan*. London: Heinemann, 1982.

South African History Online. "Poqo". https://www.sahistory.org.za/organisations/poqo (last accessed 18 January 2019).

Switzer, Les. *Power and resistance in an African society. The Ciskei Xhosa and the making of South Africa*. Madison: University of Wisconsin Press, 1993.

Taiwò, Olufemi. *How colonialism preempted modernity in Africa*. Bloomington: Indiana University Press, 2010.

Thompson, Leonard. *A history of South Africa*. Revised fourth edition, by Lynn Berat. New Haven and London: Yale University Press, 2014.

Trapido, Stanley. "Imperialism, settler identities, and colonial capitalism: the hundred-year origins of the 1899 South African war", in Robert Ross, Anne Kelk Mager, and Bill Nasson (eds.), *The Cambridge history of South Africa. Volume 2: 1885-1994*. Cambridge: Cambridge University Press, pp. 66–101.

Tshibangu, Tharcisse. *Le concile Vatican II et l'église Africaine. Mise en oeuvre du concile dans l'église d'Afrique (1960 - 2010)*. Limete: Epiphanie, 2012.

Mazrui, Ali and Christophe Wondji (eds.), *General history of Africa. Volume VIII: Africa since 1935*. Paris: UNESCO; Oxford: J. Currey, 1999.

UNESCO website for the fiftieth anniversary of the First Conference for black writers and artists: http://portal.unesco.org/fr/ev.php-URL_ID=34700&URL_DO=DO_TOPIC&URL_SECTION=201.html (last accessed 8 November 2018).

UNESCO. *Le rôle des mouvements d'étudiants africains dans l'évolution politique et sociale de l'Afrique de 1900 à 1975*. Paris: UNESCO and Harmattan, 1993.

https://web.archive.org/web/20111008183418/http://www.blessedjohn23.org/camdens_bishops.html (last accessed 29 September 2019).

Verdin, Philippe. *Alioune Diop, le Socrate noir*. Preface by Abd Al Malik. Paris: Lethielleux, 2010.

"Interviews with German anthropologists", "Short Portrait: Wolfgang Marschall": http://www.germananthropology.com/short-portrait/wolfgang-marschall/144

Wolff, Ernst. "Adam Small's shade of Black Consciousness", in Leonhard Praeg (ed.), *Philosophy on the border. Decoloniality and the shudder of the origin*. Pietermaritzburg: UKZN Press, 2019, pp. 112–147.